and now, back to mannix

JoAnn M. Paul

And Now, Back to Mannix
By JoAnn M. Paul
© 2014, JoAnn M. Paul. All Rights Reserved.
All program titles and program descriptions are used in editorial fashion with no intention of infringement of intellectual property rights.
All illustrations from Mannix are copyright Paramount Pictures Corporation and are reproduced here in the spirit of publicity.
No part of this book may be reproduced in any form or by any means, electronic, mechanical, digital, photocopying or recording, except for the inclusion in a review, without permission in writing from the publisher.

Published in the USA by:
BearManor Media
P O Box 71426
Albany, Georgia 31708
www.bearmanormedia.com

ISBN: 978-1-59393-565-8
Printed in the United States of America
Book design by Robbie Adkins, www.adkinsconsult.com

Table of Contents

Foreword (by Mike Connors) V

Dedication VII

Acknowledgements IX

Prologue (by David Breckman) XI

Introduction XV

Chapter 1—Mike Connors is m a n n i x 1

Chapter 2—The Character of the Character 21

Chapter 3—The Difference 35

Chapter 4—Heroic Matters 53

Chapter 5—Joe and Peggy 71

Chapter 6—That's Tough 93

Chapter 7—It's About the Mouse 129

Chapter 8—The Private Kind 149

Chapter 9—The Art in the Background 167

Chapter 10—Asking for Trouble 187

Chapter 11—A Pittance 207

Chapter 12—Let's Go 227

References 243

IV

and now, back to mannix

Foreword
by Mike Connors

I have just finished reading this book about the *Mannix* series written by Professor JoAnn Paul and enjoyed every page of it almost as much as I did playing Joe Mannix.

It is amazing how much thought and research she has put into this book. I thought I knew more about the show than anyone but the Professor proved me wrong.

Even though I played Joe Mannix for eight years I found the insight about the series fascinating and different. If you were ever a fan of the series or watched the show now and then I am sure you will find this book a very enjoyable experience.

                                        Mike Connors

                                        Encino, CA

                                        November 1, 2013

VI

and now, back to mannix

Dedication

This book is dedicated to

the memory of my parents,
Chris and Mary Paul,

their love endured
and so
their love endures

VIII   and now, back to mannix

Acknowledgements

This book is about a storied heroic character, one that was there when I needed him. In writing this book, certain people were also there just when I needed them. They should all feel a part of this book. Four individuals, in particular, contributed directly to both the book's contents and its author's spirit. They deserve special mention, and thanks.

David Breckman appeared when the manuscript draft was completed in an example of what Jung might call "synchronicity." He was for eight years a writer-producer on the highly successful USA series *Monk*, starring Tony Shalhoub. His credentials, combined with his strong, clear take on both *Mannix* and the book blew me away. The Prologue he wrote for the book speaks to his depth and insight. I can't thank him enough for that and for his support.

Danny Biederman, the published author, was the first person to suggest I write a book on *Mannix*. He was also there to edit the book when a family crisis occurred right after the book was accepted for publication. It was a relief to know the book was in such good hands. Thanks so much to Danny for being an important part of this project all along, including while I learned the peculiarities of the publishing world.

Special thanks to RGJ, who prefers to remain anonymous. He was the only person to read the chapter drafts before I sent them to Mike Connors. He did some light proofreading. But well beyond that, he encouraged me to write a book like no other, by unequivocally saying there was no other option for me. In the true spirit of Joe Mannix, his many contributions are of the private kind.

Finally, singular thanks to Mike Connors. Without him there would be no Joe Mannix as we know him, no *Mannix* series as we know it, and thus no book. Sending him the chapters as they were written made the writing of this book an almost unbelievably enjoyable experience. I continue to discover how much thought went into the character of Joe Mannix, how unique that character was—and still is—and how much Connors embodied that character. Like this book, so many synchronistic events converged to make *Mannix* the series it became. Those events ultimately enabled Connors to portray the knight, the hero, as so few can. I could spend the rest of my life trying to comprehend the value of that imagery and never get to the bottom.

and now, back to mannix

Prologue
by David Breckman

I once read an interview with Lawrence Kasdan in the mid-1980s. The great writer-director (*The Big Chill, Body Heat*) was grousing about the state of American cinema, about how movies were coming to resemble live-action cartoons. "And the result," Kasdan said, "is that when you look up at the silver screen these days, there's no help there."

There's no help there.

I knew exactly what Kasdan meant. He was talking, primarily, about motion picture *heroes*, since at the time the interview took place, the soldiers, cops, spies and PIs who perennially dominate the multiplex were undergoing a major overhaul—becoming bigger, tougher, faster, stronger…and damned near invincible. This was a time when Stallone and Schwarzenegger's 'roided up, sometimes robotic (literally and figuratively) protagonists were laying waste to legions of bad guys all by their lonesome, and barely stopping to reload…a time when every hero on the big and small screen was suddenly "ex-special forces" (these days he's a former Navy Seal) and was, in all the ways that mattered, essentially perfect—unstoppable and infallible.

But that was back in the 1980s, and the trend has changed considerably in the last thirty years.

It's gotten worse.

Take, for example, Matt Damon as Robert Ludlum's amnesiac super-spy Jason Bourne. In all three of his outings, Bourne is portrayed as preternaturally fast and resourceful (as well as fashionably brooding and angsty; think 007 by way of The Actors Studio: "Dean. James Dean."). This is one hero who is never overmatched, never stumbles, and is never wrong.

How relatable.

Actually the phrase "one hero" isn't remotely correct, since, by gum, today there are any number of infallible heroes kickboxing their way across the media landscape. There's Neo in the *Matrix* movies… and novelist Lee Child's quasi-superhuman former MP Jack Reacher (played onscreen by Tom Cruise)…and Denzel Washington displaying near God-like speed and lethality in *The Equalizer*…and the unerring sleuths of the small screen such as Simon Baker on *The Mentalist*, Poppy

Montgomery's eidetic crime buster on *Unforgettable*, and James Spader on the recent hit, *The Blacklist*.

Since these folks and others like them never make mistakes, audiences clearly have developed an appetite for perfection.

And that's a pity, since what we really need from our heroes isn't perfection, but perseverance.

Because, sure, we want our heroes to be tough; and brains and resourcefulness never hurt, either; and let's not forget about moxie and courage when we're drawing up that résumé.

But it is primarily their vulnerability—their capacity for injury, for setbacks, for failure… and their willingness to keep fighting *despite* that vulnerability—that is the real inspiration of the mythic hero.

Because all of us stumble, and fall, and fail in our lives. But true heroes, the best of them, inspire us with their indomitability of spirit, when—bloody but not bowed—they manage to pull themselves back up again.

Which brings us to 17 Paseo Verde in Los Angeles—the office and residence of Joe Mannix—and the book you now hold in your hot little hands (unless you're reading this on some sort of electronic device, in which case that last phrase was just a metaphor).

During his eight years on CBS, Joe was shot and stabbed, mugged and drugged, mauled and bludgeoned, beaten and blinded…and always soldiered on. Indeed, Mannix personified the verities of the quintessential, hardboiled PI as laid out by Raymond Chandler (creator of Philip Marlowe) in his famous essay "The Simple Art of Murder":

"Down these mean streets a man must go who is not himself mean, who is neither tarnished nor afraid. He must be a man of honor, by instinct, by inevitability, without thought of it, and certainly without saying it. He must be the best man in his world and a good enough man for any world."

And that was Mannix. "The best man in his world, and a good enough man for any world."

How good, exactly? Well, for starters, he often worked for nothing. If a friend needed help but couldn't afford to pay, Mannix was there for him. (Oh, hell. If a stranger needed help but couldn't afford to pay, Mannix was there for him, too). And once he was hired on a case, he stayed hired until it was over.

So what exactly animated this tall, swarthy guy in the tweed sportcoat and Ray Ban shades? What made Joey run? Naturally, JoAnn Paul addresses this question (and many more besides) in the magnificent book you are now holding (metaphor again)—but I'll take a fumbling stab at it anyway: I believe it comes down to knight errantry.

Like Phillip Marlowe before him, and Robert Parker's gumshoe Spenser, and John D. MacDonald's boat bum-slash-private detective Travis McGee, Mannix represents the apotheosis of the private eye as knight errant.

And while he would surely deflect the question with a wry quip before blasting off in his convertible GTS for another round of mayhem and adventure, Joe's mission in life (whether he's aware of it or not) is to right wrongs, protect the innocent and confront evil.

He simply has no choice. Knight errants never do.

And the "dragons" he does battle with are usually almost as tough as he is, and occasionally get the drop on him. (And how often do you see this happening to Jason Bourne? Answer: Never. Bourne's invincible, remember?)

But Joe always gets back up again. Always.

And the mysteries he investigates are wonderfully intricate (and brilliantly plotted, too, courtesy of producers Ivan Goff and Ben Roberts), and Joe will sometimes—wait for it, gang—make a mistake or two along the way before unraveling them. (And how often do you see the Mentalist being wrong about anything? Answer: Never. The guy's infallible, remember?)

So, the toughest PI in town…but he can be hurt. The smartest, shrewdest detective in the business…but he can be fooled. Who knew? And why is that valuable?

Read JoAnn's book and find out. It's all here.

Because while it features all the trivia and behind-the-scenes anecdotes a fan could ask for, this is not your typical episode guide. *And Now, Back to Mannix* serves as an eloquent and highly readable consideration of *Why Mannix Matters*.

Thirty million Americans tuned in each week not just for the movie-quality production values (*Mannix* boasted more camera set-ups than any show of its time save *Mission: Impossible*)…or the precision-crafted stories…or the effortless charisma of the great Mike Connors in the title role.

All those things were important, sure, but it's what Mannix *represented* that counted most.

What's more, JoAnn makes her insights personal, drawing from her own unique experiences to illustrate how Mannix's virtues of bravery, nobility, dignity and good old-fashioned American toughness are as relevant to our own time, and our own lives, as ever before.

In fact, one would be hard pressed to finish this book without wanting to sit down and watch the whole series from beginning to end on DVD.

Mannix solved his last case almost forty years ago, and—incredibly—seems all but forgotten today. And he shouldn't be. *Mannix* was, and remains, the finest private eye show ever seen on U.S. television. (And this is from a guy who is enormously proud of *another* PI show— one he contributed to for eight years: *Monk*, starring Tony Shalhoub).

But what they used to say about the great Sandy Koufax—*He's pitching in a different league*—also applies to *Mannix*. And here's hoping this book gets more people talking about it.

They ought to. It's a wonderful show.

And there's help there.

David Breckman

Sherman Oaks, CA

December 28, 2013

Introduction

On September 16, 1967, *Mannix* premiered on CBS Television, starting an eight-year run that overlapped what may well be the single most creative period in American television. It was the dawn of color TV, at a time when the movie studios were challenged—for both viewers and quality—by what was appearing for free on a weekly basis. Television sets were commonplace for the first time and Baby Boomers were being branded by what they saw on TV, whether they realized it or not. The television industry did not yet really know what worked well, especially in color. The genres that would dominate the next generation of television were not yet established. The popularity of westerns was coming to an end perhaps in part because color TV seemed more real, casting shadowy images of black-and-white heroes of the distant past back into the shadows and demanding that our new heroes be more than distant caricatures. It was also a time of transition between the WWII generation and the Baby Boomers, with the Vietnam War as a backdrop. The energy of great generational transition was ready to hit the streets in the form of protests and even landmark concerts—all signifying great gatherings. A thirst for individualism was in the air, even if it was carried out by the Baby Boomers in large groups where the single biggest difference between any two individuals was that no two tie-dyed shirts turned out alike.

Mannix was the last production created by Desilu Studios, which was formed when Desi Arnaz and Lucille Ball purchased RKO—a once great movie studio—and turned it into a television production facility. RKO happened to be physically adjacent to the Paramount lot, another great movie studio. The last three television productions from Desilu are *Star Trek*, *Mission: Impossible* and *Mannix*. But while *Star Trek* and *Mission: Impossible* went on to obtain cult followings, subsequent series and even subsequent movies, *Mannix* had a hard time making it to DVD release, seeming to require no less than a 2007 *Washington Post* article where a fan who happened to also be a writer for the newspaper wondered what happened to the series.[0.1] Season 1 of *Mannix* was released on DVD the next year.

The difference between the legacies of the three series would not seem to be due to inherent quality. *Mannix's* original run was longer than either of those other shows—longer than any single Desilu created drama. *Star Trek* ended after three years (on NBC) and *Mission: Impossible* ran for seven seasons (on CBS). *Mannix* ran for eight seasons, won awards for the series and both of its major stars, was syndicated in over seventy countries during its first run, and finished its fifth season in the top ten. It hit #1 for the week, overall, on several occasions and, amazingly, found its eighth season one of its strongest in the A.C. Nielsen ratings. That year it climbed back up into the Top 20 for the season and hit the week's Top 10 several times. This occurred after two challenging seasons where it had been put up against some of the strongest competition the other networks had to offer on Sunday nights.[0.2] Since there was no notion that the eighth season was going to be the series' last, it did not garner those ratings for some sort of nostalgic re-connection to its fan base, but rather because *Mannix* is one of those rare shows that never got stale, never got tired, and never degraded in quality.

Other metrics of the success of the series include the way it re-invented the basic model of the TV private eye, which can be seen directly in at least four other shows that were contemporaries in its later years—*The Rockford Files, Cannon, Barnaby Jones* and *Harry O*—and in quite a few that came after the series ended, including *Magnum, P.I.* Its maverick, individualist, personalized crime-fighting main character of Joe Mannix could also be considered the basis for all other cop-centric shows that followed, in which the main character mattered as much as the story being told each week. In a real sense, all modern TV crime fighters can trace their roots back to Joe Mannix.

One reason you knew cared about Joe was because he got hurt—a lot. And when he did, you cared. Over his eight-year run, Joe Mannix was shot seventeen times and knocked unconscious fifty-five times, by at least one count.[0.1] The number of fistfights he was in seemed virtually infinite. The injuries seemed even worse for the way they were distributed over the course of the series. During the first, second, sixth and eight seasons, Joe Mannix was hardly bloodied at all—but he made up for it in the four other seasons, during which he seemed unable to escape bullets, deadly poison, car crashes, explosions, beatings, being rolled down hills after being shot, being left for dead on the streets after being shot, and even an airplane crash in the middle of the mountains.

Mannix was framed by its action in an era when there was no CGI (computer-generated imagery) and more of a willingness to take risks, all around. The show routinely had scenes with cars that were blown up and rolled down the sides of cliffs—real cars, real fire, real cliffs. They even used real fire on the sets back then—something unheard of today. Its star, with an athletic background, did enough of his own stunts so that you wondered about the insurance that Paramount (which purchased Desilu in 1968 and so took ownership of *Mannix*) must have carried on him. This is especially true since he was in virtually every scene and there was no real supporting cast to carry even one episode without him (at least after the first season, save loyal Peggy, wonderfully played by Gail Fisher).

The show featured scripts that kept you guessing, innovative directing, great acting, stunts worth re-watching in slow motion (just to see the many that were performed by Connors, himself), the destruction of cars, all sorts of car chases, some of the most iconic convertibles of any TV series, a visual record of the Los Angeles area where so many of its outdoor scenes were filmed, signature sports jackets (sometimes referred to as "*Mannix* jackets"), one of the best scores of any television series, and one of the best visual openings of any television series. The *Mannix* team even had a propensity to "hide" nude art—which was occasionally worked into the series' set designs—from the network censors, forcing them to visit the set instead of just screening the scripts (such art can routinely be seen on the DVDs). And, while I enjoy all of those things, none of them is the real reason why I love the show so much.

The character of Joe Mannix embodies a collection of some of the best, timeless themes I have ever seen put together in one character, themes that reflect the values of the generation that produced the series. The result is one of the most quintessentially American characters ever produced in any media. The evidence for this claim arises from a brief examination of what *Mannix* wound up being all about for most of its run, and the unique way the series evolved around its star and main character.

During its first season, *Mannix* was a typical gimmick show. In the sense that each gimmick is different from the next, there is no typical gimmick show, and yet, all shows that have some gimmick can be lumped together in the category of gimmick-driven shows. *Star Trek* had outer space (and all of the many assumptions that go with space travel), *Mission: Impossible* had the missions (and an assortment of technological inventions that made them a bit more possible than they might really be), *The Fugitive* had his pursuer (and a lot of people who were willing to help him evade a policeman with seemingly no other duties), and shows like *I Spy* had the buddy concept—an ongoing gimmick where the heroism seems somehow secondary to the relationship with the buddy. *Mannix* was initially no different, being pitched by Richard Levinson and William Link, creators of *Colombo*, as a show that was supposed to be a sort of partial parody of Lew Wasserman, a high powered talent agent in Hollywood. One of the main characters in the first season of *Mannix*, Lew Wickersham, was even named after Wasserman. In the spirit of such power and the large organizations that tend to go with it, there was a detective agency in the first season of *Mannix*, named Intertect, that Joe Mannix worked for, and the show was almost named after it. Intertect's gimmick was its computers, which in that day took up entire rooms to do what we consider by today's standards to be incredibly simple things. But, back in the late 1960s, the capabilities of computers were big unknowns to most people and, combined with the large organizations it took to even have one in the first place, man vs. machine seemed a great way to bring the rugged PI—and individualist—back to TV.

The concept didn't really work, for a variety of reasons that make sense, in retrospect. But, something about the main character did, so that even those episodes in season 1 have incredible quality and charm. Despite low ratings, Lucille Ball saw something in the character that she liked and she, famously, in one of her last acts as head of Desilu, saved the series so long as it re-tooled itself and changed its concept so that Joe Mannix went to work on his own. In sharp contrast to the type of character she played through at least four situation comedies on the small screen, Lucille Ball knew something about being a tough individual—and Joe Mannix appealed to her.

Curiously, instead of simply finding another series for Connors, the second season of *Mannix* saw Joe Mannix going out on his own with only brief mention of where he had spent the previous years of his life. The show changed producers, from Wilton Schiller in season 1 to the playwright team of Ivan Goff and Ben Roberts in seasons 2-8, with Bruce Geller remaining executive producer, even if just in name in later years. Even the studio changed that year when Paramount purchased Desilu. Thus, at the start of the second season of *Mannix*, the only real connection it had to its origins was Mike Connors' concept of the main character—and some of the action-packed, *Mannix* style. With no real "concept" for anyone to hang their hat on, no gimmick to explore or write around, the show had nothing to lean on. It's ridiculous to invent a new gimmick for a show already on the air, and yet the writers had to write about something and the directors had to figure out the tone for the series. So where it wound up going was character exploration, so much so that the solving of the case could become secondary to character development, a new concept for a show ostensibly about some combination of action and mystery.[0.3] After all, character was the reason the show was renewed for its second season—just because Lucille Ball liked the character. So far, *Mannix* had a main character that could be defined as a tough individualist, who would rather trust his instincts than a machine, and who was willing to quit his job in order to find the time to help someone rather than sell himself out for any kind of steady employment. So far, so good. But, how far does that really go?

After a surprisingly strong second season of episodes, in which character development is sweetly subtle but ongoing, *Mannix* finds itself early in season 3 producing what some consider the signature episode of the series, "The Sound of Darkness." In this episode, Joe Mannix is blinded, perhaps permanently, by a shot to the temple that scares him enough that he suffers from psychosomatic blindness while a killer is still on the loose, and after him. This episode, while ostensibly about catching a killer—and finding a big pile of buried money—is really about Joe Mannix, the man. They even forgot to let the viewer in on what happened to the giant pile of money that was supposed to be fueling the entire situation. Theories abound to this day as to whether the money was ever found and, if it was, what Joe might have done with the reward for finding it. We will never know because the writers didn't bother to tell us. By the time you are done with the episode, you aren't thinking about the money, aren't really even thinking about the story anymore; you are moved by the characters—not only Joe, but Peggy and Adam Tobias, played by none other than series semi-regular, Robert Reed, who, in contrast to his experience starring in ABC-TV's *The Brady Brunch*, seemed to actually want to be a part of *Mannix*.

What is this, a detective series where the viewer forgot about story and even what happened to a big pile of money? It does not seem like American television. But, it is the beauty of *Mannix*.

The series evolved so much along character development lines, especially in the early seasons, that reruns of earlier episodes of the same season stood out like non-sequiturs, in spite of there being no ordering among episodes from an overarching storyline. It was as if the actors playing the characters were living the roles out, seeing where they went and letting that change them—and why not, since they were not beholden to a gimmick or concept? The point of the show became the ongoing illustration of a character with some core attributes reflective of the kinds of things we wanted to see in our heroes at that time, and the show's producers and stars got to explore what that meant as the stories were lived out.

This ownership and exploration of character also has a lot to do with the fact that the series never got tired, stale, old or worn out. It was as strong when it was canceled as it ever was—and even the cancellation was an absurd reflection of the show's very success. Another network—ABC—wanted to run *Mannix* in late-night—right up against *The Tonight Show Starring Johnny Carson*. Paramount sold previous seasons of *Mannix* to ABC, just for that purpose, but without the approval of CBS. When CBS decided that ABC's late-night reruns would weaken the appeal of its first-run episodes, it canceled the series while it was still going strong, ranked among the Top 20 shows over the course of the entire season. During the summer run of its final season, when it was briefly moved back to the Wednesday night timeslot it had in its highest-rated season, it reportedly hit as high as #3 in the weekly ratings. The syndication of a series that was still in production was new then—something that would not get in the way today. Beyond this, network syndication deals were (and still are) very rare, especially when the syndicating network is a direct competitor to the network on which the series continues to air first-run episodes. ABC wanted *Mannix* badly enough for its late-night run that it, apparently, was willing to let those airings serve as an advertisement for the first run of the series, had CBS let that happen.

Mannix was a great success and pioneering in all sorts of ways. But other darlings have taken the place of Joe Mannix, which are, arguably, significantly lesser heroes and anti-heroes. Joe Mannix was a tough individual who was willing to get hurt—sacrifice—in pursuit of doing the right thing. He could give as good as he got, so long as he was fighting the good fight. He answered primarily to himself, as true individuals do, but in such a way that he stood not apart from the system, but beside it, always in order to do the right thing, the thing the viewer saw as self-evidently, tacitly, the right thing to do. He was even known to break the law, on occasion, embodying the way the truth is sometimes only revealed by the individual who has the guts to see things as they really are and knows that sometimes he is the only one who can do anything about it. He gets up the next day, healed and ready to engage again, no matter how many times he's been hurt. His energy seems to come from the same place his individuality comes from—from the guts to face reality, often all alone. Episode after episode illustrated this, artfully, beautifully, convincingly.

Along the way all sorts of compromises were made to the art form, of course. Joe Mannix, famously, healed from some pretty severe bullet wounds by the next week, and never seemed to be the worse for wear for the physical punishment he took. But *Mannix* hearkened back to an era when we were more comfortable with that kind of symbolism, before we started to become the computer Joe Mannix despised so much, not by using computers, *per se*, but by analyzing everything in a technical, literal sense, distilling everything we can to logic and reason. The end result is just the same.

I've seen many comments written about the DVD releases to the effect that "*Mannix* is the one series that you loved as a kid that has held up as an adult." That is the power of this series—it worked on so many levels that it appealed to the kid, the car lover, the person who liked to look at beautiful and stylish people, the person who liked mysteries, the person who liked action. But it held so much more than that, often working subtly, below the surface. So many of those subtle things are only possible to see now, on the uncut DVD releases, because of the way syndication so heavily edited them away.

Mannix had an impact on me that I did not fully realize until I started to re-watch the show in its uncut form, for the first time since it originally aired. I did not have access to very many of the cut, syndicated runs, which mostly aired on *TV Land*. Regardless, because of the style in which the show was done—understatement, tight editing, emotion conveyed in reaction shots (often the first to be edited out for syndication)—edited *Mannix* is not *Mannix*. When I saw what was really in the show, forty years later, it surprised even me, someone who had loved it way back when. Of course, as a kid, I was different then too. In the meantime, I pursued life's issues and read fairly broadly, to include psychology, philosophy, and religion. And so, I was stunned to see that timeless themes, especially those of individuality, toughness, struggle and spirituality are woven right into *Mannix*. I was even more stunned to discover how those themes had affected me all along the way, how much better I was when I was more connected to those themes and also how much better life seemed when we embraced those themes more than we do now. My subsequent re-connection with the show has led me to a study of the importance of myths, starting with the great work done by Joseph Campbell and Bill Moyers.[0.4] I feel better because I have my myth of choice back—I not only feel better, I am better.

None of my experience matters to the *Mannix* fan, of course. Nor, in a way, should it. But, *Mannix* is a show about an individual with guts and, in a way, the only true way to honor it is to be an individual with guts. If there is a closet for me to come out of, it is the closet of the once proud intellectual who has to admit that a lot of the way they see life is because of the way they once loved a childhood hero. But what is wrong with that? Not only do I wish I was more consistent with my own myth of choice throughout my life, I wish there were more people around like him—even as *Mannix* was more popular in its day than some lesser shows from that time that now have more of a following. What bothers me is that many of the themes of *Mannix* seem to be both great and generational. We are not as comfortable anymore with responsible individuality, risk taking, and symbolism as we once were. We are not comfortable standing beside the system, as true individuals. Instead, we seem to either completely self-identify with the system, buying into how it views and values us, or completely alienate from it. That's more than a pity—it may well be dangerous.

As I go through the evolution of the series, I may stop short of saying that bringing back a love of *Mannix* could solve many of our most intractable, current problems. But, if I do stop short of that, I will not stop very far short. Re-discovering the series has caused me to conclude that so many of those problems are because we identify with groups too much and with what we have too much. The two are related. We do not think enough about our identity when we are all alone, or the pain we must, unavoidably, take on when we wish to transcend, and what we ultimately leave behind. Heroes stand alone in helping us do those things. Our myths matter to us, both as individuals and as a culture. We just don't know it, unless we really pay attention to how—and why—we come to define ourselves though the myths we found and loved. Only by paying attention to them, their impact and their relative content, can we have a hope of finding better ones that allow us to do more and be more, because only then we will be more comfortable with facing up to, and even asking for, the difficulty—the struggle—that is an inherent part of any good life. Great myths allow us to be comfortable with those things, because they are comfortable with those things.

And now, back to *Mannix*.

XXIV and now, back to mannix

Chapter 1
Mike Connors is m a n n i x

Normal star billing goes like this: "*Mannix,* starring Mike Connors." But that is not the way things are billed in *Mannix.* Instead, the opening credits for all eight seasons of the series have, "Mike Connors *is Mannix.*" Such unusual billing, then or now, does not seem to have been accidental. Articles from that time period discuss just how much Mike Connors inhabited the character of Joe Mannix, to include discussion of how the two were difficult to distinguish at times.[1.1] The original premise of the show meant that it could just as well have been called, *Intertect,* after the agency Joe Mannix worked for in the show's original format, in season 1. Apparently, the series was actually almost called that.[1.2] But, when the show's producers quickly realized who the star was going to be, the show was called *Mannix.*

The opening got it right in more ways than just the name and the billing. The classic *Mannix* opening has all sorts of action shots, and not just one at a time. They are framed inside black blocks, intended to give the viewer the impression that action is happening in multiple dimensions, with some scenes covered by multiple camera angles, seemingly inspired by the Picasso-like notion that multiple viewing angles could be translated to two dimensions. Only, in *Mannix* this does not result in a still life. The opening portrays scene after scene of action, so much action that it seemed to be coming out of the screen, all set to the classic ¾ time Jazz Waltz that remains one of composer Lalo Schifrin's signature compositions. Especially in the early seasons, the action was not a collection of just any stunts, but ones done by Connors, himself. One of these is the iconic image of Joe Mannix running across a bridge, presumably being chased by a car—one of the few scenes in the opening of *Mannix* that does not have its origin in an actual episode. The message is clear—this is a man of action.

But, action, in and of itself, can appear to be just so much moving around. A key part of the success of *Mannix* is revealed in another iconic part of its opening sequence. Framing other scenes in the opening are images of Connors' eyes, illustrating that he is looking at some things he is doing in other blocks. The close-up on the eyes is so tight that the rest of his face is actually cropped in the image. The implication is clear. This is someone living a very fast-paced, highly energetic, highly engaged life, but, at the same time, he is paying attention to it. Those eyes are an important part of *Mannix*.

Another part of the *Mannix* opening that gets it right from the very beginning is somewhat less obvious and might even be accidental. When the words "Mike Connors is" are revealed, one colorful block at a time, those colors are lined up horizontally, red over blue over apricot. They happen to be the colors of the Armenian Flag. The apricot color is not among the many other colors used in any of the other blocks that make up the opening and closing sequences, over all eight years of *Mannix*.

Not accidental is that Connors decided, from the very first season, that Joe Mannix would be Armenian, since Connors himself is Armenian-American. Never mind that Mannix is an Irish surname. In season 1, Joe Mannix spoke Armenian and was identified as such in most of the remaining seasons, continuing to speak Armenian, quoting Armenian proverbs, and even visiting his parental home where his Armenian father (played by Victor Jory) worked in the vineyards. I've seen *Mannix* fans reconcile the surname issue as one of those Ellis Island mistakes that some families never correct. Their idea is that the supposedly correct, Armenian version, Manian, was lost due to transcription error—one of a few inconsistencies in Joe Mannix's back story that fans have fun reconciling.

Right from the beginning, even before the show was successful, Connors seemed to want to bring more of himself to the role of Joe Mannix. By the time the show was a big hit, after a highly rated and Golden Globe-winning fifth season, Connors gave an analogy for how he'd learned to crawl into the character as being similar to the way a man puts on a pair of long underwear.[1.3] In effect, he was describing himself only a thin surface layer away from *being* his signature role.

When you think of Mike Connors, you think of Joe Mannix.

One category of actor encompasses those who disappear into the many different roles they play, displaying great technique to take on and mimic a wide variety of human behavior. When you think of Meryl Streep or Dustin Hoffman you think first of what great actors they are and then the many parts they have played well, but not really any one role in particular. Another category of actor plays a more limited set of roles, but with a focus of bringing a certain type of character to a variety of settings. When you think of John Wayne or Lucille Ball, a clear character type comes to mind, but that type is represented across a variety of instances. No clear single instance comes to mind, only a clear type. A third category of actor inhabits a single role so much that when you think of them you think of that role. When you think of Kelsey Grammer, you think of *Frasier*. That is the way it is with Connors and *Mannix*.

The analogy goes further. Kelsey Grammer's Frasier Crane started out as a small role on *Cheers* (NBC-TV 1982-1993) that was supposed to cover only a few episodes, and with little character definition. The highly successful series *Frasier* (NBC-TV 1993-2004) wound up being written around Grammer's interpretation of that single character, as Frasier became ever more defined by Grammer over the years. There, the actor drove the concept that became the series. In the transition from one series to another, Frasier Crane stayed in the same profession, but changed setting, job, and supporting cast. Only the core elements of the character remained. Those elements were defined by Grammer. Similarly, in the re-tooling of *Mannix* from season 1 to season 2, Connors' Joe Mannix retained only his profession, changing setting, job and supporting cast for the second season of *Mannix*. Only, in *Mannix*, the behind-the-scenes crew changed as well.

Mannix really wasn't a PI crime drama. It was really all about Connors' interpretation of this guy, Joe Mannix. To see this, go down the list of TV shows for the past fifty years or more, and consider how they might survive if their star left the series. Many shows would survive on the basis of continuation of their concept, gimmick, setting or premise by bringing an equivalent or replacement character in with some type of plot twist. Some even just use a different actor to play the same part. These situations happen when writers or producers first have an idea for a certain concept. They then try to find an actor to fill, or re-fill, the role that makes the concept work. Actors normally fill roles defined by others—not the other way around. But with *Mannix*, like *Frasier*, the series was really all about the actor's definition of a character. In *Mannix*, that was coupled with going against type.

The original foundation for Joe Mannix might be thought of as an amalgam of two previously existing genres, that of *film noir* and the super agent. The *film noir* part of *Mannix* comes from the crime-drama driven story that a PI investigates, case by case. The most iconic example might be Humphrey Bogart's Sam Spade. The super agent part of *Mannix* comes from the high-tech organization that employs an individual, a maverick of sorts, who gets things done with a lot of physical action. The most iconic example is probably James Bond. In season 1 of *Mannix*, you have a PI-driven crime drama story of the week, but the PI is also a kind of super agent. He wears a sharp sports jacket, drives a custom sports car and clips an automatic gun right to the front of his belt. He is the go-to guy on the tough cases, the one who seems to be able to get things done in spite of the organization. The super agent part forces the action, the energy—but in *Mannix* the action is combined with the darkness of human nature that drives *film noir*. Joe Mannix, the PI, is not out to save the world, super agent style, but to solve one case at a time, to deal with one heart of darkness at a time. In season 1, *Mannix* combined the two genres.

Notice something interesting about Sam Spade and James Bond. They are both emotionally detached. They need this detachment for different reasons, but the end result is the same.

Sam Spade is detached because he's seen too much of the dark side of life. His premise is that he has to be that way in order to endure it all. Sam Spade is more a central figure to a type of story than he is a hero. He belongs to a class of crime dramas with cops and PIs that were somewhat interesting, but still secondary to the story being told around them. Their continued presence from story to story serves as a familiar backdrop around which other stories can be told, rather than their own. You don't really even want to know more about them, because they don't seem to want to know more about themselves.

James Bond is detached in order to be able to carry out his missions, in a technical, even cold and calculating, way. He is all about getting it done—and getting it done is best accomplished by just doing it without thinking about it too much. He is more central to the story than Sam Spade, because you want to see him succeed in his quest. But, especially by 1967 (in the Bond film series), you never really get to know him any better than Sam Spade. You get the sense that if he thinks too much about himself, he might no longer be able to carry out his missions.

As part PI and part super agent, Joe Mannix should be especially detached.

But, Mike Connors specifically wanted Joe Mannix to have emotion.

Connors got an opportunity to go in this direction due to a curious kind of flaw in the basic premise of *Mannix*, in its season 1 incarnation. There, Joe Mannix was a lone maverick in a large computer-oriented organization. But, he wasn't an organization man, nor did he particularly like computers. As a kind of talented, highly individualistic misfit, he wound up going against the organization—a lot—to the point of quitting several times and doing cases that his boss, Lew Wickersham (played by Joe Campanella and modeled after Creative Artist Agency's Lew Wasserman), did not want him to take. This seemed to happen every week.

If Joe Mannix was going to go against his boss and organization so much, he had to have a good reason. Viewers would only accept this if he was somehow on the right side of things—and so you had to care about his reasons enough to accept that they were more worthwhile than the organization's goals. That made no sense unless Joe Mannix was someone you cared about as a humanist at heart. Put another way, the tough guy with the heart big enough to quit his job and to put himself in personal peril to help someone in need had to have a pretty big emotional component.

In season 1, Connors seized those scenes.

In the process, Joe Mannix started to become his own, entirely new, type of character.

Within even just a few episodes, *Mannix* became a series where the viewer might well tune in and see what Joe Mannix was up to, instead of tuning into see a certain type of crime story or some action-driven plot. This became even more possible—and apparent—during the next seven seasons of *Mannix*, after Joe Mannix went out to work on his own at the start of season 2. After poor ratings nearly ended the series after the end of the first season, Lucille Ball saved only the main character of Joe Mannix, forcing him—and Connors—to figure things out completely on their own.[1.4]

It does not take much to watch season 1 of *Mannix*, enjoy the episodes, enjoy the character of Joe Mannix, and think that if they take away Lew Wickersham, the organization, the computers, the super agent angle and the simultaneous man vs. machine and man vs. organization angles, then the show is not likely to last very long. This is especially true in hindsight, informed by the track records of decades of television programs that did not survive such extensive re-tooling. Sure, Joe Mannix was likable in season 1. But few series survive even minor re-tooling. Lucille Ball wanted what amounted to an entirely different series. She thought people did not understand what the computers were all about. While that was largely true, what they did do was give Joe Mannix a reason to quit a lot—they gave him something against which he could stake his humanity as well as his maverick individuality. Of course, that was ultimately going to be the problem of the original premise of *Mannix* if nothing was done. How many times could Joe Mannix quit before he started to look like he didn't have enough guts to go out and work on his own? The original premise wasn't consistent with Joe Mannix's own nature. But, there was an interesting humanistic foundation in the character of Joe Mannix, mixed in with toughness. Lucille Ball could see it. She wanted to see more of the character.

So, in season 2 the premise was stripped down to be almost as bare as it could be, with Joe in an office with an upstairs apartment. His new office location moved to what amounts to an upscale shopping and business complex called the Paseo Verde—bare bones compared to the downtown office building that housed Intertect. Also gone was the custom car. It was replaced with a simpler (but still classy—now iconic) convertible. The gun became simpler as well, but only after a few episodes in which he still used the old one, still clipped to the front of his waist. Bringing something from his previous series, *Tightrope* (CBS-TV 1959-1960), Connors soon started to have Joe Mannix hide his new .38 revolver behind his waist the way his *Tightrope* character, Nick Stone, used to hide his gun when he worked undercover. All of the regulars and semi-regulars from season 1 were gone as well, including Wickersham, Pender, Parker and any of the other agents and secretaries who used to appear in the Intertect offices. Now, Joe only had Peggy Fair (Gail Fisher) in the office out front of his own, with her image taking the place of Joe Campanella in the new *Mannix* opening sequence.

Aside from Connors, the basic structure of the opening is one other thing that remained with the series as it moved into its second season. This was odd since the original opening would seem to have been stylistically inspired by a computer panel of that era, but the computers were now gone. The block colors, outlined in black, that rapidly change pattern, interspersed with black blocks and real-life, action images would seem to have been an artist's rendering of a computer panel changing its pattern of multi-colored, square and rectangular indicator lights on and off as the computer processes data. Even the rapid paced opening theme would seem to be stylistically capturing the audible pace of data processing on the large computers of that era. The idea of the opening seems to be that this man of action somehow merges with the machine. The classic *Mannix* grid that opens and closes each act of the episodes would thus seem to have been inspired by the same concept. In the first season of *Mannix* this made perfect sense, since man and machine are working together. After Joe goes out on his own, away from the computers he despised, how did this continue to make sense?

Aside from the unique style that was already identified with the show, one reason may be that the classic opening also kept up the image of all of that multi-dimensional action in those blocks. But it was also a way to keep Joe's eyes watching over it all.

One required revision in the opening gave the opportunity to include more action shots—and also more character definition. In the season 1 opening, the computer card that came out with "mannix" spelled out, all in all lower case, which introduced the name of the show, was replaced with the individual letters m-a-n-n-i-x spelled out one at a time with new action shots behind each one. The action shots were largely taken from season 1, and included the classic "*Mannix* roll" for the "m," taken from a stunt where Connors, himself, rolls out of a dune buggy onto the sand and comes up ready to shoot the bad guy. You can see his face in it, right behind the "m," and this was retained for the remaining seven seasons. Also, behind the second "n" is a frame of Joe mishandling some burnt toast in his new apartment. This is no longer a super agent; he is something of a regular guy now. But, right in the very name spelled out, that every man still has the credentials of a man of action—he's done that stuff already, bringing his season 1 résumé with him, and you can see it, right in the opening.

Here was Connors, essentially re-starting his series from scratch, playing a character starting his private business from scratch. But the character had the track record of being a super agent, and so he had to carry that into every scene, playing a combination of confident and vulnerable that seemed somehow real. Connors, himself, had apparently planned to do the series for only a few seasons in order to help his movie career.[1.5] Prior to *Mannix* he had both lead and supporting roles in several theatrical movies, but now he was working with actors and others who were associated only with TV. In those days, crossing over from movies to TV was rarer than it is now, but the effect only seemed to add a touch of realism to the way Connors was able to liken himself to Joe Mannix, with his résumé behind him.

Another change in the season 2 opening was the replacement of Joseph Campanella's image with that of Gail Fisher as the only regular supporting cast member. Otherwise, the rest of the opening stayed the same, except for that spelling out of the title one letter at a time and the inclusion of some racing scenes—done up with multiple camera angles.

But, the opening was different enough. A friend who remembers watching season 1 in its original run speaks of how shocking it was to see the opening of season 2 for the first time and to realize what it meant to see the computers disappear and the spelling out of m-a-n-n-i-x.

How could this series possibly survive?

Connors, in concert with the show's new producers, Ivan Goff and Ben Roberts, decided this guy Joe Mannix would have emotion. But, emotion was precisely what Sam Spade and James Bond did not *want* to have. Emotion was problematic because it left them vulnerable—and vulnerability in their jobs meant that they could get hurt—in both emotional and physical ways.

At this point, if someone forces a bet on this series, I'm betting against it making it to season 3.

Here was a series with a main character that was now separated from its basic premise, and with a star who wanted to try to bring emotion and vulnerability to a PI who is the central focus of a collection of dark stories and plots with lots of action. It sounds like a recipe for disaster. But Goff and Roberts were on board with the idea. These two men, drawing upon their backgrounds as playwrights, ultimately supervised and even re-wrote scripts over the next seven seasons.

The character did not change overnight though. Rather, he seemed to grow into becoming more emotional, more vulnerable, more relatable, and ultimately more heroic, over time.

Mannix was still supposed to be a show about mysteries and plot-driven action. The character exploration and development came at the margins—it was never supposed to be the basis for the show, how the show was classified. Character evolution was done so subtly that it was often conveyed in only purely visual ways, succeeding due to how fully the actors owned their characters. The way their faces and eyes responded to what was happening was often more revealing of character than the dialogue in the script. Viewers learned about the nature of character by paying attention to these non-verbal, visual cues at the margins of what the characters actually did, in a true parallel to the way we learn about the nature of character in real life.

By the time you get to the end of season 2, the character of Joe Mannix has evolved to the point that it almost appears as if he learned, even grew, by living out what happened to him and around him in each episode. This made him more human and more confident, simultaneously. Connors, as Joe Mannix, seemed to take on the changes a real Joe Mannix might if the fictional character lived out the episodes in the real world. He played the character as if he was paying attention to the life stories his alter ego was living.

Joe Mannix ultimately became more interesting to follow than the stories told around him.

There is a *TV Guide* article called "Six Authors in Search of a Character." The issue in which it appears features Connors on the cover in an action shot, showing time-elapsed movement.[1.6] Inside, the article has him sitting up on a gurney—they sure got that right—surrounded by some of the *Mannix* writers. The article consists of those writers discussing the writing process, relating it to their backgrounds. They do not state the obvious. This is a show where authors are in search of a character precisely because this is not a "concept show" any longer, not since the original concept of the series was dumped at the beginning of season 2. This show exists because its leading man interprets stories scripted with incredibly simple dialogue in ways that are entirely compelling, appealing to the audience—and if the writers are going to be successful, they need to fit to what they already see on the screen, giving fuel to its continuation and growth.

This is an amazing article, actually. One of the writers actually says he sees Joe Mannix as "The Christ Figure." He did not mean anything particularly religious by this, and it was said in a time before religious fundamentalism hit the mainstream in the U.S. and elsewhere. Back then, such a statement would not cause the angst it would today—from one point of view or another. People were more comfortable with religious and ideological pluralism. And if Joe Mannix invoked such rich symbolism in a modern-day setting and made it all seem fun—even appealing—what could the harm be? Viewers could always tune out.

People found it appealing.

For its first four seasons, the series was buried in what some consider one of the worst timeslots of the week, Saturday nights at 10:00 p.m. In those days, there was no way for viewers to record TV shows, so people had to be in front of their sets in order to see *Mannix* on the one night of the week they were most likely to go out. Yet the ratings for *Mannix* rose each of the next three years, and went higher still when the show was moved it to its best timeslot, where it stayed only one season, on Wednesday nights at 10:00 p.m. It was clear that people wanted to see Joe Mannix be Joe Mannix, and to discover what that meant. By season 4, Connors won the Golden Globe for playing the character.

There was Joe Mannix driving around in that convertible on the streets of L.A.—side streets, never the freeway—getting shot at, never seeming to get paid, escaping all kinds of harm after being knocked out so many times and in so many ways that it does not seem possible to have an exact count. Somehow, it wound up being believable because you *wanted* to believe it. It wasn't just because of the things this guy did. On some level, the viewer got that the real heroism was not just in the deeds, but also in a self-awareness that led to emotion which in turn led to vulnerability.

Joe Mannix seemed more aware of it all than Sam Spade or James Bond. A more self-aware hero is a more vulnerable hero. If he can find ways to keep engaging in the tougher stuff of life despite being vulnerable and emotionally involved, then he seems an even bigger hero.

It rang true. The exploits of Joe Mannix, in effect his résumé, while never mentioned in the later episodes, seemed to build into his reputation, and ultimately changed the way Connors played the role. It was almost as if the things he did as Joe Mannix gave him confidence as an actor which, in turn, gave the character more confidence. But the confidence was never the "above the fray" or cocky kind. He managed to stay everyman.

It probably only helped that the show was about a tough individual, and the show, itself, was demanding. Episodes were shot in six and a half or seven working days' time, with Connors in virtually every scene. Beyond this, *Mannix* was known for extremely tight editing, credited to executive producer Bruce Geller, who developed the show since series creators Levinson and Link departed soon after pitching the initial season 1 concept. This resulted in the need for around fifty camera set-ups a day compared to the average drama which would have around thirty camera set-ups a day.[1.7]

The filming wasn't tough just because of the schedule. *Mannix* combined all that action with all of those close-ups—which is where Connors seized the visual, emotional reactions in the plot-driven scripts.

As a single-camera drama, *Mannix* was filmed like a movie where each scene is broken down into parts filmed one at a time. This meant that scenes with interleaved shots had to be done in multiple takes where only part of the acting was filmed. For example, two actors' lines are interleaved by the editor later, with the camera first filming all of one of the actor's lines while the other actor is off camera, still saying his or her lines, and then the other way around. The resultant workload is much greater than when multiple cameras are used to surround a bunch of actors that fill a stage and act out a scene with each other. Combine that with all sorts of location shooting, action scenes, stunts, and the tight editing that resulted in the show having so many scenes to begin with—along with the grind of having to produce an episode in what amounted to a little over a week—and it meant that each on-camera take had to be accomplished in just one to two tries, just out of practical necessity.

What was conveyed in those close-ups had to be lived out right on the set.

The scripts, themselves, didn't have a whole lot in them. *Mannix* scripts are surprisingly thin. They contain dialogue that seems simple and predictable with just the barest kinds of description of setting. What's more, the scripts contain little, if any, description of what the characters are supposed to be thinking and feeling when they say the lines. So much of the heroic quality of character wound up right in those single-camera close-ups, in those single-take shots, right on the face, with emotion so often conveyed with no words at all. Since a crime drama was being subtly turned into a character study, making character the reason viewers tuned in each week, qualities of character had to be both strong and consistent at every opportunity.

A friend who was once a devoted fan of *The Fugitive*, the ABC-TV series from the 1960s, can't stand the ending of that TV show. He goes even further to say that the last episode actually ruined the entire series for him so that he can't even watch it on DVD anymore, despite once loving it. In that final episode, Richard Kimball's *Les Misérables*-inspired version of Inspector Javert, Lieutenant Philip Gerard, is finally convinced of Kimball's innocence. But, Gerard is wounded in the leg with the one-armed man trapped at the top of an amusement park tower. With Gerard handing Kimball his gun, Kimball goes up the tower to get the one armed man. My friend claims that had he stayed true to character, Richard Kimball would never have gone up the tower to get the one-armed man. The logical thing to do in that circumstance was to wait for the police to come—the guy was trapped up there. It made no sense to go up; just keep the gun down there and go get the police. Kimball's demeanor through the five years he was on the run was to be calm, logical. This was a move based more on passion.

I pointed out to my friend that Joe Mannix would have gone up that tower because Joe never waited for someone to come when he could take care of matters himself. If there was a bad guy there, Joe was going to go get him. A running gag at the end of many episodes of *Mannix*, one that began with Lt. Adam Tobias (played by Robert Reed), is that Joe always got the bad guy and had things under control by the time the police arrived. The standard joke went something like Joe saying to Adam, "One of these days you're going to be just a few seconds too late," to which Lt. Tobias would reply with a brilliantly understated kind of near-shrug. This is, of course, just another example of Joe being Joe. You tuned in each week to discover what that was, and see it in action. You learn that Joe is passionate. He is independent. He is vulnerable. He is a maverick. And he can take care of himself.

Mannix fans just knew that, each week, Joe was going to be Joe. Watching the show during its first run, from week to week, the thought never once occurred that it was possible to see Joe do anything inconsistent with his own nature. How could he?

The *Mannix* season 1 DVDs have some "extras." These include voiceovers for a couple of the episodes and promos for the series. In addition, they have Connors doing audio introductions, probably recorded in early 2008, which amount to *TV Guide* synopsis-level descriptions of each episode. Curiously, when he describes an episode, he routinely says, "In this episode, I ..." or, "In this episode, my ..." referring to Joe Mannix as if it he was referring to himself. It comes across in a completely genuine, almost off-hand, way—not the least bit wry.

One of the captions for *Mannix* that is still out there is that Joe Mannix takes beatings and bullet wounds in stride. You get the sense, right on his face, and right in his demeanor, that Connors lived that way, was the product of a tougher kind of America, where tough was not the same as powerful or mean, but just that—tough—not for sale, always ready to take a beating for a good cause, but never stopped by that beating from fighting the next time. His fight is coupled with a curious kind of acceptance of it being a part of a larger process of living a good life. Connors is quoted as saying that he used to fight in school on a weekly basis, the result of growing up Armenian-American in Fresno.[1.8] In *Mannix*, that spirit not only comes across, but you wind up *getting* it—even if you don't always get it right away.

There is a scene in a season 3 episode, "A Penny for the Peep Show," where Joe, Peggy and a client are held hostage in Joe's office by three thugs with guns. When one of the thugs starts to handle Peggy, Joe grabs the guy and punches him right in the gut, causing the guy to grab his gun and point it at Joe, ready to shoot him. Joe avoids getting shot only because one of the other thugs stops it.

Okay, it's cool that Joe stood up for Peggy like that, but you'd think Joe would have learned his lesson—he is outmanned and out gunned. He escaped harm this time only through sheer luck. Only a few seconds later, when a different thug goes after the female client, ready to take her up to Joe's apartment, Joe grabs the guy and pushes him into another guy, thereby knocking down two of the thugs, only to be knocked unconscious by the third. The scene ends with Joe lying on the ground, knocked out when the classic *Mannix* grid appears to end the scene. It hardly seems to have helped for him to fight like that, only to wind up that way.

But you just can't watch that scene without somehow loving the fight in him.

He fights not for the sake of fighting, but because people he feels protective of are being mistreated right in front of him. He conveys the spirit that what happens to him is less important than the fact that he fights for others in those circumstances.

I had watched that scene for the first time during its first run, when I was eight years old. A more solid memory of it—since faded by the passage of time—was undoubtedly formed during a later viewing, probably sometime during the ABC syndication run. When I watched that episode again in early 2011—after a passage of thirty years or more—I wound up saying right to the TV screen, out loud with no one there to hear me, "That wasn't too smart, Joe."

Of course, that was said with a big smile on my face. After all, I felt so much smarter than my hero, my myth of choice, in that brief moment.

The moment of intellectual superiority did not last.

Because right after saying that, sort of stunned at my own reaction, I thought about my own life, the countless times I did things that were similarly not too smart, but which had just that kind of fight, often for reasons of utter unfairness, sometimes even anger at that unfairness, just as depicted symbolically in that episode. Some of those times I was often, metaphorically, knocked out. The utter likability of Joe Mannix in those parallel situations is probably what enabled that better part of me to exist in those moments for which I am now so grateful.

That likability worked to even greater effect, ultimately getting to the viewer in even deeper ways, when Joe Mannix wound up in physical peril. When Joe was blinded, drugged, shot, beaten, or involved in some sort of vehicular crash (from car to airplane—both were in the series), you always—*always*—knew he was going to get out of it, and even be healed by the next week. But, you wanted to see how he felt about it, how Peggy felt about it, how Art Malcolm and Adam Tobias felt about it. All of the characters demonstrated depth of emotion that seemed to convey acceptance that all sorts of stuff was going to happen to Joe just because of the way he was—an implicit awareness existed that he could be seriously hurt or killed at any moment. If that happened, everyone cared—including Joe. But it was somehow simultaneously accepted as a part of his life. Joe wasn't Joe unless he got into those situations in the first place. Joe wasn't Joe unless he wound up getting hurt in the process of engagement. And Joe wasn't Joe unless what happened to him and around him mattered to him. In addition, his supporting cast conveyed ways they cared about what happened to him that mirrored your own. What happened to him was going to happen to you—if you could manage to find that better part of yourself and risk being really engaged in life. Since the way that all worked out in *Mannix* seemed strangely beautiful, it made the truly difficult seem truly desirable.

You get it because he gets it. You can see that he gets it, right in the eyes—the eyes that remained in the opening titles for all eight seasons.

The eyes were so important in *Mannix* that one entire episode of season 7 was built around them. While many story types are re-done across different episode-driven series through the years (hero goes blind, is falsely imprisoned, goes back to his hometown, loses his memory, etc.), there is one *Mannix* storyline that, to my knowledge, has not been tried by any other series. In season 7, "The Dark Hours" has Joe Mannix shot and dumped down a hillside, left for dead, right in the opening scene. Even his great buddy, LAPD Police Lt. Art Malcolm, thinks Joe is dead when he is discovered in the morning, and is diverted from being taken to the morgue only at the last moment when an ambulance attendant sees a couple of fingers moving. This might be considered shock value—and it is shocking—let alone that the theme is pretty darn close to portraying someone rising from the dead. But it also serves to set up what the episode is really all about—Joe lying there in a hospital bed, trying to figure out what happened the night before, and actually even trying to help someone else. Through flashbacks, interleaved with scenes of Joe in that bed, we mostly see close-ups of Connors' eyes. There is a mask covering his nose and mouth almost the whole time, so Connors has to act all sorts of things *with eyes alone*. Undoubtedly, that episode is a main reason he was nominated for an Emmy that season, which was late in the series' run.

In most of the episode, Joe can't even speak; he says very few words from that hospital bed before the final scene, and barely moves a finger or even his head. There is virtually no facial expression he can make. The flashbacks that are interleaved with the hospital scenes are just that—flashbacks. They do nothing to tell the story of what Joe is thinking in that bed.

His acting in that episode was so good that you could see not only the pain and confusion about what happened to him, but you sensed what it felt like for Joe to be trapped in that bed because he was so severely injured. You got the sense that he hated being there not because he was afraid to die, but because he couldn't move. He had work to do—unfinished business. It was all conveyed in the eyes.

Now, just think about this—you got the sense that the hero you identify with is not afraid to die, but just hates being in a situation where he can't move and can't help. You see this right in his eyes. No words convey this, but it is there for you to get, if you let yourself.

In that same episode is one scene where Joe wakes up after being out of it the night before—we come back from a commercial break where the last we saw Joe he seemed to not be doing so well. The doctor greets him with a line, "Welcome back, we almost lost you last night." But that is only after Joe wakes up. And when he does, he does so very, very slowly, conveying in every way that the previous night was a struggle for which he wasn't even awake. This is the slowest we've seen Joe wake up over the entire series run, wordlessly conveying the extremity of his situation—and we've seen him wake up so many times in the series that you'd think you'd have seen every variation by now.

Most actors playing scenes where they regain consciousness tend to open their eyes and start talking, just saying their lines, sort of getting it over with. They seem to need to do this because they seem most comfortable only when speaking dialog.

Since few people in series TV have been knocked unconscious as many times as Joe Mannix, few people have awakened on screen as many times as Mike Connors. When Joe Mannix wakes up, Connors does it slowly, always conveying a sense of world weariness and acceptance right in the eyes. This generally takes up many seconds of airtime, when no words are spoken at all.

Of course, waking up is always about the eyes. Those eyes tended to convey a general sense of confusion, a kind of "Where am I?"—although that phrase is rarely uttered—along with a general sense of a "Here we go again" kind of acceptance that says, in effect, "This is life, and it's just happened to me again—and it won't be the last time either."

How much more symbolic does story get than the need to wake up in the first place?

Another signature episode of the series, the one that many believe defined the show and took it to the next level, is "The Sound of Darkness" from season 3. In this episode, a bullet that grazed Joe's temple leaves him psychosomatically blind—scared to the point he couldn't stand what he saw, so his "eyes closed." With no idea if or when his sight will come back, we see Joe blind for most of the episode—only to set up one of the very best episode endings in all of series TV. This episode is so powerful that some who are not familiar with the series know of it as the episode where "the guy goes blind."

Curiously, the main hero going blind is a standard kind of episode, especially in those days. But the way it was handled in *Mannix* was so different that a direct comparison between *Mannix* and the way other series handled the same kind of story reveals just how special *Mannix* is. In the episode, after being shamed by his loyal secretary, Peggy—a real gutsy move on Connors' part where reality and story merge—Joe winds up trying to take on a killer on his own, even while blind. Some speculate that a short lived series, *Longstreet* (ABC-TV 1971-1972), was inspired by this one episode of *Mannix*.

"The Sound of Darkness" is, in many ways, the complete opposite of "The Dark Hours"—even though both are all about the eyes. In "The Sound of Darkness," Connors' eyes are expressionless for most of the hour. His handicap in this episode—an expressive actor prevented by the story from using his eyes to convey emotion—aligns with Joe's handicap as an investigator unable to use his eyes to assess his surroundings. This ultimately makes the episode more poignant. Plenty of actors who play blind just put on a wooden face to make it seem like being blind and being emotionless go together. By contrast, Connors manages to convey all sorts of emotion on his face while playing blind, ranging from self-pity to frustration to happiness. We see some of this emotion in a famous scene with him and Peggy walking on the beach—a scene that includes an oft-examined sunbather that seems to have an entirely nude breast right in the foreground of one of the shots. He somehow makes his eyes stare off into space while this is going on, thereby avoiding having to look at the breast.

Still, in the episode, you can't help but notice how he looks so different from the way he normally does, despite allowing his face to convey all sorts of emotion. So much of him is missing because he can't use his eyes. At the end, when he looks like himself again after regaining his sight, just seeing him back to using eyes again winds up being moving—you can see how much they really mean to him. Both actor and audience are relieved that Connors has his eyes back for acting purposes as well—so that he gets to play a sighted Joe Mannix again. If it wasn't established before, by the time "The Sound of Darkness" is over, you are watching *Mannix* because of Joe Mannix. What did happen to that big pile of money that was supposed to be in that building where Joe was shot anyway?

Connors was asked what he thought might have ultimately happened to the character he created after *Mannix* ended. His reply was that he thought Joe Mannix was still out there, working somewhere; that he was a "decent, dignified man."[1.9]

Now, the word "decent" is fairly consistent with virtually all of the role models on TV. Decency is really just a way of saying that behavior meets established standards of morality, however invested some heroes are in achieving those standards. But, decency only goes so far.

All sorts of people can manage to think of themselves as decent and rationalize not doing very much, especially when confronted with injustice. Decent people, by and large, can get away with being decent simply by doing no harm, at least by today's standards.

But that word "dignified" is so much harder to define. Definitions vary, as they tend to, with dignity ultimately connoting nobility, coupled with self-worth.

Consider that for a moment.

Dignity implies a kind of nobility not just due to having been born into a station in life, but being a higher class of individual, set apart, because of a combination of deeds and self-recognition.

The coupling of these two seems essential to dignity—the doing and the seeing of oneself in the doing.

Dignity requires a combination of deeds with enough self-awareness in order to properly place one's own value on those deeds—one without the other results in something so much less, even monstrous. The implication is that in order to achieve both, the deeds have to be deemed worthy by the person doing them—not by any organization, or really anyone else at all, just the individual.

This is quite a high standard really.

In order to have dignity, we have to come up with something that we fairly and independently judge as being both worthy of our doing as well as personally difficult for us to do—and then actually do it.

Dignity requires true independence of thought in coming up with our own definition of something worthwhile to do in the first place, as well as overcoming our inner demons in order to survive all sorts of push back and failure so that we can persevere in so doing. In this process, we need to fairly evaluate ourselves, so that we can say that what we did was both consistent with our gifts, but also challenging for us, personally.

Beyond that, our own ability to fairly see ourselves takes guts. And so, it takes guts to grant ourselves our own dignity, because, since self-awareness is part of it, no one else can grant it for us.

Dignity only comes on purpose. It only comes to the self-aware individual, the person who can see themselves fairly, as if looking in from the outside. It takes guts. It never comes without cost, a struggle—and probably ongoing struggle at that.

If we want to live a dignified life, we are surely going to get hurt along the way, and need to find a way to not only be okay with that, but to get up the next day, ready to engage again.

It is curious that Connors would have used this word to describe his creation.

Dignity really is such a difficult concept to define.

You really only know it when you see it.

and now, back to mannix

Chapter 2
The Character of the Character

In season 8 of *Mannix* is a scene from the episode "The Survivor Who Wasn't." The basic story is that Joe Mannix is hired by Mrs. Anderson, a woman who has issues of her own with trustworthiness, to find out if her husband, who ostensibly survived an airplane crash requiring face-altering plastic surgery, was really her husband. Joe is curled up on the couch in his Spanish-Mediterranean styled office, having come down from his upstairs apartment to meet his friend, police Lt. Art Malcolm. Joe is in his pajamas and bathrobe, holding a towel filled with ice behind his head. The night before he had been taken from his office by a couple of thugs to a warehouse and hit over the head with a piece of pipe. Art, one of his best buddies on the police force, had found him.

In this scene, the next morning, Art tells Joe he can no longer help him in the way he usually does, because he is getting pressure from both the FBI and his superiors in the police force to stay off the case himself. Art was also told to warn his friend to stay off the case, and specifically told to tell Joe to "Get interested in another case. They don't want to see or hear any more from you—and they meant it."

After some pushback, Art starts to yell at Joe, who is trying to cover his ears, presumably due to a headache, "You're off the Anderson case. And you'll stay off because you'll get no more help from me, or from the Feds. You're solo—against a brand-new roughhouse Syndicate!"

After more concerned yelling at Joe—sweet reward for those came to know and love these characters over the previous six years—Art leaves. On the way out Art tells Peggy, who is in her customary outer office, to make sure Joe gets some rest. Art is still yelling all of this, which is atypical of Art's normal calm demeanor.

As soon as Art leaves, Joe calls for Peggy, who comes in from her outer office. Joe wants to find out if Peggy knows the whereabouts of an underground figure they once helped, and who might be able to help them this time. Now Peggy starts to yell at Joe, who is still in the fetal position on the couch, "Joe, for heaven's sake, didn't you hear what Art just said?"

Joe replies, "Yeah. He can't help us anymore."

Joe continues to ask Peggy to pursue the contact.

Peggy replies, "Joe, he said you're off the Anderson case."

Joe replies, "Yeah, so did Anderson. I'll tell you what I told him. My client is *Mrs.* Anderson."

The next scene quickly cuts to Joe, back on the case, meeting with Mrs. Anderson.

And so Joe Mannix gets beaten, bloodied, admonished by his best friends, and warned by two governmental organizations to stay away. He has been hurt and he is alone. People are still after him, willing to hurt him some more. And yet, he is willing to put everything he has on the line, including his reputation and his life. He does so not to save the world, or because some organization told him to, or even so that he does not disappoint his friends. He can't even fully trust his client, since there is some question about her mental stability. Her presumed husband warns Joe that he should not believe his own client, and makes a good case for that. But because her stability is merely an open question, not fully assured one way or the other, Joe tells Mrs. Anderson, "You're my client. I'm trying very hard to believe you."

If Joseph Campbell was right and heroes do, indeed, have 1,000 faces, with those faces going back to the very dawn of civilization,[2.1] the next question is, do the differences in those faces matter?

The scene has a police Lieutenant (Art Malcolm), a widowed single mother supporting herself (Peggy Fair) and Joe Mannix. It wouldn't be too far a stretch to say that, by today's standards, both Art Malcolm and Peggy Fair, who appeared in the series more than any character other than Joe Mannix, qualify as heroes. During the course of the show's run, they did brave things, each of them, at different times. They didn't run from danger. They had high ethical standards. They showed some toughness. They were always there for Joe, one way or another. Why was Joe Mannix the clear hero among them, even in just that one scene, set apart from the other recurring characters in the same series?

It goes well beyond the writers of the episodes pointing to the character of Joe Mannix and saying, in so many ways, "He is the hero of this show—the one you want to follow." Even if the writers used devices to point to Joe Mannix as the hero, there is a reason they could do that. You see him as the hero just because you do. You seldom ever consider why. And in turn, it orients you in ways that often go far deeper than words can describe.

If we really can, and in some ways must, implicitly rank the bigger hero among the mythical characters in that one scene, then we must implicitly rank the mythical heroes we see throughout our lifetime in movies, on TV, in plays, in cartoons, in books, or even just in stories told to us before we could read. If we do that within the confines of one episode of one TV series or even across all of the heroes to which we are exposed in one lifetime, then it seems plausible that heroes could have subtly different faces from one generation to the next, with subtly different qualities. If that is true, then when heroes in our popular culture become less, we become less.

When I was growing up, *Mannix* was just there, one of many popular TV shows of its era that I watched. I happened to like it more than anything else I saw, and there was not really a close second. But I found it in the same way I subsequently found other characters that appeared in the popular culture, and implicitly evaluated them, one against the other, in my highly impressionable mind. In a strange sort of parallel to my growing into adulthood, subsequent characters in the popular culture seemed somehow smarter, or move evolved than Joe Mannix.

One example is Jim Rockford, of *The Rockford Files* (NBC-TV 1974-1980). He seemed to be, even to me, somehow an evolution of Joe Mannix. He seemed wiser because he was far more cynical, more of an anti-hero, and, despite the show's many car chases that may have been inspired by *Mannix*, preferred using his wits to outsmart the villains without getting hurt so much, without risking himself quite as much. He lived in a trailer and seemed more down to earth than Joe Mannix. That, somehow, seemed smarter, more realistic. My budding adult mind found it hard to refute: Even I, someone who could not have loved *Mannix* more, thought *Mannix* must be kid stuff. Apparently I was not alone. A search of The Web finds numerous descriptions of Jim Rockford as an "evolution" or "perfection" of Joe Mannix. Baby Boomers would seem to identify with Rockford far more than Mannix.

It is telling that Jim Rockford exists as a "negative reaction" to Joe Mannix. *The New York Times* obituary of the creator of *The Rockford Files*, Steven J. Cannell, explicitly discusses this, describing Jim Rockford as a "reluctant detective who would rather crack wise than fight." The article credits the series as "helping to signal a cultural shift away from the perfect physical and moral specimens of the movies and early television and toward more realistic heroes, the kind viewers had come to expect, given the harder-edged reality they saw on the evening news." It also quotes Cannell, from a 1999 interview: "Culture changed, and as that happened, so did our need for a hero. That square-jawed good guy began to look like an idiot to us." [2.2]

The square-jawed good guy idiot was, apparently, Joe Mannix.

Cannell's *Wall Street Journal* obituary also quotes the *Rockford* creator: "I was watching a show called 'Mannix,' the private detective of the day. A little girl came into Mannix's office and told him her mother was missing. She says 'I need help finding my mother' and he listens to her tale of woe and finally says 'Let me see if I can help.' The little girl says 'How much does it cost?' Joe Mannix says, 'How much do you have' and the girl pulls out a quarter. 'Exactly the right amount,' he tells her. I watched that and I thought to myself what a pile of bull sh—. I thought my guy would say 'Did my Dad put you up to this?'"[2.3] Never mind that this scene never does happen in *Mannix*. Joe Mannix never asked any kid how much money they had to pay him. He did work for kids, for free, as a highly qualified professional who does *pro bono* work will sometimes do. Cannell further goes on to describe Rockford as a guy who always wants to be paid and who quits every time he's threatened.

So here, side by side, are two heroes to be compared, virtual contemporaries. One, Joe Mannix, was more valued by what Tom Brokow has called "The Greatest Generation," who survived The Great Depression and helped to win World War II. The other, the Baby Boomers, defined all their lives as a cohort of children, identify better with a reluctant hero who always wants to be paid and runs when threatened. Rockford is, simultaneously, a reflection of who we became, as well as a reinforcement of it. That is the way cultural myths work. This feedback effect is one thing that makes them so powerful.

But, I could never get my love of *Mannix* out of my head, and never did find ways to like Jim Rockford or any of his cohorts or follow-ons. They seemed to be cut from the same mold as a kind of "gifted child," cracking wise and staying above or outside the fray—anywhere but completely invested. Those wise guys seemed, to me at least, to substitute cleverness for real wisdom. And they wound up being all around me in my real life, taking over positions of power as the Greatest Generation passed the baton to their economically Booming Babies, who seemed to want their myths to confirm a sense of entitlement, rather than to inspire them. We still seem to be living out this parent-child relationship, even into the next generation, caught in perpetual psychological youth.

An example that examines a single character in a movie, and the implications of a moment in that movie, illustrates how certain qualities of heroic character help us achieve psychological adulthood while others cannot. By focusing on a single character, the example separates heroic properties from different instances of heroes. *A Few Good Men* is a 1992 movie about a smart, young and gifted lawyer, Lt. Daniel Kaffee (played by Tom Cruise), who knows Col. Nathan Jessup (played by Jack Nicholson) is a bad guy. The challenge for Kaffee is how to bring Jessup to justice. In this story we go through Kaffee's struggles to figure out how to nail a guy we know is guilty. We want Kaffee to succeed—he is the clear hero of the tale. We get to the climax, where Kaffee is cross-examining Jessup on the stand. Kaffee brings in a potential bluff, and makes one attempt to outwit Jessup. It almost works—but not quite. There are two parts to what happens next.

The first is the way Kaffee almost manages to trap Jessup. He employs logic. And, this is clever. The first time I saw the movie, I could not believe I did not see this argument coming. Kaffee really was quite gifted to come up with this argument—and he was the only one that did. His cohorts, Lt. Cdr. JoAnne Galloway (played by Demi Moore) and Lt. Sam Weinberg (played by Kevin Pollak) did not. If all Kaffee had to do was make this clever argument in order to get Jessup, it would have made for an entertaining movie. Kaffee would have gotten the bad guy and been the clear winner. We should all want to be like him; he is smart, he used his gifts to good ends, there was something of a struggle, and he won. He did not risk much in the process; it was seemingly a clear-cut intellectual feat. And had the story only gone that far, I might have seen that movie a single time and, once I knew the argument, probably never have wanted to see the movie again.

The second part of that climax is why I want to see the movie over and over again. Because the second part is established by the premise that if Kaffee goes after Jessup, and does not get him, he is going to pay with his life. He may not die, but he is going to be subject to court martial and most likely dishonorably discharged. He will be ruined.

Even the fiery Galloway tells Kaffee, right before the climactic scene, to not go after this guy if he is not absolutely sure he can get him. Galloway, in her official duties, would have to go after Kaffee if he tries and fails—and there is a lot of doubt about Kaffee's ability to succeed.

The movie establishes how Kaffee fails to get Jessup the first time he tries. At this point, the third defense lawyer sitting in the courtroom, Weinberg, shakes his head "no," right at Kaffee, to warn him to go no further. He is trying to protect Kaffee. The judge has warned Kaffee that if he continues to go after this highly regarded senior officer, Kaffee is going to face severe consequences from the court. In addition, the lawyer for the prosecution of the two guys Kaffee is defending, Capt. Jack Ross (played by Kevin Bacon), is Kaffee's friend and he warns Kaffee, knowing that if he goes too far, his friend is going to pay dearly.

All of this leads to a moment. Nothing is said. Kaffee just stands there. It is silent and it is visual. It all comes down to him.

Kaffee is all alone. And he has to choose. He either risks everything and goes after this bad guy, or the two men he is defending are going to pay with *their* lives—and those guys are already risking everything in order to try to expose the truth, which is that they are being framed by a powerful military officer. Furthermore, an evil man, who does not seem to be able to distinguish right from wrong, will continue to be in a powerful place, potentially doing more harm in the future if Kaffee does not do something more. This man's very power is the reason Kaffee can't go after him without extreme risk to himself.

This moment, this point in this move, is a basis for comparison of different heroic molds. Kaffee got to this point precisely because he has special abilities—special intellect and training. He is gifted. If he did not have those gifts in the first place, then he would not hold the potential key to getting this guy—the key that, if it does not work, will ruin his very life. Those very gifts are what placed him in this particular position of responsibility. But intellect, cleverness, and cracking wise only get Kaffee so far. He comes to realize this.

In a moment, he separates from the myth of the gifted child to the myth of a heroic adult. He decides to risk everything in order to do the right thing. When he does, he becomes a psychological adult, a bigger hero than if he had been able to get Jessup by using wits alone. Had the movie ended with Kaffee able to get Jessup using the wits he displayed just prior this moment in the climax, it would have been like so many others in our popular culture these past forty years, depicting heroes that outwit, outsmart, out-clever their foes. Those movies depict heroes that confirm our desire to feel special. They send a message that overcoming is tantamount to displaying cleverness, and life is seen as a kind of game to be won, and if lost, then not all that much is really lost.

But the second part of the climax, the one that includes the decision point and the willingness to risk everything in order to do the right thing, is in the same spirit as the entire series that is *Mannix*. *A Few Good Men* has been described as a "coming of age" movie—a term used when a child becomes an adult. The whole point of the movie is that very few people would actually do what Kaffee does. The implication, all too real, is that too many people never quite become psychological adults. When the movie began, Kaffee was the myth of the "gifted child." His wits and ability to skim the surface of life by using them are well established. If the movie had played out only to the first part of the climax, he would have stayed a gifted child. But because he had the guts to put himself, and all of those gifts, on the line in order to do the right thing, he became a man—in the symbolic, mythical sense. In that moment, Kaffee becomes a bigger hero. And because Joe Mannix is not only willing to risk himself in order to do the right thing, but actually does get hurt in the process, he is a bigger hero, still.

Only as an adult, only after facing all sorts of trials over a long life, did I come to realize that my long-held view of *Mannix*—that it was kid stuff and *Rockford* was a more intellectual, more adult, more evolved view of a hero—was completely backwards.

Joe Mannix is a mythical hero for adults, those who transcend the realm of the clever, gifted child. The series portrayed the beauty and desirability to have the guts to put oneself on the line as a tough individual who does the right thing, come what may, amazingly, in so many different ways, that it never got tired, stale or old. *Mannix* took the premise of the tough individual to the next mythical level—that the hero was vulnerable enough to not just risk but also actually get hurt along the way, including both emotional and physical pain. A willingness to endure pain in the pursuit of some greater good is what may be at the very heart of becoming a psychological adult, the process Carl Jung would refer to as that of individuation.[2.4]

I see all kinds of people who have all sorts of gifts, and who "struggle" with them—to a degree. They may try to do the right thing—and certainly do a great job convincing themselves of that—all the while preserving so much of what they have. But as a culture, as a nation, as a people, we don't value struggle anymore—not our own, nor even that of others. We prize outcomes, and pretty much only outcomes. We seem to have come to believe that the more intelligent a person is, the more they should be able to enjoy outcomes that provide high quality of life, particularly in the absence of struggles that risk that very quality of life.

How ridiculous that is, even on the surface. But that is the message in any myth that portrays sufficient goodness in learned skills, inherent talents, or some other excuse to be above the fray.

Of the many important properties of myth, perhaps the one most significant is that the myths that surround us, especially the popular ones, while we are most often not even aware of their impact on us, can create *setpoints*. A setpoint is, roughly, a point that allows a kind of separation to take place on either side—sifting things from one side to the next, with more going to one side or the other, depending upon where the setpoint is. I heard someone describe recent politics as tantamount to the process of reading setpoints more than actually setting them. This makes the primary role of the politician that of tapping into and reading the general feeling of the public more than affecting it, thus more about collective interpretation that requires cleverness and focused on winning, than personal investment that requires risk and focused on doing good.

These past decades, things that seem smart to us may not really be.

My chosen field is not only a highly intellectual field but also historically one of the least welcoming for women and with no answers for this in sight. Its culture is bad and the culture lacks heroes.

Through the lens of time, it is clear to me that I never would have gone into this kind of professional field if I wasn't heavily influenced by my childhood myth of choice. I seemed to pick up on the symbolic foundational properties of that myth more than the more superficial ones, and so I was ready to do something hard, take my lumps, hang in there and fight back—at times. In addition I was willing to do this alone—to the extent that was possible. Without painting myself out to be more than I really am, while I am proud of when I did do those things, it is also clear to me now that I could have done much, much better along the way had I better understood the properties of my childhood myth, as well as how his absence affected me, especially in the presence of the changing myths in popular culture that seemed to send a very different message about how to live a good life.

When I made my choice of profession, I knew it would be hard, especially because of the culture. But I had faith that, even if there were a lot of "bad guys" out there, there would be sufficient good guys to make it worth my while—worth all that I put into it, and all of the risk that entailed. I never thought that the good guys would outnumber the bad guys, but I thought there would be enough truly good guys, just enough heroes, just enough of a setpoint to make a difference.

Now, I didn't expect to see Joe Mannix there. Even from an early age I understood the broad dramatic outlines of mythical character, as most children do, and must. But I expected to see more people with some of the qualities that prompted the existence of a character like that in the first place. Another property of myths is that they don't pop out of nowhere. Their foundational elements arise from qualities already in the culture.

I went into my current profession later in life, having had a family crisis affect all sorts of things for a long time. Being at the tail end of the Baby Boomers to begin with, the older Baby Boomers were already established in power. Now I can reflect on the TV myths, "in the room" with the room representing a typical meeting place, symbolic of a powerful subset of the people in my particular department or area of specialization who might get together and review things—people with all sorts of ability to influence outcomes, quite subjectively.

There were all sorts of buddy combinations in the room. Buddy combinations seem to enable people to do the right thing only to a limited extent—to the extent the "right thing" is already defined. For example, buddies do a great job helping each other enforce "the law" but not a great job recognizing injustice in the first place—deeper levels of injustice. That next level of awareness of the "right thing" seems to arise solely in individuals who learn to think for themselves, and who also have the guts to do that in the first place, all alone.

Buddy combinations are notorious for being stable configurations, so anyone who wants to get in there and go against the grain is going to need to stay away from them. Individuals are unlikely to appeal to buddies and may even make them angry because individuals make buddies take a look at themselves, however subconsciously. This effect is even worse for groups. When many people form a common identity, their common enemy tends to be individuality.

It surprised me to go back and think about the more individual myths at work behind the people in the room, those who were not paired up, or who did not give themselves over to group-think. And so I thought of those TV characters of the late 1970s and early 1980s that I knew.

Kojak was in the room, for sure, and probably running the meeting. If you shaved the heads and gave a lollipop to a few of those guys, you'd get the same thing—loud, to the point, the center of attention, lots of personality of a sort that appeals to the impressionable. They enforce the law of the land.

Rockford was there, aplenty, those who were not only reluctant but disdainful, distancing themselves from complete investment by viewing life as a parody. They wanted to be paid and wanted to run from fights.

Magnum was definitely in the room—lots of those. I've seen websites use the word "puerile" to describe Magnum. It seems to fit a hero type who drives a fancy car he does not own and lives in a mansion for free while he hangs out with his "good ole' boy" buddies a lot—which seems to fit a generation whose very name is derived from being the children of another.

At the opposite end of the spectrum from that of the "good ole' boys" is that of the intellectually entitled individual, and those were also in the room, aplenty. These are guys like Colombo, guys who dressed a little differently, just to maintain some uniqueness, and were too clever by half. They could take people down, but tended to do so as more of a game. A myth dominant in the present day is that of the creative and talented person who is simply identified by others for being so brilliant and thus lauded for possessing some innate, special ability. Baby Boomers are passing this view of specialness and entitlement on to their offspring. They tend to want their kid to be considered "special" for some innate reason far more than they want their kid to work hard to do the right thing, despite the consequences. Parents seem to want their offspring to be born into good lives, rather than struggle to actually lead them, let alone struggle to understand what leading a good life even means.

Operating under the "gifted child" myth, the people "in the room" would produce work that pleased others, which made it, by definition, nothing very special—but very rewarding. They seemed to fail to consider that, through all ages, over all time, the only truly significant intellectual work anyone has ever done has come only after someone has (a) struggled with themselves to arrive at something truly new, and

(b) struggled with the backlash that always comes from putting some truly new idea out there.

I never saw Joe Mannix in the room—nothing like him, over all of those years. Even calibrating for the huge variances that are likely to go with the type of person attracted to my profession of choice, if I am honest with myself, I expected to see something of his ilk there. But I never did.

No one seemed to have a priority of doing the right thing—come what may, and at personal risk if not personal cost—and to fight injustice when they saw it. They did see injustice, at least some of them. But they seemed to feel that injustice was not their problem.

Incredibly, for many of these people the actual personal cost in absolute terms for fighting injustice would have been minimal—not only no bodily damage of any kind, they wouldn't even have lost their jobs. Yet they simply weren't willing to take a beating of any kind, to go against the grain, and certainly not willing or able to fight for much of anything that wasn't directly in their own self-interests. If they couldn't be perceived by the powers that be as somehow clever, or a part of a club, they simply walked away and let whatever was going to happen, happen.

And so, after decades of wondering what the heck must be wrong with me to have put myself in a situation like this, in a world dominated by other myths that reinforce far easier forms of existence, I re-discovered my childhood myth of choice. To my astonishment, he contains values that not only I did not encounter in my profession, but which I wish I had in greater measure myself, even as I had some of them, all along, buried deep, well below my awareness.

As will be described in more detail later, *Mannix* has some authenticity behind it. This includes the reason Gail Fisher is even a part of the series to begin with—her presence, and the way Mike Connors put his own series on the line in order for her to be in *Mannix*, was enough to solidify all sorts of things for me. That kind of behavior is something rarely, if ever, encountered anymore.

I wish there were more Joe Mannix types around and not just because they might have helped me.

If life has no meaning without struggles and our preferred heroes are the ones who manage to avoid real struggle through some special gifts or wit or attitude, then what does that say about us?

One thing it might say is that whatever gifts we have been given, we're not using them enough. If that is the case, then the reason may be that we are not motivated to do the hard things by our myths anymore. Our tastes in heroes have changed, ultimately affecting us in ways that are not immediately obvious.

Joe Mannix is a hero who is not out to save the world; his client in the scene described above is just one person, and her situation would seem to be important only to her. Nor is he always able to defeat his foes using wits alone—he gets beat up and even shot a lot. Nor is he part of any kind of group—the point could not be made clearer that he is all alone, time after time. Nor does he have superhuman powers or abilities—he is an ordinary guy. Nor does he have access to special gadgets—all Joe really has are Peggy finding information on the phone, his car, his fists and his gun. Nor did he emerge from any kind of elite school or training—he didn't go to Harvard or emerge from Special Forces training. Nor does he use detachment to succeed—he takes quite a bit of punishment, both physical and emotional. Nor does he subscribe to or enforce a collective ethical directive—he goes against the law and uses his fists and gun when he deems they are needed, relying upon his own, internal moral compass.

The real mystery here is why you identify this guy as a hero at all, at least by today's standards.

And yet, here is a hero who is entirely comfortable not only being alone in his opinion, but going against what would seem to be the "better judgment" of today's standards—the very root of which might be based in an assumption that by being smarter, we can avoid really being engaged, and so avoid pain. This hero seemed to understand that taking beatings wasn't a reflection of failure on his part, but a part of the process of doing something right.

As a result he had incredible energy, and never seemed to let even his own setbacks get in the way of moving on. He acknowledged the power and necessity of organizations, but he never let them rule who he was or what he did. He did not even let his own lack of credentials get in the way of doing heroic things. A private investigator is a seamy kind of profession, even described as such in the show. He certainly made money, and was concerned about being paid. But money did not come first. Doing the right thing was first.

Joe Mannix embodies the properties of a spiritual individual—one who is engaged in the world. That's a pretty loaded sentence; it contains the words "spiritual" "individual" and "engaged." If you can put those three things together, you can live a pretty good life.

But if spiritual issues are too much for you, then consider it from a far more practical, even technical or logical perspective.

Western culture relies upon on invention and re-invention—ours is a culture that needs creative solutions to problems and creative contributions of all sorts. When creativity becomes less, we become less. And all true creativity is done utterly alone, with plenty of metaphorical "beatings" along the way, requiring the will to overcome all sorts of difficulty and setbacks. Creative people must stand beside systems, not entirely with them and not apart from them either. The creative individual sees things just outside of the way the establishment does, thereby advancing it.

That kind of desire comes from a place deep inside of us, a place we find only because we once saw it clearly, and recognized it as a transcendent way to live, as a heroic way to live.

Joe Mannix is the prototypical mythical tough individual who is willing to put everything he is on the line for that one person—which is metaphorical for that one idea, one concept, one artifact. He is comfortable being alone and not hiding in a corner, but being engaged—getting up the next day fresh, even if he was wrong or beaten up the day before. He is who we were, far more than we are now.

He, more than any other hero or myth I have ever encountered, made it seem as if being comfortable getting hurt, risking oneself, in the pursuit of doing the right thing was not only noble, but the utter secret to life. He embodied personal, individual courage, coupled with grace, week after week.

When *Mannix* left the air, nothing quite like it ever replaced it, despite what might be unprecedented levels of exposure to mythical characters that have been churned out in cookie cutter fashion. Perhaps this even makes sense, since the multitude of outlets for characters in all sorts of movies and TV shows can tend to reduce quality.

Also, *Mannix* is the product of one individual, Mike Connors, as well as a group of people who were creative because they had to be. They were not simply taking models from previous iterations of heroic molds and dressing them differently. There was no mold for this kind of character yet in modern-day, weekly TV.

The reasons would seem to go beyond that. Our tastes in myths have changed. It seems somehow less intelligent to watch heroic figures who are always getting knocked unconscious, shot, drugged, and having to use their fists to fight their way out of bad situations they are always getting themselves into. We now think intelligence is tantamount to the ability to get through life with minimal pain and struggle. We define success as accrual while encountering a minimal amount of difficulty and risk.

Nothing could be further from the truth of what intelligence and success are really all about.

Mythical heroes allow us to survive all sorts of things that happen to us because they allow us to connect with imagery that puts our immediate, threatening surroundings into perspective. In that same vein, they can also inspire us to consider our actions and lives in the context of timeless themes.

When our heroes become less, they can confirm our being less. We seem more concerned with how our actions please others, than with how well those actions stand up to scrutiny from our own inner voice, a voice that tends to transcend our immediate surroundings. In turn, we so often do not have the guts to put what we are on the line for what we know to be true, in so many daily outcomes, large and small.

How can that result in anything very good?

Some myths can enable us to find that inner voice.

Great myths can inspire us to heed it.

Chapter 3
The Difference

We are only as good as the mythical heroes our culture produces, and those we choose to define us. Mythical heroes allow us to see our behavior within our immediate environment as transcendent, even as we live in that environment.

My childhood hero got beat up, shot and knocked unconscious—a *lot*. It got to the point that I used to tune in each week and when he somehow escaped unscathed, I wound up disappointed. You'd think I might do a better job picking heroes, or at the very least I might root more for him to get away with heroic kinds of deeds without getting hurt so much. But I was drawn to watch him. Not only that, TV being what it was in those days, I was my own recording device, playing back episodes in my mind during boring grade school classes in the era before DVD, DVR, the Web, and VHS recordings. Even the coming attractions of each next week's episode would cause my imagination to run wild, filling in all sorts of things to bring the sixty-second previews up to a complete story. I was able to conjure stories consistent with qualities of character because I knew those qualities so well. The characters in that series were virtually a part of me.

Mannix overlapped my grade school years. Its debut occurred during the same fall season that I entered first grade, 1967, and its original series run lasted until I finished the eighth grade in 1975. It was there at the dawn of my awareness and into the dawn of my adolescence. Nearly forty years later, in January 2011, I discovered how much it remained a part of me and what a difference it made to me all along.

More stunningly, I also discovered how its absence from my conscious awareness affected me.

If mythical heroes allow us to see our lives as transcendent, somehow allowing us to do and endure more than we could otherwise, then losing them makes the difficult that much harsher.

It is not an exaggeration to say that the contents of some relatively small, relatively inexpensive collections of plastic cases that hold plastic DVDs did for me what nothing else could for decades. It not only helped me make sense of my life, making the choices I made seem entirely different than they did before, but it helped me to make more sense of life, in general. Through that lens, ultimately motivated by wanting to understand my experience more fully, I discovered how heroes and myths, especially the ones we find on TV, are foundational stories which both reflect and shape a society. They affect us in ways we so often do not understand. When they change, so do we, as a culture and as individuals. This change, often dismissed as mere evolution of societal self-concept, is not always for the better. We are never so aware as a society, or as individuals, as when we are aware of the contents of our myths.

I've also discovered just how good *Mannix* really was—and is. Because of the great volumes of stuff most people my age watched on TV growing up and that has appeared in reruns over the years, there is an overwhelming tendency to think that shows we loved as kids don't hold up so well. And this is largely true. Many shows and characters become, in essence, parodies of themselves as we watch them all these years later. Movie re-makes of "classic" TV shows hardly even need to work very hard to cast caricatures into comic relief, which also seems to be the main contribution of the movie versions of characters we used to watch weekly, religiously—just to give us the reason to look back and see that what we used to think was story was really only parody to begin with. The message seems to be that we were dumb then and we are somehow smarter now—such easy money, to just reinforce our deep cultural desire to think of ourselves as smart.

For this reason I was hesitant to even open the DVD package for season 4 of *Mannix* when it arrived on my front porch on its release date of January 4, 2011. I was in the middle of a tough personal time, near—but not quite at the end of—an over four-decade-long struggle on both personal and professional fronts. It was time to put the holiday decorations away, and I was about to stuff the *Mannix* DVDs for season 4 (I always purchased two sets of the releases for some reason) into a pile to store away with other DVDs that I had collected over the years.

Something made me put the season 4 DVDs of *Mannix* into the player before I put them away.

In 2008, when the season 1 DVDs of *Mannix* came out, I had opened them and played them, but just a bit. I was still in the middle of some very tough times and the format of season 1 of *Mannix* is very different from that of seasons 2-8, the seasons with which most fans are most familiar. Season 1 wasn't the *Mannix* I remembered so well and so I watched very little of it. Perhaps because of this lack of immediate connection, it seemed as flat as everything else in my life at that point. When the subsequent seasons came out on DVD—with season 2 released on January 6, 2009, and season 3 on October 27, 2009—all I did was purchase a couple of copies of each and immediately put them away, unopened.

I did, however, continue to search for information on *Mannix* on the Web. This practice started in an occasional way virtually as soon as it was possible to search for anything on the Web that wasn't strictly related to computing. This practice occurred mostly on dark nights in my office after working long days and wanting to have a little fun before dragging myself home. Aside from news, weather and sports, I'd occasionally search for news on *Mannix* DVD releases. I used to chalk it up to nostalgia for simpler, happier times. *Mannix* was the only series I searched for in this way.

In this process I discovered that DVD releases for series tend to stall for unforeseen reasons not always pertaining to DVD sales, and that these stalls can often mean the end of the series release. Leading up to January 2011, with tough times for me escalating, I continued my occasional nightly searches and found that people were woeful that the rest of *Mannix* would never be released. Announcements of subsequent season releases tend to come less than four months after a DVD set for a season has been released. The announcement for season 4 of *Mannix* came a full eleven months after season 3 was released. The release dates of October 27, 2009 for season 3 and January 4, 2011 for season 4 span more than fourteen months, unusual for classic series that tend to have their season releases six months or less apart.

I took this in from a curious distance, still wanting to follow, collect and eventually—someday—view the series again. But I followed its delayed release with a general sense of malaise. *Mannix* was just something, buried somewhere in the deep recesses of my mind, that would occasionally come up as some sort of lark.

This delay in the release of the series was a part of the reason I never opened the boxes that contained seasons 2 and 3. I did not want to be disappointed by getting to see part, but not all, of the series I once loved so much as a kid.

But on a snowy, post-holiday, early-January day, the darkest time of the year in many respects, something made me decide that having season 4 might be enough, even if I never saw any more of the series released. It was a time during which I seemed incapable of digging into anything else new, so it seemed worth risking the possible disappointment from two potential directions—that the series would not hold up very well or, if it did, that I might never see the remaining four seasons. I expected a brief nostalgia trip to officially end my holidays.

I put in one of the DVDs for season 4.

Nice menus—the great *Mannix* theme and cool graphics to go with it that really capture the spirit and style of the show ... curious too, because they changed that from the season 1 format. Gee, I remember those episodes that those menu clips came from ...

I watched one of the episodes.

Then another ...

And another ...

Almost instantaneously my brain seemed to light up with an energy it had not experienced in a long, long time—back to a time that almost seemed to be beyond words. Those images—they were doing far more than just allowing me to re-visit my youth. Much to my surprise, the stories seemed to hold so much more than I expected—the individual vs. the group, the toughness, the way the guy not only seemed to endure so much, but understand that enduring is a big part of life. Amazing.

I opened up the DVDs for the other seasons I had not yet opened—seasons 2 and 3. The same thing happened. I started to flip around for specific episodes, even specific scenes I remembered, in many cases held in my mind for over forty years probably due to the way I had memorized and played them back as a kid. I became aware that this practice continued throughout my life, where I would sometimes reflect on moments from the series in moments of quiet or crisis, without even being fully aware of it. This reinforcement gave me a specific memory of certain scenes that was nearly perfect. Other scenes I conjured over the years were oddly distorted by time, but not by very much.

Clearly, that character had stayed with me all of these years, despite my denial of his importance as I became ever more educated by a combination of books and changing conventional wisdom—ever "evolving" myths.

As someone who typically needs a lot of sleep, I went through a weeks-long period where I routinely got only three and four hours of sleep a night—and that was all I seemed to want or need. I just could not get enough of the re-connection to the series. I'd finish one episode and want to go directly to the next one, often shouting and laughing recognition right out loud, right in the middle of the night. I was up watching episodes of the first four seasons of *Mannix* into the wee hours of the morning and fought to stay awake until I could no longer force myself to keep my eyes open. Then, incredibly, I'd be up only three to four hours later, feeling completely refreshed.

In the process I was stunned to discover something I had not known before—I had actually seen most of the episodes of the first season of *Mannix*, before it changed its format. Season 1 had not been previously syndicated in the U.S., and so there was no way I could have seen all of those episodes since they first aired in 1967-1968, when I was six to seven years old. Yet when I watched those DVDs, so many scenes were familiar in virtually every episode of that season; I clearly had seen them before, when I was such a different person, one that could not even read or write. In some cases I even knew what was coming next; the soon-to-be fifty-year-old was seeing what the six- and seven-year-old saw with forty-three years of life lived in-between.

I had just never before put together that the show I came to love in its subsequent format was one I had seen from its very beginning. Curiously, as a kid, around 1970 or 1971, I had used my allowance to purchase a book on TV. My memory is that it was called, *The TV Book*. Inside was a picture of *Mannix*. I never purchased the "kid stuff" that was connected with the series, going instead for what seemed like a book an adult would buy so that I could have something in my hands connected to the series. Intellectual rationalization starts young.

Under the picture of Joe Mannix standing by his convertible wearing one of those late 1960's scarf-style ties, the caption discussed how Joe Mannix went out on his own in the second season, after having worked for something called "Intertect" during the first season. My ten-year-old heart sank. There was a piece of *Mannix* I was missing. I yearned to see that season so badly; I wanted to know everything about that character that I could. So when *Mannix* did go into syndication, which famously ended its prime-time run, the only thing I consoled myself with was that I would finally get to see all of the history of the show I loved. But it was not to be, as the syndication package of *Mannix* eliminated the first season entirely, and most of the seventh season and all of the eighth season as well. *Mannix* fans griped about this for nearly four decades, until the DVDs for all of the seasons were finally released.

Then, in January 2011—forty-three years after season 1 first ran, forty years after buying that book, and thirty-five years after hoping to see the first season when the show first went to syndication—I finally got to see the first season of *Mannix* again, with a lifetime lived in between. I sat there, in the middle of the night, and viewed one episode at a time, mostly screaming at the TV "I *saw* that" and laughing right out loud with almost pure joy the whole time.

The energy levels in my brain were palpable—unmistakable, undeniable.

What was happening to me?

That kind of energy that I had from watching that show, the kind that took me from someone who seemed exhausted at pretty much all facets of life and wanting to sleep all the time, to someone who could not get enough of this particular activity—where did that come from?

It wasn't nostalgia.

It was recognition.

It was getting an invaluable piece of myself back.

In those episodes I saw so much of what formed my views of life at the most fundamental of levels. In those episodes I also saw how losing connection to those views hurt me—ultimately making me a lesser person during those times I did not feel connected to them—and how having them back had the power to heal me and make me a better person.

How can such a thing happen?

How does a college professor—a female who works in a profession dominated by males from all sorts of cultures, who focuses intently on what many people consider some of the driest topics imaginable, and who spent a lifetime dealing with some pretty extreme and chronic health issues of a family member—find healing by watching episodes of a more than forty year old TV series that mythologizes the exploits of a private detective who runs around L.A. in a convertible, gets into fistfights, gets knocked unconscious, and gets shot a lot?

The change in energy level I experienced wasn't because of a drug. It wasn't due to a new job. It wasn't due to coming into a pile of money, a love affair, a new lease on life. There was no change in my medical condition other than the fact that the energy allowed me to resolve a long overdue need to lose a lot of weight—which I did, effortlessly. I also started to go for walks every day. In this day and age, people wanted to know my secret.

I mean, this was just a bunch of images on a collection of DVDs. I'm a scientist, a researcher and an engineer. I study topics related to the meaning of life in my spare time. I crave the deep stuff.

But when I watched those DVDs, all of a sudden my life was turned upside down—everything looked different. That is exactly what great myths can—and should—do.

My childhood hero, a character I could not have loved more as a kid, didn't exactly have an easy time of things, nor did he even *want* to! He seemed to think that getting hurt was a part of doing the right thing, even a part of the process of leading a good life. Furthermore, he often wasn't even recognized or appreciated when he did do the right thing. Still further, despite his many abilities, he wasn't exactly loved by a throng of people or put up on some sort of pedestal for being so special.

Yet you, the viewer, could see that he was special by what he did. He had just a few friends who could see that as well—but only just a few. He wasn't the most popular guy around, nor did he seem to want to be. He really only answered to himself, but he did not make that look so easy. It seemed like more of a responsibility, even a burden, than a gift. And he seemed so graceful, so dignified.

Being, fundamentally, a researcher, I had to know more—about both my reaction to seeing it again, and the show, itself.

I started by searching the Web for information on *Mannix*, and found that the series has a deep, loyal following. I also discovered that many shows that were its contemporaries have much larger followings. Still, I discovered multiple places where the love for the series has been expressed in written word, often by individuals who do not seek group affiliation, much as one might expect from a show about a tough individual. Some managed to express better than I could what I felt when I first saw those DVDs, such as: "This is the one show you loved as a kid that does not embarrass you as an adult."

Thus, it helps that the series is simply outstanding—it has much higher quality than many give it credit for. To this day it continues to carry the label "one of the most violent shows on television" and it was famously discussed in U.S. Congressional hearings because of its level of violence.

Could that have contributed to the series falling off the radar of many Baby Boomers? If so, then we are paying a price for not understanding symbolism anymore. Evidence of this would seem to be how we have become so literal-minded that we are now surrounded by reality TV and absurd techno-driven dramas. Some might say our art has devolved from dealing with meaning, or mythos, to dealing with cause and effect, or logos.[3.1] And that can make us significantly less than we once were.

Labeling *Mannix* as violent is a bit like labeling Christianity—or any religion—as violent. The violence in *Mannix* is not gratuitous; it is actually necessary in portraying something of fundamental importance on a deep, symbolic, psychological level. Inside all of our heads, as we become adults and then for the rest of our lives, is a violent struggle to define ourselves—to be individuals as we attempt to make sense of everything that is happening around us. Those who succeed ultimately find violent struggles when they stand up to all sorts of things, as individuals must. Those adult, individual struggles are no less violent when they result in potential job loss or being ostracized from a profession or any other organization. Those struggles are always a part of standing alone when trying to do the right thing.

Fairy tales are violent. *Harry Potter* and *The Lord of the Rings* are violent. Probably the most gut wrenching viewing experience I had as a kid came when I saw *Bambi* in a movie theatre.

I discovered that some researchers and thinkers believe the violence in our foundational stories, such as fairy tales and mythical heroes, actually helps us be less violent on the outside, in our real lives—because the connection with heroic myths who struggle with violence actually helps us to sort out and deal with conflict inside our own head without playing it out in the real world. I discovered that this process may actually be even more significant for highly creative types—the kind our culture relies upon.

What is crucial is how the violence is portrayed in the context of the hero, so that we can access the hero in ourselves and face up to the symbolic violence that is all around us, in all sorts of daily encounters. The symbolic content of *Mannix* started to intrigue me as well—the symbolism, the mythology, the heroism.

But before that, I realized how badly I wanted to see the release of the rest of the series. Having four seasons simply wasn't enough. I knew there were four more seasons out there, and I knew that the quality of *Mannix* never, ever went downhill—a rarity in a series that ran for eight seasons, especially one built around a single leading character.

Almost desperate to see the rest, I realized one way to facilitate the release of the rest of the series was to help the DVD sales. In theory that should drive the studio, CBS/Paramount, to release the remaining seasons. But this was not a sure thing. Even series that have sold relatively well have stalled, for reasons those of us on the outside of the industry can only speculate about.

The answer seemed to be to start to write about the series. I wrote my first article on *Mannix*, an Amazon review of season 4, and put it on the Web on February 4, 2011. The title of the review is, "This is the best television show, ever." Well, it's to the point anyway.

But what was I doing, and why was I doing it? My name was on that review (as JM Paul) as a by-product of my Amazon username, and so what if people discovered I had this incredible fondness for an old television series that a lot of people consider either violent or superficial?

I have something of a reputation as a serious person, as a deep thinker, and I want to think of myself that way as well, having worked hard, virtually my whole life, to earn that right. I am also a PI—a Principal Investigator—of research awards that all too often tend to be funded on the basis of reputation more than actual content. I went for my newfound daily walk the same day I posted the Amazon review and thought about taking the review down. My heart actually started to race at the thought of someone discovering I put that over-the-top writing out there with my name on it. But I ultimately decided to leave it, with the rationalization that I deserved this kind of frivolous lark at this point. It would be easy to explain away by contrast to the otherwise serious nature of my life.

Rationalization can be the next best thing to real discovery.

At the same time, I continued to search for information on *Mannix*. I remembered a discussion group that used to be out on the Web, put there by fans of the series. I found it, and joined it. I made a post—a clumsy, really kind of stupid post.

I found Mike Connors on *PBS's Pioneers of Television: Crime Dramas*, an episode that ran in early February 2011. He was interviewed, and the coverage of *Mannix* discussed how Joe Mannix was unique because he "had emotion" unlike previous iterations of PIs. He also discussed how the show had a unique style of editing that made it seem to "move" and also made each hour seem to contain more content than the typical hour-long series in those days. That was interesting.

During those dark nights in my office, in the preceding years, I had found another group that discussed the DVD releases of various classic TV series. There was a thread, started on September 20, 2007, called "Mannix is Coming!" on the Home Theatre Forum (HTF). The first post said, in effect, that there was a rumor that *Mannix* was being digitally re-mastered in preparation for an eventual release. The impetus for the rumor seems likely the by-product of research for a *Washington Post* article, which was published in November of that year.[0.1] It seems all too coincidental that, around the same time the paper would have started to ask questions about why the series was gathering dust, rumors were leaked that a planned release was in progress. The article, written by a fan of the series who happened to be a *Post* writer, lamented that the series had not been released. I monitored the HTF over the years, on an irregular basis, to include reading posts that were grim—it hurt to even read them—questioning whether the rest of the series would ever be released on DVD, especially during the long period after season 3 was released. I would leave my office on those nights in a kind of despair, but one that sat below the level of consciousness. On the surface, it was just one more thing.

The fourth season was finally released in January 2011, and the announcement of the fifth-season release came on April 18, 2011. Someone posted on the HTF that the release of season 5 of *Mannix* was a "50/50 release." I posted a simple question, "What makes you say this is a 50/50 release?" hoping to obtain just a bit more information about why the release was regarded as a coin-toss decision.

I discovered, much to my surprise, that my real name was included in the post.

I had joined the forum in February, but never posted there before. I had thought that only my username, jompaul17, constructed out of an abbreviation of my first name, my middle initial, and my last name, with 17 added for "17 Paseo Verde"—Joe Mannix's address—would be associated with my posts there. But my entire real name was put right under that, a practice the HTF seems to have since changed. I was nervous to even make that simple first post. It was never replied to in the thread. People who knew each other were replying to each other and they just ignored my question.

Somewhat irked that my question was simply ignored, I posted again the next day, this time with a much longer post, praising the series. Since the previous release was rumored to be a coin-toss decision, I wanted to say positive things, hoping to positively impact subsequent releases. That was how it began. During the next sixteen months, I made well over 500 posts on the thread, some lightweight and conversational in tone, but others far more substantial.

I started to look forward to posting there, and found that I was looking forward to it more than other things I was doing, even more than anything else I had ever done before. It became my way of writing, in real time, my appreciation for the contents of the series—its foundational elements and execution, as well as discussing its significance to me. Deeper themes emerged in that process. Those themes were the product of my trying to reconcile the intellectual in me with the clear, deep emotional response I was having to a childhood myth I once loved so much, lost, and re-found.

Aside from that, I found that people kept commenting on the changes that had taken place in me—how different I looked, and not just because of the weight loss. Some said my eyes looked different. They wondered why and, wanting the same thing for themselves, guessed that various ordinary reasons were behind it. I responded that the changes they observed were due to "a strange reason." I really had no idea what else to say, and was not at all comfortable with revealing the truth to anyone who had known me previously. How could I explain this?

And yet, through this process, I learned more about myself and life than at any other time of my life.

I've watched a lot of TV, not only while I was growing up, but really throughout all of my life. That both helped and hurt, because it allowed me to discuss how Joe Mannix related to so many other heroes and mythical characters, TV and otherwise. I discovered that trying to relate the properties of Joe Mannix to other mythical TV heroes causes some people to become angry. In retrospect, this makes perfect sense—heroes matter to people in ways we so often do not understand, but ways that run very deep. After all, that is what happened to me.

I was also trying to understand why *Mannix* became so badly mislabeled as a violent series, had a hard time making it to DVD release, was threatened to be stalled in that process, and does not have the same kind of following in the Baby Boomer generation as other series. So I was always positively, and deeply, comparing Joe Mannix's qualities to that of other heroes, many of which seemed far more suitable for people who sought to find ways to reconcile good lives with doing and sacrificing less, or who perhaps felt entitled to less challenging lives. For them, Joe Mannix must look kind of odd. But for me, the wisdom he seemed to convey to a kid remained an essential part of me. So many years later, I simply could not refute that wisdom. It held up.

Aside from exposure to so much TV, which some seem to think makes a person out to be of weaker intellectual ilk, I discovered that that I am a very visual person—at least when it comes to myths. I seem to prefer my myths visually rather than on the written page. Some things simply do not translate well to words. They need to be seen, and ideally reinforced in the way only a weekly relationship with a TV character can do. Only then can they reach a level of affectation where they can be generalized to one's own life, as both fictional hero and TV viewer experience ongoing struggles. I understand words, but I *see* symbolic behavior. My dreams are largely visual. Visualization is projection and so visual myths are powerful ways to allow us to project ourselves into larger themes.

I also discovered that I had a strong foundational relationship to the fundamental qualities of my childhood hero before I could read or write. It isn't just that this gave me an early start or that the foundational elements of the hero run so deep; it told me that the symbolism of some myths really does run deeper than words can convey. But this makes perfect sense. To this day, watching even just a few minutes of *Mannix* can brighten my mood, bringing all sorts of foundational elements of the hero back in only just a few seconds of time, really much like a piece of music that also goes beyond words.

Even as music and symbols are timeless, so are the themes in great myths, like *Mannix*.

You got the sense, when you watched this man, that he was engaged in the world, put there for a reason—but one that did not come from divine intervention in the "gifted child" sense. He embodied "to whom much is given, much is expected." His essential goodness is what caused him to want to get out there and engage over and over again, to risk, and endure getting hurt. His gifts were not something that allowed him to rise above the fray. His gifts were the reason he felt the need to get in there and use them to some greater purpose, ultimately risking them in the process.

He was called upon when individuals were in times of crisis, and he gave everything to help them, holding nothing back. This is, of course, precisely the reason he got hurt so much. He also struggled to endure and overcome all sorts of situations where people did all sorts of things to him, trying to hurt and kill him just because he was trying to do some good.

The show was bold in these timeless themes, in your face with them and, incredibly, carried them out in a modern-day setting. *Mannix* got away with it because you believed this man, this character.

It wasn't just what he did. You could see it right on his face. In the midst of all of that so-called violence, you could see—right on that one face of 1000 heroes[2.1] that stayed with me all of my life—that his response made a kind of perfect sense. For a show that was supposed to be about action and violence, so much of it wound up being about very subtle expressions on faces conveyed in close ups, especially through the eyes. The response to the violence was what mattered. Reaction shots meant so much more than dialogue in *Mannix*.

In series like *Mannix*, which was a single-camera show, there was a mix of action with close-ups, and in those close-ups were visual responses that were artistic interpretations of how the main characters responded to their situations. Here was an unabashed blend of action-driven life and soul. Here was a character with a lot of energy to engage, not reluctantly, in sharp contrast to most modern-day heroes, but with complete awareness of the potential consequences of what it meant to be so engaged.

Sadly, those close-ups, those reaction shots, were so misunderstood by those who edited the series for syndication that they cut them, sometimes in fine-grained editing that removed only a few precious seconds at a time. But the series is so well acted that the DVDs reveal those precious seconds as being so rich that you want to slow them down, freeze the frames, and just see the reactions on those great faces. Some of those faces, especially in the context of the characters, take pages to describe. The detail is there.

The "evolution" towards "reality" in TV really started in the mid-1970s, when the anti-hero arrived on the small screen and continued through a phase where cameras rolled around the scenes, making you feel as if you were walking around in a real setting, witnessing what was going on. The idea was not to understand the soul any better, but to be exposed to a lot of stuff that was somehow more truthful because it did not interpret, did not reach for depth in the faces of the actors so much as it made the viewer feel like a voyeur, looking into a window. Currently, the nearly absurd level of emphasis on reality has resulted in staged dramas being called reality—a true paradox.

The common message seems to be that deeper kinds of heroic themes are silly because they are, on the surface, untrue. Never mind that myths are not supposed to be analyzed on the surface. This shift towards a kind of false literalism, as opposed to a deeper kind of symbolism, in what may be the single art form most responsible for storytelling in our modern culture, may be a more significant cause of a sense of emptiness, malaise, violence and discord than most people realize.

Viewing myths in a superficial way is like reading a page and considering only its esthetic qualities, considering only the fonts and the way the words are laid out—but not what the words mean. Another analogy might be the way an animal watches images on a TV screen—seeing only light, color and noise, but unable to interpret meaning. Therein lies a spectrum, between reality and symbolism, and when we are less comfortable dealing with symbolism, we become more mundane.

It remains a mystery how we can find meaning in words on the page or images inside DVD cases that are played out on a screen in patterns of light and sound. That mystery, to me, now seems so much more significant than reality.

It is enough for me, as a researcher, a scientist and an engineer, to step back from my own life and see the power that myth has had over me—even to be a better researcher, scientist and engineer. It is enough for me to respect that and hope that others can relate to my experience, to include my desire to understand more about it. Still, realizing that so many will find my love of the series misguided, my reaction out of proportion, or my desire to know more about it a waste of time, one more example may be in order.

There is a scene in a season 6 episode of *Mannix*, "Light and Shadow," where Joe is in his office right after Peggy leaves. Some thugs come in, bringing Peggy back with them, and Joe is punched in the gut, right in front of Peggy. After the thugs leave, Peggy does the usual, "Joe, are you all right?"

And what is Joe's response?

He tells her to relax, "We must be doing something right."

Now, in and of itself, most people would probably take this scene in with little awareness or fanfare—even as I did as a kid, watching it, taking it in, and not really thinking about it very much. This scene is simply consistent with Joe Mannix's nature, and so you take it in stride, especially once you have a picture of his character in mind.

Really think about that one scene for a moment.

Just keep it in mind.

Flash forward thirty-seven years. Let's say you find yourself in academia, and have spent nearly your entire career, your whole life really, basically putting yourself where you weren't wanted by the silent, and sometimes not so silent, majority—the informal groups that dominate all cultures and sub-cultures, often behind the scenes.

There are two reasons for not being wanted—one is being a minority (being a woman), and that reason is superficial, but all too real. The numbers bear me out, for those who cannot see the reality. The second is because you find that you tend to challenge conventional thinking. For those who think academics sit around and when they see a good idea just nod their heads and agree, think again. History is full of people who have been right about fundamental truths, but who spent truly difficult lives fighting for their ideas, often alone, only to have their ideas accepted after they were dead, if then.

There is actually a structural reason for the often difficult kinds of lives led by non-conventional thinkers in science and academia, and a famous, classic book has been written about it.[3.2] Beyond that, however, is another reason—science is filled with all sorts of unbridled egos, and, if you challenge those egos, they are going to fight hard to protect their self-images.

Through generations, those who fit the mold of what people want, whose ideas fit in with a powerful group, will be rewarded—on the surface of things. But if you are not one of those people, you can find yourself, at age forty-nine, having taken quite a few lumps along the way, still very much on the ropes, what some might say is way too over-invested in a career (however noble the intentions), wondering if there isn't something wrong with you because you aren't like your generational cohorts who seem to have the common purpose of living lives as comfortably as they can, somehow justifying that as wisdom. You start to question your need to challenge—both yourself and others. You start to think maybe your more conventional cohorts are right and that there is something wrong with you, ultimately finding yourself watching one entire season of *Dancing with the Stars* and lingering on the Food Network a little too long. You become a little too intrigued by the way *The Barefoot Contessa* cracks eggs on the kitchen counter. You actually buy a crockpot. You find yourself going back to your apartment at night, just a little too fascinated with how the food turns out, eight hours later.

You are headed towards the abyss, so deep, you may never get out.

Things are so bad that when the season 4 DVDs of *Mannix* arrive, you barely take notice. You think that childhood heroes are just that—for children. Anyway, even though you used to love *Mannix* as a kid, like no other series, surely this series, more than any other, would not hold up well.

But after cleaning up the holiday decorations one January, you pop in the DVDs for season 4 . . . and then 3, and then 2, and then 1 . . .

What you find in there is amazing. In there are elements of the stuff of psychology, philosophy and religion, the stuff of reading done in various metro stations, airports, and hotel rooms these past twenty years or more. But there is also this one element of the nature of this particular hero, one that used to define us as a culture so much more than it does now.

Joe Mannix was not only willing to take a beating; he actually felt that when he took one, he must be doing the right thing!

And so, almost as if in an instant, everything I did, everything I endured, looked completely different. Now, if I went to my grave tomorrow, the things I would be proudest of have nothing to do with any measurable, absolute outcomes, as assessed by the crowd. Rather, they would be those times I had the guts to go up against people with the power to make my life miserable in order to make the point that I belonged. They would be those times I had the courage to pursue ideas and works that I knew mattered, even when that went against the grain and ruffled dangerous egos. I am so, so grateful I did those things. Before I watched those *Mannix* DVDs in January 2011, I did not realize that I felt that way, or why.

Almost in an instant, I came to realize that I can't control outcomes, or what people think of me, but I can control how I respond to situations, including when I go into them in the first place, knowing how difficult they will likely be. And I am so thankful that there was something there inside of me that was willing to continuously put myself in those situations because I felt I was doing the right thing, come what may. I honestly do not think I would have done that, to nearly the same extent, if at all, were it not for my love of my myth of choice.

Some think the future of the U.S. would benefit from more minorities, including women and non-conventional thinkers, participating in science and technology. If so, don't put *CSI* on the air, or any other techno-drama. If you want people to get in there and do things that really matter, like advancing fundamental knowledge through research or fighting injustice, then don't put any of the so-called reality shows on the air.

Put the likes of Joe Mannix on the air, and give people the courage and the desire, individually, to be alone and take a beating in order to pursue that one idea or do the right thing, ready for the repercussions that inevitably come in so doing.

Having that, deeply, symbolically, inside of me was essential to virtually all of the things I did that I wound up valuing the most in my life, which includes placing a higher value on *doing* than on *having*.

That is the power of myth.

And that is why Joe Mannix is one great myth.

So go ahead and beat me up for writing this.

If you do, I must be doing something right.

Chapter 4
Heroic Matters

Classic heroes do the impossible; they reconcile pain with beauty. They do so by casting the value of entire lives into single stories, often single moments within those stories. In such moments, they completely transform who they are into what they do—being into deed, material into spiritual.

Such heroes are often depicted as handsome figures, and always with enviable attributes of some kind. After all, heroism only matters if the hero sacrifices something of material significance that they have for something non-material that matters to them more. They always do so by conscious choice. Deeds are only heroic if they are done on purpose, only if the hero is aware of what they are sacrificing, and why.

Classic heroes have enough self-awareness to place a value on what they are, what they have and what they can do so that they come to see the value of their gifts as a mixed blessing. They realize they have been given something of value. But in recognition that life is transient they realize that they will not own it very long. So classic heroes come to a point where they become capable of facing the difficult, the inevitable and the painful on their own terms, ultimately placing their own value on their own gifts by consciously transforming them into something else. When they do so, they inevitably open themselves up to experience pain. But, in a true paradox, they also realize that the pain of heroic engagement—deeds done for some higher purpose—is significantly less than the pain of leading a meaningless life, one based upon accrual, comfort and societal rewards.

Accordingly, classic heroes show us that pain is not to be avoided, but rather is part of the process of life. By coupling good deeds with the pain required to carry them out, they give us the secret to leading a good life—since we are going to experience pain anyway, as an inevitable part of any life, they show us that the best lives, the most beautiful ones, are those that render pain transformative. For this reason, such heroes tend to be energetic and engaged in life, regardless of the circumstances.

Classic heroes are energetic not because they always win, because they do not always prevail along the way. They do not merely overcome all obstacles, as all-powerful Supermen. Rather, they are heroic because they are not afraid of pain in the many forms it can take, ranging from physical to psychological, so long as they are in concert with their self-identified sense of right and wrong. The hurt they encounter really does hurt. But they show us how something matters more than the pain, something that makes enduring the pain worthwhile. When we are in concert with such heroes, we discover that the pain we experience in life is not personally directed at us, not punishment meted out by any deity, and not random, but rather is a part of a process that leads to something beautiful, something transcendent, something ultimately spiritual, as meaningful things are.

In season 7 of *Mannix*, the episode "The Gang's All Here" has Joe Mannix taken from his office by a gang of young kids. They intend to kill him on the street in front of a rival gang, the idea being that if they kill Joe Mannix, who has a reputation for being tough, then they will obtain a reputation for being tough. But, as group courage tends to go, when it comes time to kill Joe—after he was knocked silly, as usual—the leader of the gang gives a gun to the gang's newest member, a young kid, instead of the leader doing it himself. The gang leader presumed that the kid, Arlie, would be motivated to do something he would not otherwise do on his own because he wanted so badly to become a member of the group—the gang. But Arlie is the son of a former cop who was killed only a few years earlier, presumed to be on the take at the time. Arlie, being disillusioned about his father, wants to belong to something larger than himself. He can't seem to orient his life around the memory of his dead father, especially since the father was presumed to have gone bad.

But when the time comes, when fire engines come into the area, summoned by the gang to drown out the noise of the gunshot, Arlie can't shoot Joe. Something stops him. Instead, the leader of the gang shoots at Joe after Joe—having regained some of his wits—starts to run away as the fire engines pass en route to their destination. The shot hits Joe in the side.

Most of the rest of the episode follows Joe as he struggles to survive while slowly bleeding. We follow him on the street and in run-down, deserted buildings. He is hiding from the gang that still wants to kill him. He can't get away from them, because he's been shot. He can barely move and is surrounded. All he can do is try to get the word out that he is there, and hope people come to find him.

Loyal fans of the series get to enjoy seeing Peggy and Art first discover that Joe is missing, then that he's been shot. *Mannix* did these scenes so very well—understated, but with feeling that made it back to the viewer that the primary reason Peggy and Art were concerned was not because Joe was their friend, but because of who Joe was. The idea comes across to the viewer, in a clear but subtle way, that the loss of Joe would mean more than just the loss of a friend.

That is, of course, the whole point of larger-than-life characters, or myths. They point to value beyond the immediacy of tangible things like friendship, or any other kind of reward, save the kind of reward that can only be associated with behavior that belongs to another realm. Great myths, classic heroes, give us the sense that this is a realm to which we would like to belong. Through our myth of choice, we also come to know that this type of behavior is never easy, by its very definition.

Joe Mannix is a mythological character, the product of story. As such he is not real and yet contains far more reality than so many situations we live out to which we pay so little attention. When we pay close attention to Joe Mannix, we are really paying attention to ourselves. By capturing our imagination, mythological figures allow us to place our own valuation on what a good life means, including our own. But, since their properties are different from each other, mythological figures have the power to affect us to varying degrees. Only those mythological characters that inspire us to be better versions of ourselves are true, classic heroes.

As a culture, and as individuals, we need such heroes so badly that we project heroic properties that do not exist onto real people. Children do this for their parents. Countries do this for their politicians and rulers, past and present. Companies do this for their founders. Groups do this for their leaders. We can become disappointed, even disillusioned, when we discover the reality behind the projections, the myths, completely missing the point of why we need that kind of story in the first place.

At the heart of what it means to be human lie two dilemmas: how to think and how to behave.

From our earliest moments on Earth, we take our cues from those who immediately surround us: our parents, siblings and any other caretakers. These individuals give us the opportunity to mimic so that we may learn how to survive. But even before we are completely aware, we begin to process things symbolically. We abstract what is around us, projecting what we know about anything—from objects to people—into new situations so that we may learn how to live independently. Our caretakers can only take us so far in life, and from our earliest days we somehow know this. Accordingly, we look outside of our immediate environment for answers to the dilemmas we face.

This ability, in humans, to process symbols takes on its highest form in stories. Mythological stories are made-up projections of answers to life's dilemmas that some parts of the human race are communicating to other parts. But the description of story as a made-up entity, with connotations of artificiality, has mistakenly become a way to de-value the importance of story. Stories are abstract representations, models, but they represent things that are all too real. When we ignore their impact on society, or what they represent to us personally, we give up something important about what it means to be human.

Only in recent history have we tended to think of symbolic, abstract descriptions of life's issues as somehow having less value than supposed real ones. Intelligence has recently been connoted with the ability to get to the bottom line, where all value is presumed to be distillable to a single type of currency, monetary or otherwise. That which does not directly affect the bottom line is considered personal whim; qualitative rather than quantitative.

Curiously, while this type of mindset affects all sorts of decisions in the business practices of science and engineering, as in so many other businesses, those very disciplines which would seem to be the foundation of this kind of thinking would not be possible in the first place without the ability to manipulate the abstract, the symbolic. The success of science and technology in transforming our world has been enabled by mathematics, and mathematics is a self-consistent, highly abstract and symbolic representation of the world, one that can, at best, approximate reality. Belief in irrational numbers is, in some ways, less rational than belief in story. The calculation of the area of a circle relies upon the existence of an irrational number, *pi*, divined via a simple relationship that would seem to point directly to the infinite. And yet the circle exists. Through the use of mathematics and the abstract thinking that enables it, individuals can model highly complex systems that no single human being can build. They can do so because each instance of such systems does not need to be built in reality in order for us to understand its properties. In so doing, we can far more efficiently build much better systems the first time around, with the limited materials—time and space—that we have in which to build the systems.

Similarly, story is the powerful abstraction through which we can model, and evaluate, the relative merits of individual lives without having to live each one in reality. In so doing, we can lead far more effective lives, should we take the time to consider what is behind the stories we encounter, the ones that move us, and why. Story is similarly as powerful, if not more powerful, than mathematics. Both are highly symbolic, highly abstract. Both are powerful representations of reality. When we do not consider how powerful mathematics is in modeling and allowing us to affect the physical world around us, we become so much less. When we do not consider how powerful story is in modeling and allowing us to affect the spiritual world within us, we become so much less.

Stories take on a wide range of forms, including cartoons, fairy tales, books, opera, religion, television programs, movies, and even songs. The description of some aspects of religion as story is not a commentary on the veracity of the content of any religion—it is only to say that all religion has some elements of story that are an important form of expression of its deeper meaning. Meaning is most powerfully conveyed in story precisely because we can project ourselves into story in a way that we cannot project ourselves into someone else's reality. Any individual's reality includes specificity which tends to preclude our ability to call it our own. Stories, by contrast, are open for all of us to consider, and to claim. Some stories are more useful, more widely applicable, and ultimately more enduring than others. The extent of spatial and temporal universality of these stories—their widespread, timeless qualities—qualifies them as myths.

The content of recurring myths and the structure of the human psyche have been observed to be related as archetypes—or psychological patterns that are so built into us that we seem to recognize myths, more than learn from them.[4.1] This recognition is ultimately what allows us to powerfully address the dilemmas of how to think and how to behave as individuals, because we get to pick and choose and thus act deliberately instead of in a merely instinctual way—should we choose to do so. Archetypes allow us to see ourselves in other forms because we recognize the similarities, thus casting those similarities into greater relief. The process of seeing ourselves in some archetypes, but not as much in others, is what allows us to pick and choose. Ultimately, through story, we realize we *can* pick and choose.

Beyond recognition, story can compel us to aspire to behave according to principles that transcend our very existence. Classic heroic myths tend to be defined by a willingness to put their lives in jeopardy, or even sacrifice them entirely, so that they can live in accord with a higher purpose. Some real people behave like this.

But heroism cannot be learned. There is no manual to read, no prescribed set of skills, no exam and no rules to follow that will result in anyone becoming a hero. The process of becoming a hero is as tacit as the process of learning a language, or learning how to swim.[4.2] We only discover we can do these things by observing others, trying, failing, and ultimately, putting ourselves in the loop, paying attention as we try to do the thing we wish to do, or become the person we wish to be.

Learning can only take us so far. People we love, and who love us, can influence our behavior and thinking by example and by telling us what to do. These things can even make perfect sense to us. And not only do we reject them, in many ways we should reject them. Humans are less when they only mimic and follow. The best answers to the fundamental questions come from individual choice—when we are in the loop, aware of the significance of the choices we make about how to behave. We are the only ones that can ultimately judge our own behavior, and we find it easier to live with ourselves when our behavior is more consistent with patterns we admire, should we objectively view ourselves from the outside, as if our lives were a story.

Because we contain the structural elements to recognize a wide variety of archetypal myths, we get to discover who we are by exposure to a similarly wide variety of myths on the outside without having to live through all of the situations those mythological figures encounter in stories. Thus, we can discover who we are through myths as if we were living other lives spiritually, without having to physically live them.

In this way, story allows for greater efficiency in evolution of the human race. Humans do not have to rely on reproduction in order to evolve. Genetic evolution, the generational process of "survival of the fittest" or natural selection, is incredibly slow. But story allows us to evaluate and define new standards of behavior within single lifetimes, instead of across many. Through story we experience virtual lives, giving us the opportunity to pick and choose how best to behave. Our ability to evaluate—and value—ourselves and others on the basis of behavior, the choices we make more than our genetic properties, separates us from animals. We can choose to identify ourselves with characters whose authors have little in common with our genetic composition. We identify with the same archetypes they do. We seem to recognize who we really are through story into which we can powerfully project ourselves.

This recognition has the potential to allow us to become true individuals, identifying with themes that are far removed, physically, from where we are or have even ever been before. Story is what enables us to stand up to the crowd, to do what is right even when we are the only one who can see the right thing to do and despite the potential consequences to ourselves. When we see, and embrace, our mythical heroes doing something in a similar vein, we want do to the same. We want to be like them in a more meaningful way, the less superficial we are. But in order to do so, we must make myriad projections to the specific circumstances of our own lives, to the situations we encounter that matter to us, as well as to our own skill sets—what we have that makes us, symbolically, handsome or otherwise attractive. We must first discover the best we have to offer in order to act in accord with the myths that move us. Accordingly, the greatest myths are those that inspire and enable us to think for ourselves, to evaluate our own behavior against the many prototypes we have seen and heard in story before, and to have the courage to behave as true individuals, as classic heroes, when it matters the most.

An important corollary is that, if mythical figures in story can allow us to become individuals so that we can act alone, then those figures operate at a more powerful level than those people we experience around us, directly, in reality. Significantly, myths can even act to sustain us when those around us fail us, as people so often do, especially when they fail themselves.

By capturing our imagination, myths transcend the immediate. We might go willingly to our death for a family member, because they have immediate, tangible benefit for us. We come to love them as a result of those benefits, and we feel that their lives are worth the sacrifice of our own. Animals will sometimes do this, because they perceive direct, immediate consequences for the loss of those beings they perceive as part of their pack. But myths can compel us to willingly sacrifice our so-called quality of life, ourselves, or even put our loved ones at risk for a higher ideal of what it means to behave well—so that a *principal* may not die. That principal may affect people we will never meet, and those people may well be ultimately grateful to us, even if they never met us, even if our lifetimes did not overlap.

Through myths we can place a value on the only things we can control in our lives, what we think and how we behave. This includes placing a value on our entire existence, our physical being, as secondary to our spiritual choices—to the good we must first imagine.

Classic heroes portray the power to cast the value of a single lifetime into a single moment. Myths have the power to capture our imagination. Classic heroic myths have the power to put the value of our entire existence into perspective, come what may. Since they have that kind of power, they also have the power to be there, and to never fail us, throughout our entire lives.

As with anything powerful, myths are not universally good. Like technology, myths are neutral; they provide the basis for great good as well as great evil. Hitler tapped into myths—that is where his power came from. But the people who fought him were enabled by their myths as well. People tend to follow the myths that are easiest to find in their culture, the ones most readily available to them.

In order for myths to move us in the first place, we must find them. And in order for us to find them, they first had to be there. A cynical culture, one that lives in the concrete view that only what is seen and what is real has value—the bottom line—is likely to be one that values myths that reflect the imposition of will, rather than ones that reflect individualism, transcendence and the importance of struggle. When this happens, the culture becomes more angry, depressed, and even violent.

My personal experience serves as impetus for writing this book, as well as an example. As a kid, when I was in concert with my myth of choice, who happened to be there for me at precisely the time I needed him, I was able to endure things that, in retrospect, are doubtful I would have endured as well, if at all. But, in keeping with my myth of choice, on some level I understood that the pain I was experiencing was completely in keeping with the dignity of my hero, and even transformative. My family, which was where the problem originated, could not help. Peers were not helpful and, if anything, were a part of the problem. My myth was more powerful to me than the reality that surrounded me. In turn, he had the ability, by having meaning to me, to positively affect my reality. Later, when I became immersed in career and other issues, and lost connection to my myth, I became less.

The less we have exposure to certain kinds of myths, the more likely this is to happen. According to Joseph Campbell, when our myths become less, we become less.[0.4] Furthermore, if we do not reflect upon our own story, in the context of our myth of choice, we can come to behave and think badly—both towards ourselves and towards others. Mythological choices can become limited by cultural restriction (group-think or imposed barriers), lack of individual exposure (either through self-imposed limitations or inability to symbolically process myth), or lack of development of myth in the form most appropriate for the culture. The more limited mythological choices are, the more cultures and individuals become self-destructive. When we do not find meaning—higher purpose—in our behavior, we seem to want to sabotage our very existence, sometimes through hurting others. When we cannot aspire to higher purpose, we seem to need to transmit the pain of our lack of meaning to others in any way we can, often very subtly.

When a life is placed into a broader context, it is far easier to live. It also becomes more our own, because we can only choose how to think and how to behave—but not what results, nor the circumstances we encounter, nor even our abilities. Paradoxically, the most powerful heroes have the most universal qualities, even as they enable us to distinguish ourselves as individuals. Those universal qualities tend to facilitate our ability to separate what is significant from what is not, allowing us to amplify the value of self-reward and doing while attenuating the value of group reward and having. For example, classic heroes tend to not have aspirations for higher position, or greater titles, or more money or even marriage or children. These are things that a hero might be rewarded with, or not, in the course of events. But they are not the goals of a hero because those are not guaranteed by-products of good behavior. For a true, classic hero, the behavior—the doing—is all that matters; transcendent behavior is its own reward. Such behavior is transcendent simply because it is. Why it moves us defies explanation, similar to the way we cannot say why singing is more moving than speaking.

The classic, heroic themes are perhaps all the more exposed in *Mannix* because *Mannix* really did not start out to be a series about a classic hero. Its origins have so much more to do with some combination of Sam Spade, James Bond and man against machine. The series and character are richer because they grew into something classic, and so it was possible to watch the evolution. By the time season 5 comes around, loyal viewers got the chance to witness Joe Mannix endure all sorts of situations, from becoming blinded to being shot (many times) to having only hours to discover the antidote for deadly poison. Each time, you could tell the hurt affected him—and yet he pressed on, often all alone. Surrounding these events, where he was completely on the line, were countless situations, virtually at least one per week, in which he would put himself directly in harm's way, but not always get hurt. He always found the will to press on, to keep engaging. He seemed to find his energy in his belief that he could positively affect the world, and from nothing else.

Essential was the impression that his behavior was not unconscious, not mechanical—not the product of living out the wishes of his father, or some organization (such as the government), or anything else which would have given him an excuse to be less than aware of what he was doing from moment to moment. Those behind the show seemed to be aware of the importance of self-awareness in the construction of a classic hero.

In season 5 is an episode, "A Button for General D." In it, Joe's friend, Monty, is killed in the opening "teaser." We never do get to know Monty very well, only that he seems very troubled at the time of his death. The person who killed him, Cindy, did so accidentally, in self-defense. She becomes a love interest of our hero. Just prior to this happening, Cindy picks up a book, one of a collection of books that turns out to be a key to the mystery behind the cryptic words uttered by Monty right before he died, words which also form the title of the episode. Cindy notices that one book has a passage underlined in red—the passage is actually shown on screen:

"It is the bitter sorrow and regret of a man who knows that once he had a great talent and wasted it, of a man who knows that once he had a great treasure, and got nothing from it, of a man who knows that he had strength for everything and never used it."[4.3]

These are poetic words, moving in their own right.

Cindy starts to read the passage, and then Joe comes in to recite the phrase from memory starting at "he had a great treasure…" Cindy replies that Joe's recollection was "word for word." Joe, clearly moved by the very words he remembers so well, goes on to say that he and his now dead friend once "kicked that around one night." The look on Joe's face belies that he, himself, has thought about the meaning of having great talent, great treasure, and great strength—heroes, after all, tend to have those things, in one form or another, even as we all do, in one form or another. But heroes also are aware of what it means to waste those things.

Joe Mannix gives every impression that he was aware of what it meant to waste those things. The way *Mannix* distinguished itself from other series, most especially ones with reluctant heroes, or anti-heroes, is that Joe Mannix gave every impression that his greatest fear could well have been wasting the gifts he was given. All other fears were secondary to that one. When we waste what we are, our gifts, what we have been given, we are the ones who render our own lives meaningless.

In addition to Carl Jung and Joseph Campbell, Viktor Frankl describes how meaning is crucial to leading a good life. His great work recounts how he survived life in a WWII concentration camp by attaching meaning to his suffering.[4.4] He also observed that others who survived the camps did so because they were also able to find meaning, even if their meaning was very different from his own. His logotherapy concept describes the importance of attaching meaning to sacrifice and to suffering. How else can this be?

Frankl approached his philosophy in a way an Engineer might solve a practical kind of problem—he observed what worked, then generalized it. For Frankl, it was enough to say that attaching meaning to circumstances made a difference to behavior. His definition of meaning was left up to each individual to decide. Heroism is similar in so many ways. Meaning is essential. Only the individual can decide what the meaning is. But the meaning must permit us to accept suffering, to continue to struggle when faced with pain. Otherwise, the meaning is not transcendent.

Classic heroism is, quite simply, useful as well as spiritual.

Heroes set forth an example of behavioral beauty that we find so compelling that we want to find ways to be in concert with it. Once we see that, we never forget it, even if it becomes buried deep within us.

And now, back to the episode, "The Gang's All Here."

Joe winds up sitting at a table in a deserted dance hall, last used to celebrate New Year's 1969—the streamers are still hanging from the ceiling in the dark, now run-down hall (the episode first aired in the fall of 1973). It's now been several hours since Joe was shot and seriously wounded; he is slowly bleeding to death. A few hours prior, he encountered an old drunk, a derelict who is living in the deserted dance hall. The derelict had worked there when the place was last used. He happens to tell Joe about Arlie's father, the now dead policeman who was thought to have been on the take at the time of his death four years ago. While Joe is trying to clean up his wound in the deserted men's room of the dance hall, the derelict tells Joe that he witnessed Arlie's father being set up on that fateful New Year's Eve. Joe manages to find some dimes in the repositories of the pay toilets—much to the derelict's surprise. After Joe sends the derelict off to make a phone call to the police, the derelict goes off and uses the money to buy a drink instead. Joe is, once again, alone and left to die.

In the meantime, Arlie is having second thoughts about not having the courage to kill Joe the first time. He finds a gun from one of the girlfriends of an ex-gang member, and this ex-gang member happens to be the one who planted the phony evidence on Arlie's father that New Year's Eve. The girlfriend is vengeful, because Joe killed the ex-gang member earlier that same day in a shoot-out. She sends Arlie off to kill Joe, whom she discovered to be in the dance hall because the derelict, now drunk in a bar and telling stories, revealed where Joe was.

Arlie goes off to find the courage to kill Joe, with this gun, but by himself this time. When Arlie encounters Joe, now sitting at a table, with his head down as if he does not possess the strength to move anymore, Joe asks Arlie for a last cigarette, clearly a ploy because *Mannix* fans know that Joe was supposed to have kicked the habit two years earlier. Joe tries to appeal to Arlie's better nature. But it does not work. Arlie, while still listening to Joe, wants to feel like a man. His current model of what this means is to become one of the gang—the gang is an immediate way to satisfy his need to connect with something larger than himself. In order to do so, Arlie believes he needs to find the courage to kill Joe.

But Joe knows who Arlie's father was, and he now knows what no one else but the derelict knows; that Arlie's father was not on the take, that he died a good cop and was set-up. Joe has to find a way to convince Arlie that he knows this and is not just making it up in order to try to save his own life. He tells Arlie, who initially does not buy it. But Joe happens to know that cops sometimes carve initials on the handle of their guns, and he asks Arlie to look at the gun in his hand. Arlie finds his father's initials there. He tosses the gun away. In that moment, he decides the image of his dead father is more powerful than the more immediate rewards of living up to the expectations of the gang.

Joe, somewhat relieved that he isn't going to be shot dead at that moment, but still needing help, starts to leave the dance hall, with Arlie's help. But two other gang members discovered where Joe was hiding in the meantime, and they get there before Joe and Arlie have the opportunity to get out. Joe hides in the men's room while Arlie stands up to the two gang members, telling them that he let Joe get away. Arlie has now, of course, become much more of a man than he ever could have by killing Joe or joining the gang. But Arlie is now going to take a beating, or worse, as a result of this choice. Joe, knowing this, finds a way to throw a lit bottle of cleaning fluid across the hall, setting part of the dance hall ablaze. This breaks up the beating, initially saving Arlie's life, because the two gang members quickly leave the burning dance hall behind, with Arlie in it. Their mission is accomplished if Arlie burns to death anyway, and Arlie is now on the floor of the burning dance hall, unconscious. He is also, from Joe's perspective, behind a wall of flame, since the men's room is near the entrance of the dance hall and Arlie is towards the middle of the room.

Now on his last legs from the hours of bleeding, Joe goes back in to get Arlie, dragging him out, barely able to do so because of his own gunshot wound. He's coughing due to smoke inhalation, clearly struggling to do something he would normally very easily do—get Arlie out of the building. He manages to get them both out in time. Both are presumably found by the arriving fire trucks we only hear. Joe finds a way to save not only himself, but someone else as a result of his own plight. This theme is a recurring one in the series—what else would you expect from *Mannix*?

But the story does not end there.

The next scene, consistent with the tight editing that was a big part of the *Mannix* style—heroes, after all, do have a sense of style—cuts quickly to show Peggy at the end of a hospital corridor, glancing up at the heavens, thankful Joe was found alive. She is nervous and clearly waiting for something. She is waiting for Joe.

A stretcher comes from around the corner, and Peggy does not initially notice that it is Joe on the stretcher. But then she does, and she pushes off the wall and darts over to intercept the path of the stretcher as it rolls down the corridor, stopping the orderly from pushing it along. She goes to touch the stretcher, seems to think better of it, lest she hurt Joe, and then simply says, in the great way Gail Fisher was able to convey so much emotion with simple, often single, words, "Joe," almost in the form of a question—implicitly asking how he is in the very tone of her voice, laden with concern.

In response, in the similarly great way Mike Connors was able to convey so much emotion with simple words, Joe says, "Hi, Peggy." But he is clearly struggling to say it, or much of anything at all.

Peggy smiles the smile of relief and happiness that Joe wound up alive that night, can recognize her, and has conveyed to her that "it happened to me again" kind of acceptance of his way of life.

She next informs Joe that she called his father, whom Joe was supposed to visit that evening to celebrate his seventy-fifth birthday. His father is instead coming down to L.A. from Northern California, she tells him. Joe replies with a bit of sarcasm, "Some birthday."

Peggy softly shakes her head and says in reply, "It's the best ever. You're alive."

The words, so simple, say nothing compared to the facial expressions on these two, and the tone in their voices. In keeping with the kind of transcendence that is the hallmark of classic heroism, these characters convey a warmth and deep affection for each other that seems to transcend normal bounds of friendship and even romantic interests, the latter of which they did not have, or at least did not culminate, over the years the series ran.

Uncomfortable—presumably due to how Peggy just expressed how important Joe was to her, but also presumably due to thinking about things some more, as well as due to being in some pain, with all of that conveyed on his face at once—Joe replies, "How's Arlie?"

Peggy replies, very softly, almost in a whisper, seemingly in order to try to keep Joe as calm and relaxed as possible, "He's fine."

Joe, in thinking about things some more, still says, "That Dietz report Peggy, you're going to have to re-type type it." He does so by slurring his words, repeating "type," as if it is difficult to say it at all. He's been shot, been bleeding most of the night, and was presumably medicated by now.

Dietz is the ex-gang member that Joe killed earlier that day, the one who set-up Arlie's father. Peggy was completing the report when she found out Joe was missing and shot.

Peggy has a momentary look of shock on her face—perfect, and something the viewer most likely barely noticed when first watching the episode, something far more easily seen by freezing the DVD. It is far from the only time such transient but moving expressions have appeared on those character's faces.

She has no idea why Joe wants the report re-typed, has no idea what Joe found out that night, and is not thinking in any other terms than being grateful Joe is still alive, coupled with the knowledge that he has not yet been treated for his wound. She seems to think Joe is just not thinking straight. But then she softens just as quickly, one emotion transforming to another with no words in-between, and then says, also softly, beautifully, in a firm way, "Later, Joe."

Then Joe, in thinking about Arlie, and presumably that he, himself, might not make it through the night, seems to have a small spurt of energy and says, "No, it's important, Peggy. Now. Now..."

He slurs these words, too, having to work to get "Peggy" out, and as the second "Now" trails off, he passes out, putting his face away from Peggy in order to do so.

The conversation being over at this point, the orderly wheels Joe away, presumably to be treated.

We see Peggy in the last shot, with a look of utter admiration, and even awe, on her face, her eyes half-closed as her gaze follows the stretcher down the hall, and she says, for no one there to hear it, "Tomorrow, Joe."

It is, again, uttered with rich emotion, all things conveyed in melody of voice and imagery. The scene is not sappy, not over-done. Nor does it make light of the heroism of the moment. It does not brush the behavior aside, rendering it small. In true *Mannix* fashion, it is unafraid to reach the heroism. It hits a sweet spot.

The *Mannix* grid appears, ending the episode on Peggy's frozen gaze of admiration and awe at Joe.

The scene is like a song. It moves you—and it's difficult to completely say why. It is especially moving for those who had a relationship with these characters since their very inception. Because, you, the viewer, can relate to what Peggy must be feeling. You have witnessed all of the things Joe has done, as she has. You know her admiration for him is real—it goes beyond compassion for a close friend. Joe is more than boss, colleague, friend, even lover, belonging more to the world than to any one person, as heroes must. Like a song, the scene can be watched over and over again. Each time, you can think about it just a little bit more. Each time, it sinks in just a little bit deeper, if you let it.

And when you let it, then you want to be like Joe Mannix, just a little bit more, just in your own way. You can't be just like him—that would be pointless anyway, and even wrong. Heroes, by definition, cannot be copied. True heroes must find their own meaning, and contribute in specific, unique situations, each according to their own gifts. Copying results in mere imitation and that is not heroic, is not consistent with the first step of heroism, which is self-awareness.

But, in terms of qualities of character, you want to be something like the hero who, in that moment, had the courage, the dignity to think of the kid who almost killed him—twice—but who could not quite bring himself to do it, despite intense peer pressure, despite being otherwise alone in the world. You want to help the same kid, whose father was a good cop but set-up when he was killed trying to do his job. You want to do it despite whatever cost it presents to you. You want to do it despite being in pain, despite bleeding to death, and despite not knowing whether or not you are even going to make it through the night.

You know that Joe Mannix could not stand to live with himself if he did not do just that—if he did not put Arlie first, even though Arlie almost tried to kill him twice, even when Joe was barely able to speak himself, even when he barely survived, even when he was about to pass out. And when you see it, you know that kind of behavior is transcendent, and that the pain, and even fear of death, is secondary. You get the sense that Joe's own death meant far less to him than his telling what he found out that night, placing his life second to helping the kid who wound up finding the courage to not kill him.

As a kid, I used to re-play that scene in my mind, as so many other scenes in *Mannix*. The scene was mysteriously comforting, even though it seemingly had little to do with what was happening around me, or to me, or with my plans for my own life. But it was somehow easy to reflect upon, even natural to do so, as an old song that once moved you comes to mind when you least expect it.

That scene, and so many others like it, had a lot to do with the pain of things that happened to me over the years being just a little more endurable, and the desire to do the right thing despite the consequences just a little easier, at least on some occasions. But I also know that, over the years, my loss of connection to what was behind that scene was tantamount to denying myself and what I knew, on some level, really mattered most. Somehow that denial was connected to ever more education and participation in the supposed rational world.

As an engineer, I am in awe of that scene and its immense, useful, practical value.

As a human being, I know I will never completely understand why it moves me.

But I am so grateful that it once did.

I am glad that it still does.

Chapter 5
Joe and Peggy

Heroes do not need witnesses. But heroism takes on additional significance in the presence of a credible witness. Such observers bridge behavior to its evaluation. Credible witnesses in story imply that heroic deeds might have timeless qualities worth re-telling. Accordingly, witnesses imply the need for us to better observe ourselves for evaluation of the potential timeless qualities of our own behavior.

To this day Joe and Peggy have what may be the most unusual relationship in TV series history. There was obvious chemistry between them, clear deep affection. They got about as close as they could for two single heterosexual people of opposite gender who had no reason to not get any closer, except for the times.

Prior to 1968, few blacks (the term used then, and so the one I will use), male or female, had leading roles in TV series of any kind, where leading roles are defined by the appearance of the names of the actors in the opening credits of the show. Bill Cosby famously co-starred with Robert Culp in *I Spy* and Greg Morris was a member of the IMF team in *Mission: Impossible*. But those shows largely ignored race, to the point of affecting the plausibility of the undercover missions. In 1968, there were three black actresses in prominent roles in series TV. One was Diahann Carroll who played the starring role in the sitcom, *Julia* (the NBC-TV series from 1968-1971). Another was Nichelle Nichols, who played Uhura in *Star Trek* (the Original Series). *Julia* was criticized for portraying the black lead character as, essentially, a white woman who was only incidentally black. The situation was similar in *Star Trek*, where Uhura is famous for opening hailing frequencies and having a forced inter-racial kiss with her captain. The third was Gail Fisher, who played Peggy in the re-tooled *Mannix*, replacing Joseph Campanella in title credits when Joe Mannix left Intertect to go out on his own, at the start of season 2.

Of these, only *Mannix* acknowledged the race of the leading character as a plausible disadvantage. Only *Mannix* included episodes that explored that difference. Only *Mannix* permitted the leading character to have open, deep affection for her white co-star.

Gail Fisher was a black woman who was not merely playing some pre-existing type—black or white. The spirit of character inventiveness that was the hallmark of the season 2 renewal of the series applied to Peggy as well as it did to Joe. As a result, her qualities wound up being critical to conveying the heroic qualities of Joe Mannix. Since Joe got hurt a lot, the way she felt about it mattered, and made him seem more human by virtue of being human to her. The fact that Joe hired a black woman in 1968, and that he treated her, in many ways, as an equal, made the way she came to care about him all the more believable, all the more moving.

When *Mannix* was re-tooled for Joe to go out on his own for the opening of the second season, Joe needed a secretary. The show's executive producer, Bruce Geller, was open to the woman having any kind of background.[5.1] Nichelle Nichols was tapped to fill the role, but she was still committed to *Star Trek*.[5.2] Gail Fisher had limited acting experience, having been the first black woman to be cast in a commercial.[5.3] But she had won several beauty contests. And she was expressive. Since facial expression was Connors' hallmark, going back to why he was discovered in the first place, she fit. Connors is quoted as saying, "That personality hits you right away—she's so alive."[5.1] True to the character he played, this appealed to him rather than intimidated him as an actor. Even though his role would not work unless he always came across as the biggest guy in the room, he seemed to realize that the role would be even larger if the guy he played was comfortable being challenged. This made it into the on-screen chemistry between Connors and Fisher who, for her part, credits her success in her role as Peggy to working with a "great guy."[5.4] Something else may have also helped this chemistry.

Both Connors and Executive Producer Bruce Geller went to the CBS brass and stood up for Gail Fisher when the brass thought a black woman would hurt the show in the South. But while Geller had another show at the time (*Mission: Impossible*, which was going into its third season), Connors not only had no other show, but his career had hit a downturn. He even took a singing and dancing act to Mexico for a time, after his earlier TV show, *Tightrope*, was canceled after one season, but remained popular in Mexico. *Mannix*, itself, was almost canceled after its first season. Connors put his series on the line anyway, so that Fisher could be a part of it. Did this touch of behind-the-scenes reality help?

The relationship between Joe and Peggy quickly evolved during Fisher's first season, so fast that the second half of season 2 almost looks like a different series. The first episode produced for season 2 (but the fourth one aired since *Mannix* episodes were not aired in production order) is "To the Swiftest, Death." There, Peggy is just a traditional secretary, even serving lunch. The one and only exchange between them in the entire series that is painful to watch occurs in that episode—where Joe addresses her as "honey." Luckily, this practice ended as soon as it began. We never do get to see when Joe hired Peggy, or when he quits Intertect, for that matter, but the first time we do see Peggy there is at least some indication that she is going to be more than a pushover for Joe.

The first time the viewers see Peggy, in the first episode aired in the second season, is the first time they also see Joe's new office, at 17 Paseo Verde. He just shows up there, without explanation, and is presumed to have quit Intertect. She is in only one scene of that episode, one in which Joe is being Joe by aggressively questioning a woman who has witnessed a phone conversation that indicates someone is about to be killed. The woman is deaf and Joe is pushing her to remember the rest of a phone number. When Joe pushes too hard and the woman breaks down, Peggy gets upset—actually glaring right at Joe in that very first scene. Of course, Joe simply takes it in. Joe is big enough to take it in, and to take it in not only from the likes of his secretary, but a black one at that—in 1968. For those with no context of what 1968 was like with respect to race relations, it might be worth asking for a refund on your high school education.

So enters Peggy. She is now Joe's secretary—but she is not even visually typical and there she is glaring at and admonishing her boss. Still, for the next few episodes in which she appears, she could very well be white. Initially, viewers must have wondered if *Mannix* was going the direction of all of the other shows that incidentally included blacks in leading roles. But the series *Mannix* was not unlike its main character, and so about two-thirds of the way into the first season in which Fisher appears, *Mannix* has the guts to acknowledge that Peggy is black in two great episodes that run nearly back to back. Those episodes are all the more powerful because *Mannix* was not about race, after all. Peggy functions in her job in such a way that race is not an issue, filling a role both in the series and to Joe that a white woman could have. The viewer implicitly understood that she was not hired by Joe because she was black, but because she is competent, for a set of qualities he values over and above whatever consequences he may have to endure because he did something out of the norm by hiring her. Thus, it is all the more powerful that Fisher is not playing white, that her race is not ignored. This makes her one of the most, if not the most, groundbreaking black character in TV history.

Peggy also has an interesting back story of her own, which helps give her credibility in standing up to Joe. We learn that Peggy is the widowed mother of a son, and that her husband, a policeman, was killed in the line of duty. We also learn that she used to work in the police department in the DMV (Department of Motor Vehicles), and her contacts there prove useful to Joe. But she also has loyalties to the police, at least at the beginning. This beautifully evolves as Peggy changes her loyalties over time, by witnessing the qualities and exploits of her boss. She grows somehow warmer to her boss. Their relationship becomes something unique, ultimately working to great effect for loyal viewers because it is revealed right on the faces and in specific, often brief, scenes not easily rendered to stereotypical description. Credible witnesses have more value if they are won over to heroic nature, over time. But, initially, you get the sense that while Peggy likes Joe, she probably went to work for him either to get away from the police environment or because the money was better, because she seems to have mixed feelings about her boss.

For one thing, she can't seem to call him by his first name until the eighteenth episode of the second season. That episode, "Death in a Minor Key," probably not coincidentally, is one of the more masterful episodes in TV history for the way it handles race. It is also the first time Joe helps Peggy, as a friend. In so doing, and almost in passing, we hear Peggy for the first time address her boss as "Joe." She does so softly and in the context of his helping her, now as a friend. Then Joe goes off to a small, nameless Southern town to try to find out why Peggy's jazz trumpeting boyfriend has been framed with a crime he didn't commit. And when Joe, our hero, goes there, he carries his own prejudice with him—his prejudice of the South.

The sheriff of the Southern town, played by Anthony Zerbe, is actually more progressive than Joe gives him credit for, providing a twist at the end where one of his black police officers has been following Joe all along, undercover. But because you see Joe being prejudiced about the South, you, the viewer, are more comfortable with your own prejudice—we all have some form of prejudice for something, in one form or another. In typical *Mannix* fashion this is all done very subtly, via misdirection that makes something important, and of educational value, also entertaining. You just get it, without even fully realizing what happened unless you really think about it.

Our hero displays toughness in many forms in this series, but perhaps none is better than the scene in this episode with the crippled man that accused Peggy's boyfriend of hit and run. In that scene, a self-proclaimed "vegetable" says to Joe, "You don't know what *they* are like," with the "they" referring to black people. So when the crippled man accuses Joe of taking the word of the black man over his, you can see it on Joe's face, how hard it is going to be to simply say to that man, "That's right." Joe knows that in so doing he is going to hurt a man who has already been hurt, and he knows he is going to hear it back from this man and be kicked out of his house. But Joe simply takes a deep breath and says it—he does not run from the issue, nor does he become preachy about it. In typical *Mannix* fashion, he just does it, just says what he believes, and faces the consequences. Joe is tough in more than just a physical way.

This episode sets the tone for the way race was handled in the rest of the series. It is not ignored. Like everything else in *Mannix*, it was handled in a gutsy, classy way—and with some artful misdirection. Not only is there misdirection because Joe has to confront his own prejudice about the South, but this episode, which is the first one where *Mannix* acknowledges Peggy as black, breaks the "Joe" barrier.

Having Joe work for Peggy as a friend, in order to help her boyfriend, is likely not accidental in adding to the level of viewer comfort when this moment occurred. The producers found a way to have Peggy start to call her boss by his first name, getting past any problems viewers might have had with that otherwise. And without that, none of the other good things that happen between them would be possible.

It was done in an off-hand way in "Death in a Minor Key," but if there was ever any doubt that Peggy is now calling her boss comfortably by his first name, that doubt is removed in the next episode that was filmed, "All Around the Money Tree," a semi-comedic episode that is a take-off on the movie *It's a Mad, Mad, Mad, Mad World*. Near the beginning of that episode we have Peggy getting ready to leave for the day, but at the last minute she decides to check in on Joe, who is in his office behind a closed door. When she does, she says "Good night, Joe." Joe does not initially respond, being deep in thought about something they both witnessed that morning. Peggy has to repeat herself. So she says "Good night, *Joe*" loudly, and with emphasis on his name, because she is, ostensibly, trying to get his attention. But this emphasis is as much for the viewers as for Joe—the point is being made, she's calling him *Joe* now and anyone who is uncomfortable with that had better find another series. After all, Joe is so comfortable with it that he didn't even notice her doing it the first time. From this moment on, she would come to say it so well over the years, sometimes conveying paragraphs of emotion in that one word.

Which is why it is all the more shocking—for those who remember what the characters grew into—that for Fisher's first seventeen episodes of *Mannix*, her character addresses her boss as "Mr. Mannix," "Sir," or—even more impersonal—just plain "Mannix." Those behind the show must have decided early on that they wanted these two to become closer, and that there had to be some sort of transition for the viewers to accept it, because, as the second season progresses through its middle third, Peggy starts to use Joe's last name less when she addresses him. Instead, she just says nothing where a solid "Joe" would be used in later years. Without this transition to having Peggy call her boss and now friend, "Joe," the signature episodes of *Mannix* can never happen, Gail Fisher never wins her Emmy, and you can never quite see Peggy as that credible witness, which ultimately, in turn, made Joe Mannix a larger hero. Connors and the people behind *Mannix* had guts for doing this.

If the whole first name issue seems like no big deal all these years later, consider another TV classic, *The Mary Tyler Moore Show*. Interestingly, its debut on CBS was at 9:30 p.m. on Saturday nights in the 1970-1971 TV season, making it the series that was on the air right before *Mannix* ran at 10:00 p.m. on CBS during its fourth season. When *Mary Tyler Moore*'s closing music ended, after a brief commercial, the *Mannix* grid appeared with the newly added word "mannix" behind it, all in lower case and gold lettering. And there was

Mary in the previous half hour, famous for being a single woman who wanted to go out and be on her own, college-educated and working as a single woman in an all-male newsroom. But she can't call her boss anything but "Mr. Grant." Such a big deal is made of this that an entire episode is devoted to her clumsy attempts to call him "Lou"—but that episode does not run until late in the series, in the mid 1970s. In the meantime, Peggy has been calling her boss "Joe" since early 1969! So in 1970 it was possible to watch *The Mary Tyler Moore Show* and *Mannix* run back-to-back, with Peggy calling her boss Joe and Mary still too intimidated to call her boss anything but "Mr. Grant." A nine- and ten-year-old girl could just *feel* that kind of difference.

If this still isn't enough evidence of significance, the issue actually comes up twice later in *Mannix*. In the season 5 episode, "Run Till Dark," some thugs are holding Peggy hostage in her office. They are waiting for Joe to come back so they can ambush him. Joe calls in on his car phone. When Peggy answers, she addresses her boss as "Mr. Mannix" and "Sir." This, in and of itself, sends a clear message to Joe that something is very wrong. He enters his own office so warned. By now, if Peggy is calling him "Mr. Mannix" and "Sir" then something is definitely not right. They are friends, even virtual equals in a day and age where women who worked as secretaries in offices were just not treated that way.

As late as season 6, in "The Man Who Wasn't There," one of Joe's nutty Korean War ex-buddies is, yet again, holding Peggy hostage. The number of times she is taken hostage is the subject of another discussion, similar to the number of times Joe is shot and knocked unconscious, but because of the closeness of those two, those episodes where Joe needs to get Peggy out of trouble just work. Peggy was talking to Joe on the phone at the time this nutty buddy comes in, and she says "I've got company, Joe." The Korean War buddy says, "She calls you 'Joe,' ain't that nice." It was still unusual, and acknowledged as such, that she called her boss by his first name, in an episode that aired as late as early 1973. But that practice was already going on for four years in *Mannix*. And Mary was *still* calling her boss "Mr. Grant."

In order for this to work, Connors had to be comfortable enough in his presence as a larger-than-life hero to give a bit of cheap status away for something far more genuine. It also made those times when Peggy was that credible witness that much more moving—she could convey so much just by saying his first name to him. What the viewer got was deep affection—imagery parallel to the dialogue.

One of the longest examples of the great visual, non-verbal acting in the series comes in an episode that is normally not considered one of the signature episodes of *Mannix*, yet which is a very good episode in its own right, season 6's "The Open Web." In this episode, a young cop is killed in Joe's office the night before by a character played by Rip Torn (in one of his earliest acting roles), after mistaking the young cop for Joe.

Peggy enters the office the next morning. The piano music in the background, a subtle classic score, was scored by no less than Lalo Schifrin, himself. Peggy first sees a broken light on her desk, and presumably knows what happened. She picks up a piece of the broken shade and reflects upon it—someone died there the night before, and it was supposed to be Joe. She continues into her office, and notices that the light is still on in Joe's office, the one on his desk. She conveys how that is highly unusual. She goes in to turn it off—and on the way discovers Joe lying on the couch, asleep. She is, in one single moment, both surprised—clearly he is not typically found there when she arrives for the day—and relieved to see that he is still alive. She knows he wasn't killed the night before, but it's still a huge relief to see him still alive. She walks over to turn the light off. After so doing, she finds a bottle of empty scotch. She picks it up, looks at it, and then looks at Joe. In one moment, she simultaneously conveys recognition of why Joe is there, acknowledgment of why he drank the scotch, and disappointment that he did. She realizes she will probably need to wake him up, since he is going to be hung over—and she walks over and utters her first word of the scene.

And that word is, "Joe."

Joe does not immediately respond. He is hung over, after all, and so she says it again, this time shaking his leg a little to get his attention, but this time with even more feeling, "*Joe.*"

So many scenes in *Mannix* are just like that, not filled up with dialogue, not over-done with emotion, but visual expression that conveys depth of feeling and appreciation of character—most especially between Joe and Peggy. The DVDs, along with the ability to pause frames, allow viewers to actually see many of the complex expressions on faces that were never possible to see before, often right as people enter or leave rooms or when the scene changes. In many ways, *Mannix* can be seen and appreciated on the DVDs better than it ever could before, just for the ways the actors stayed so much in character even when they were barely on camera. This scene runs for over a full minute and it is all about Peggy's complex visual expressions.

So much of the success of *Mannix* had to do with the way the actors inhabited those characters. They had to pull off a lot of believability in order to make the series work, since the series was not just about the characters, but character, itself. Incredibly, they also made us believe that it made perfect sense that the relationship between Joe and Peggy only went so far.

They were both single, heterosexual, and clearly had deep affection for each other. And yet, during the seven years they worked together, from the time Peggy appeared as a relatively new hire at the beginning of the second season until the series ended in 1975, they only ever dated other people—those annoying *other* people. There was never any hint that Peggy did anything but come to the office in the morning, leave it at night, visit Joe in the hospital and worry a lot when he went missing or made himself into a target.

It just made no sense—except that she was black and he was white. Even *that* made no sense in the context of the characters. Joe Mannix wasn't going to let a little thing like race stop him from doing anything. And Peggy didn't seem to let it bother her either.

What was going on here? Did we miss something during those commercial breaks?

It's strange now to think that President Obama was born seven years before Peggy became Joe's secretary. But back then interracial dating simply did not happen on TV. There was the much publicized interracial kiss between Uhura and Kirk on *Star Trek* in 1966—but that was a forced thing. There was never any suggestion that they actually *wanted* to do it.

In sharp contrast, *Mannix* left you with the impression that Joe and Peggy actually *did* want to do it, actually leaving *you* wanting them to do it.

Now, just think about this. Starting as early as the fall of 1969, shortly into the third year of *Mannix*, there is this interracial duo of members of opposite sexes in a highly successful TV series where a considerable portion of the fan base actually would have wanted to see things go farther than they did. That had to be so much more effective in opening minds, even if in a subconscious way, than any kind of in-your-face relationship *telling* you what you were supposed to think.

What's more, there was apparently even discussion among those involved with the show that their relationship would go further—but it was decided that that would be too off-putting. It almost seems as if as if the decision to keep them just close friends came near the beginning of season 4, after some experimentation during season 3.

Leading up to season 3, the closest they get in season 2 has a lot to do with yet another treatment of race, the second classy way it was addressed in *Mannix* in the same season. In "Last Rites for Miss Emma," Joe is investigating a robbery. A supposed victim—and also supposed hero—of the robbery is a black man who threw some perfume on the robbers and got a flesh wound in the process. Peggy falls for him. When Joe discovers that Peggy's love interest is likely the inside man, Joe goes over to her apartment to try to warn her, and looks uncomfortable in so doing. When Peggy discovers what Joe is trying to tell her, she accuses him of racism. In response, Joe simply grabs Peggy by the arm, turns her towards him, and glares at her. This is completely visual. Peggy immediately backs down, realizing that she was wrong to say that to Joe—but never really apologizes for saying it either. She has enough will to not simply believe Joe, at least not right away. She is no pushover.

But still, Peggy accuses Joe of racism?

Now, in the larger scheme of things, she is probably not wrong. She has every right to think that might be a factor in the thinking of most people—but not Joe. So when Joe is the one accused of racism, especially by Peggy, and Joe is offended by that, enough to react the way he did, you get the point. Joe is not racist. You also realize there is nothing he can say to her, and nothing he should have to say to her, so he just grabs her by the arm—and glares. His denial is completely, 100% visual. And it is such a real, human response.

Heck, at the beginning of the episode we see Peggy pick him up at the Burbank airport, one of the last times she addresses him as just "Mannix," yelling his name when she sees him. In later years she would say "Joe" even in that kind of situation, and even later in this same episode she is now calling him "Joe," privately. This episode is really a kind of transition, so it has her still calling him by both names. He goes on to take her by the arm, in the manner in which gentlemen did in 1969, and they walk that way in the airport. But a white man walking that way with a black woman in such a public place in 1969 opens up the possibility for some ambiguity in the minds of onlookers, to say the very least, and so was not something people in the South, and many other places in the country for that matter, might take lightly. That scene took guts.

"Last Rites for Miss Emma" seems a kind of set-up for other good things to come in the relationship, further indicated by a seemingly casual exchange when Joe and Peggy are walking to Joe's car, which Peggy presumably drove to the airport in order to pick Joe up. When they are walking there, Peggy is offended that Joe did not notice her new dress. Just remember this when you get to the last line of "The Sound of Darkness" if, by chance, you are skeptical that the people behind the series did not pay attention to nuance, especially in these characters.

Season 2 went well enough that the series survived on its own merits, thus faring much better than season 1, which required Lucille Ball's intervention in order to survive and re-tool. This time, despite continuing to linger in a 10:00 p.m. Saturday night graveyard timeslot, its ratings were good enough for renewal. Its ratings would go up during each of the next three seasons, until it was moved to a killer timeslot. The character evolution just kept going.

Initially, this meant Joe and Peggy got closer.

"The Sound of Darkness," which first aired in December 1969, the third season, ends in a platonic, but incredibly warm, embrace. Prior to the embrace is a classic scene where Peggy lets her boss, and now friend, have it while he is blind—she tells him off in his worst moment. To think that both of these things happened in a single episode in 1969 is just incredible. Since that episode is arguably *Mannix's* signature episode, its details are discussed in another chapter. Prior to the airing of that episode, the character set-up in previous episodes seems intentional, deliberate. "The Sound of Darkness," which relied upon a presumption of closeness between Joe and Peggy, would not have worked at any point in season 2, or even at the very beginning of season 3.

But the first several episodes of season 3 have Peggy out there with Joe on cases, something that not only did not happen in season 2, it was atypical, and perhaps even groundbreaking, for secretaries of leading-men bosses. In "Color Her Missing," "The Playground," "A Penny for the Peep Show," "A Sleep in the Deep," and "Memory: Zero," which are among the nine episodes that aired in season 3 prior to "The Sound of Darkness," Peggy is starting to witness her boss in action, firsthand. She is involved with his cases more as well. In some of these episodes we see Peggy witness Joe punching out a couple of guys, right in front of her. The camera goes right to her face in such scenes, setting us up to know that she is quite literally acting as a firsthand witness to her boss' exploits.

And so, by the time we get to "Memory: Zero," which is really only the eighth episode of season 3, airing two before "The Sound of Darkness," we have Peggy acting, well, pretty indistinguishable from that of a jealous wife when Joe goes off to a trailer park to try to both protect and help jog the memory of a secretary of a fellow private eye who was recently killed. Someone is trying to hunt this secretary down and kill her. Joe spends lot of time with her in order to try to find out what she remembers. The set-up is clear. Despite the two of them spending both days and nights together in a rented trailer, the situation is platonic. Joe even goes out of his way to fend off anything going any further when the secretary kisses him. But Peggy does not know this.

In this same episode, when Peggy later expresses her displeasure at her boss for spending all this time with this beautiful secretary, she does so by referring to him as "Sir." This way of addressing him tips him off that something is wrong; only a year earlier it would have been ordinary, expected, and commonplace. (*Mannix* is now making an implicit commentary on the very ground it broke.) She goes further, saying to him on his way out the door, "Just remember, you already have a secretary, *Mr. Mannix*." By the time we get to this scene, her use of "Mr. Mannix" to address him has been cast in the form of admonishment, much like a parent calling a child by their full name. The camera stays on her gaze as it follows her boss out the door, a gaze that seems to hold more than a secretary that is worried about her job. The end of the episode has them walking off together, pretty much like a duo in a buddy show. But what are we supposed to think about this duo?

The very next episode produced after "The Sound of Darkness," but which aired in early 1970, is "Medal for a Hero" in which Peggy's late husband, a police officer killed in the line of duty, is accused of being on the take at the time of his death. Joe gets involved, of course, and proves the opposite, ostensibly on behalf of Peggy's son, Toby, who does not want to grow up thinking of his father as crooked. Near the end of the episode Joe shows up at Peggy's apartment one morning, newspaper in hand, to show the headlines to Toby—Joe has made things right. At the very end he hands Peggy back her wedding ring, which the police had taken, and flashes one of those great, warm, Joe Mannix smiles that seems to be reserved only for Peggy. She takes it—and the frame freezes on the wedding ring.

A few episodes later, "Harlequin's Gold," has Peggy the target of a kidnapping plot. In this story is a man with a weak spot that can be exploited. The bad guys can get to him because he is in love with a woman who does not exactly return the favor. In one scene Joe boldly says that he has no such weak spot. That response reflects his own presumption that he is still some sort of combination of Sam Spade and James Bond. But he discovers he is wrong. The bad guys of the episode know what Joe does not seem to. They then go on to show Joe that they have Peggy. This is not your typical PI show any more, and Joe Mannix is not your typical hero, and certainly not your typical crime fighter.

Two episodes after that, in "Only One Death to a Customer," we see Peggy come to visit Joe in the hospital late one night after he has been shot in the shoulder, ambushed by his client. The look of pained concern on her face comes right through the screen, one of those many scenes dialogue does little to convey. Indeed, that scene has no dialogue at all for what seems like minutes at a time at the beginning and end, as Peggy enters and leaves Joe's hospital room. Still another episode that same season has Joe running towards the lakeside cabin where Peggy and Toby are staying for vacation. Joe is worried they have been drowned in the lake by bad guys. When he enters the cabin, and Peggy is clearly surprised—but not displeased, the look on his face returns the favor. These two are now some kind of unique pair—but what kind?

The opening episode of season 4, "A Ticket to the Eclipse" is another one of those stories that mixes the closeness of these two with some classic heroism. It is also yet another episode where Peggy is kidnapped. Only this time, it is one of Joe's crazy ex-Korean War buddies who is serial-killing off all of his old pals. This guy also understands Joe's blind spot—that the best way to ultimately get to Joe is to get to Peggy. Everyone seems to know this but Joe. Prior to Peggy being kidnapped she visits Joe on a Friday morning to drop off some letters. She sees that his face has been beaten. She needs to know what happened. He tells her to leave and "drop it." She tells him, "Joe, I'm not leaving until you tell me." He recognizes there is no way out—this is no longer anything like the relationship they had in season 2. He tells her what happened, realizing he has no choice. She clearly has some power over him. Viewers have come to know this.

This episode ends on a trail by Joe's lakeside weekend cabin, with Joe arriving in his car, shot at by the bad guy while Peggy and Toby are being held at gunpoint. When Peggy sees Joe being shot at, she tells Toby to run—but then grabs at the gun in order to try to save Joe, getting tossed to the ground in the process. Of course, Joe has to go off and do his thing, facing the crazy on his own, leaving Peggy and Toby hiding behind the car wheels. After the sounds of the Jeep and gunshots come to an end, Peggy decides to go find out what happened, with Toby in hand. Joe stands up from behind the Jeep that just ran over the nutty buddy, and he walks over to put his left arm around Toby. Since his right arm has been shot and Peggy is on that side, she just puts her arm right around his *waist*—at a pretty familiar level. They walk off like a family would—and there can be no mistake.

At that time, you start to look for what is transpiring between them. The next few episodes have some really nice scenes in that regard. "One for the Lady" has a scene where Peggy is watching Joe shave at his desk (with an electric razor—a *Mannix* thing) after he has been let out of jail just that morning. He's been falsely accused of murder, among other things. She tells him how much he has in his bank account—not very much. He responds by saying, "not bad" and continues to go about his shaving. She responds with a look of combined exasperation, affection and concern (these two were masters at conveying looks that communicated combined, complex emotions). She tells Joe that she has a little money in the bank, and offers some in case he "needs any eating money." He stops shaving at that point, and his look is one of clear appreciation, surprise and affection. He refuses, of course, saying he has a "pocket full of credit cards."

Two episodes later, in "Time Out of Mind," we have Peggy going through Joe's books late at night, worried that he does not collect on overdue bills. Their exchange is, again, like that of a married couple—only it seems warmer than that of other married couples, at least on TV at the time. The phone rings in the middle of that conversation. It is a friend of Peggy's calling to ask if Joe could help her out with something as a favor, as she has no money. When Peggy looks at Joe in the middle of that phone conversation and realizes she is going to ask him to do something she just admonished him for doing, her look is wonderful. She knows, deep down, he is going to do it—all she has to do is ask. His helping in such a situation is completely consistent with his character—one that she, and we, have come to know so well.

After that we get to see them in "The Mouse That Died," which is another of the signature episodes of *Mannix*, also discussed later. Here, Joe is slowly dying of poison, and will be dead soon if an antidote it not found. Joe wakes up from a hallucination and, finding himself in the hospital with Peggy, Art Malcolm and a doctor looking over him, discovers the bad news. Once again, this is where *Mannix* shines—the facial expressions, especially the eyes and the eye contact. The look on Peggy's face when Joe is given the news seems so genuine, so adult. She is close enough to him at this point that she can't even completely process his predicament. But that is just the way people who care deeply for each other deal with this kind of news. After Joe is told "you're dying" by the doctor, Peggy admonishes the doctor and then just looks at Joe, who is looking in the other direction at the time. But, like all bad news like that, he can't quite believe it at first. Peggy waits—because she knows Joe is going to look at her to confirm this news. She steels herself for it. But that fails. Because, when he looks at her, she cannot look at him for very long. She looks away. That is the moment when Joe knows what he's heard is real.

Joe being Joe, he does not stay in the hospital, but tries to take matters into his own hands, and winds up working on decoding some cryptic letters in his apartment. Peggy is hanging around, presumably just in case Joe needs something—like to be taken back to the hospital. She looks at him as if she knows this person she has come to admire so much is going to die soon, and she still just can't seem to completely process it—but she slowly does by now, just a little bit more. And you see this. The tears start to run down her face, but she just stands there as Joe paces about the office. It is a scene that conveys raw, deep affection. So many TV shows and movies wind up having people over-react in situations like that, as if to try to tell you that you need to be as upset as they are. But when the worst things suddenly happen, we cannot initially completely process the bad news. For a while we keep going on, doing what needs to be done. Then the realization slowly comes. The portrayal of such processing is all the more powerful when conveyed in an understated way by otherwise strong characters. The affectation was right in those eyes. Eye contact is there at the end of that episode as well (along with a great line). You want to see these two get closer. They do—to a point.

The classic plot misdirection that was a hallmark of *Mannix* is used to deal with the evolving level of closeness between Joe and Peggy in "The World Between," which aired in November 1970. This episode, written by co-producer Ben Roberts, is simply superb. When I first saw it as a kid, I did not connect with it at all. This is actually true of quite a few episodes of *Mannix*. Some of its content was over the head of the kid version of me, who loved the series for other reasons. It worked on that many levels.

In this episode, Peggy is shot in the shoulder in the opening teaser. She and Joe are in her office and a thug comes in and demands pictures that Joe had to work hard to get, pictures that are supposed to be evidence in a case. When Joe goes to hand them over, Peggy throws a cup of hot coffee in the guy's face. While Joe wrestles with the guy, the gun goes off and Peggy is shot. We see Joe call the police as the iconic grid goes into the *Mannix* theme music.

Next, we see Joe standing over Peggy's hospital bed, pushing the button to call the nurse because Peggy is waking up. The nurse comes in and says he should be on the payroll. Peggy wakes up—to hear from the nurse that she has been shot, but everything is fine. She looks pretty put off, as anyone would be in that situation. But she's probably more than just a little put off that she was shot trying to help Joe, yet she wakes up to see a nurse there, but no Joe. Immediately concerned for her son, and probably a little disoriented, she says to the nurse, "Where's Toby?" The nurse replies, "Who is Toby?" Then we hear, but do not see, Joe answer, "That's her son." When we hear his voice, her face lights up with a smile and she looks a little bit into the distance to see him standing behind the nurse. Joe was there all along. And she responds—it is all right there on her face.

After a warm exchange that includes Joe admonishing Peggy for putting herself at risk, and his asking her to never do it again (a promise broken quite a few times in later years), he leaves for the evening. That night, Peggy has nightmares, during which she yells the curious phrase, "Joe, get the gun," which seems like something only people who live together would say. When she does, a stranger from across the hall comes in to try to figure out what the heck is going on—a black man who was mysteriously brought in the night before, seemingly in very poor condition. He looks not only healthy now, but handsome, and Peggy winds up biting him on the arm, thinking he is after her.

The next day, she calls Joe, clearly still pretty upset by being shot in the first place, and now concerned that this mysterious black man is after her. We cut to Joe's secretary office. Standing there is an attractive white woman with long blonde hair answering the phone in a sexy voice, "Mr. Mannix's office." When Peggy hears this, she is taken aback for just a second, then asks if this is the answering service. But when the blonde chick says, "This is Mr. Mannix's secretary, who is calling?" Peggy replies by saying, "This is Mr. Mannix's secretary and you tell him to call me just as soon as he shows his face."

The incredible thing is that you, the viewer, in 1970 when the episode is first shown, find that this sexy *blonde* chick in Joe's office just looks so incredibly *wrong*. By now in the series, you know that office is Peggy's!

That is only a teaser for what happens in the rest of the episode.

That evening, when Joe visits Peggy, he sort of makes fun of her thinking she's been replaced. In return, she reverts to calling him "Mr. Mannix" to his face, which turns out to be an effective means of conveying her anger. It also shows us how close these two now are, and ultimately exploits the series' very progressiveness. Take a look at Joe's face when he responds to her saying that. He clearly looks hurt. He quickly softens his gaze because, after all, Peggy has just been shot trying to help him. But he walks out of her room by teasing her again, comfortable that she is okay and amused by her overreaction to everything, including his having hired a temp.

The tables quickly turn on him.

Peggy winds up falling for the black guy in the room across the hall, who turns out to be an African Premier. He is a hunk, and very stylish to boot. She falls for him so much that she is prepared to move to Africa and become his wife. Peggy falling in love with a black hunk seems like it could be a kind of cover from the perspective of the show's producers, and a clever one at that. For one thing, it winds up enabling some of the closest scenes between Joe and Peggy in the entire series. The intensity of those scenes comes across as less than they would without the cover of Peggy ostensibly being in love with someone else, someone who makes a lot of "sense," especially to those who are racially challenged. But because Peggy has expressed love for a black man, Joe and Peggy get away with warm exchanges they might not have otherwise, on television in 1970. We see Joe visit Peggy and try to talk her out of going to Africa, but he does so without making any kind of commitment. What kind of commitment can Joe make to stop her from doing such a thing?

After trying to make the argument that she needs to consider Toby—an argument that fails—he does say he does not want to lose her, and this goes so far that it appears that he is asking her to not pursue love and marriage in order to stay a secretary to him!

Furthermore, after he says he does not want to lose her, Peggy turns her head and cries. She is clearly overwhelmed with Joe saying that to her. He actually reaches for her face and turns it back towards him—and the scene ends with her saying "I only said I loved him. I didn't say he loved me."

This is, of course, a perfect metaphor for how she just might feel about Joe. The look on Joe's face can easily reflect his awareness of that.

The African Premier is over-the-top elegant—a world leader with fresh ideas. We see Peggy with him, and we can see she's head over heels. It is also, of course, no accident that he is not only black, but African. Peggy somehow feels instant affinity to someone from another culture, from another country, from another continent just because of her race, ostensibly over and above her clear affection and admiration for Joe, thus exposing the first-order nature of race in 1970.

But we also see the contrast between the way she deals with the idyllic, heroic-in-his-own-right African Premier, and the way she interacts with Joe. Because, later, there is a brilliant scene where Peggy is being re-bandaged behind a screen and Joe is in the room, sitting there, having one of his last smokes of the series (he wasn't allowed to smoke in season 5 and beyond, because CBS banned it for the stars of its series). Peggy is upset that she was asleep when her African Premier came out of emergency surgery the night before. She is taking it out on Joe. They fight. In typical Joe fashion, he fights back a little, then re-gains the perspective on the situation and says, "Hey, what are we fighting about?"

This scene shows what closeness really is. They are comfortable with each other. Peggy can take her frustrations out on Joe and he can find ways to understand that, and forgive it. We never see Peggy react with this kind of comfort or closeness with the African Premier—for one thing, he just seems so unreal. By contrast, the relationship between

Joe and Peggy seems so real, so human, and somehow more intimate as a result. And that is the whole point.

Of course, the decision is taken out of Peggy's hands—how else can it be? Still, at the end, she seems to enter the hospital room of her African Premier love interest expressing a desire to go with him to his country but with a willingness that is somehow less than it was before—subtle, but perceptible. She seems to admire him now, but also seems to be coming out of her infatuation, perhaps having second thoughts, even if just a little. Those second thoughts quickly evaporate when she discovers the Premier is going to go back to his country to die. Sure, it's an obvious plot device. But that isn't the point. The richness of this episode was all under that cover. All of the warm scenes in this episode between Joe and Peggy can happen only because they happen under the cover of Peggy ostensibly being in love with someone else.

The last scene of this episode has Joe coming into his office while Peggy is on an urgent phone call. Joe puts the call aside and deals with her—asking her how she is doing. She says, in uncharacteristic fashion, "I'm beautiful." Of course, this is an expression of the times, but it means more than that, in this context.

As usual, it's all on the faces.

The camera goes right to Joe's face. He looks as if he knows that fact very well, and he does not say a thing—it is all visual. Joe is now in a different place with respect to Peggy, because she openly and completely fell in love with someone else. The episode marks a transition, even if a mistaken one.

The way these things work, falling in love with someone like that in a week's time, after someone has been shot, can be a reaction to all sorts of things. We are left at the end, when Joe walks back into his office to take the call, with the camera on Peggy, who is crying. Is she crying because her African Premier is going to die? Surely that is some of it. But the viewer is left to wonder if some of it might also include the knowledge that nothing is ever going to happen between her and Joe—there is, between them as well, a "World Between" after all.

Just consider how powerful it is that you wind up not wanting to see Peggy with a guy of her own race. It looks wrong. You'd rather see her with Joe. And this is in 1970! That meant so much more than any sort of contrived, interracial kiss.

This episode also sets up the relationship between them for the rest of the series, another thing provided by the clever cover of this episode's main plot. The resultant situation is, quite simply, intelligently adult. Left to our imagination is what happened in between so many scenes of *Mannix*, right after the abrupt endings, in between episodes, in between seasons, and after the series ended. What happened to Joe? What happened to Peggy? What happened to Joe and Peggy? The tight editing of *Mannix* invites our imagination so that we can each have our own version of the series.

When Mike Connors reprised his character of Joe Mannix on a 1997 episode of *Diagnosis: Murder* (CBS-TV 1993-2001), the writers seemed to leave things vague on purpose with respect to Joe and Peggy. While that episode might not be sanctioned by hard-core *Mannix* fans, because Goff and Roberts did not participate (Ben Roberts died in 1984), it did have Mike Connors, and so one has to consider its contents as much, if not more, than just another one of those lame remakes. In that episode, when Joe's friend, Dr. Mark Sloan (played by Dick Van Dyke), asks Joe where Peggy is and Joe replies that she is on vacation, Mark replies, "Why don't you join her?"

Really? On the same vacation? This meant so much to some viewers that they placed posts on the Web that they were glad to see that they finally got together. They so wanted it that they were willing to take the ambiguity in one direction only.

But viewers also pointed out that Peggy's absence from the episode made it feel somehow incomplete. Even those who watch and enjoy season 1 on the DVDs have pointed out that the episodes are good and the basic elements of Joe Mannix are there, but they miss Peggy. They want to know what she's thinking about Joe's exploits—even though she hasn't arrived on the scene yet.

Joe seems both heroic and human, through Peggy's eyes. Peggy wants her friend and boss to be who he is, yet cares about him enough so that she also wants him to play it safe. Since these things cannot be reconciled, she chooses to live with the tension and we feel that tension through her. This was especially fun to watch in the signature episodes of the series, the ones where Joe is in the most extreme physical situations. Not only was Peggy in all of the signature episodes of *Mannix*, she played an important part in them, enduring the emotional impact of witnessing the hurt and potential harm to someone she values both personally and, more importantly, in a larger context of contribution to mankind.

Subtly, but perceptibly, Peggy starts to get why Joe is Joe ever more as the years go by. The more she gets him, the more she acts as a credible witness and the more we see why she wants to be there for Joe, in a platonic way, to include enduring the potential loss of him at any moment.

And so, their relationship only goes "so far."

Or does it go as far as any relationship can—and farther than most?

Chapter 6
That's Tough

We respect the powerful. But we admire the tough. The difference is one of affinity, with the implication that illustrations of toughness can affect us in ways power can never reach.

Both power and toughness are manifestations of will, thus actualizing what we think into what we do, and ultimately what we leave behind. But power is enabled by ownership of something, from a physical object to a logical position of authority that can be bestowed by others or even merely projected onto some. Power is tantamount to having money, status or objects of force. Power is something to be sought, held, used. By contrast, toughness is a way of being that can only be earned, displayed as situations arise, even moment by moment. Toughness is manifest as resilience, endurance, or in overcoming adversity. Toughness is something to be tested, developed, achieved.

Power is wielded. Toughness is cultivated. We are made powerful. We become tough.

From its very beginnings, our society has prized toughness over power and so that relationship, more than anything else, defines who we are. The Continental Army is said to have won the Revolutionary War not through great battles, nor the imposition of power, as it had relatively far less than its foe, but by enduring long enough to attain an identity that became recognized by others.[6.1] Virtually all of our cultural legends embody toughness, from the Pilgrims to the Founding Fathers to Lincoln to the Civil Rights movement. Their legendary greatness comes from their way of being, from rising to some challenging occasion, not something they were given, innately or otherwise.

Beyond our culture, virtually all spiritual icons embody toughness, often as an answer to power, even the only answer to power, when power turns bad, as it so often does. Since toughness often demands that we put all we are on the line, and always tests our personal limits, even sometimes causing us to pass beyond some break point, it tends to go bad only when we wish to self-destruct, and we only wish to self-destruct when we cannot reconcile our personal will with our personal definition of goodness.

The desire to be tough more than powerful tends to cause us to want to identify with something beyond the merely material. Toughness does not deny the importance of the material world. Toughness transcends it. Power is material, embodied in an object or mechanism, something outside of oneself. Toughness is spiritual, embodied in myth, something that we identify with on the outside and then find within our very selves. The mechanism for transmission of power from one generation to another is the passing of something, an object, respect for a hierarchy, for procedure, or for organization, whether written down or informal. The mechanism for transmitting toughness from one generation to another is admiration for singular examples with which we yearn to identify.

At the heart of *Mannix* is one tough character. Joe Mannix is a good-hearted, tough individual first, a private investigator second. Because *Mannix* wound up being a character exploration, by virtue of losing its gimmick after season 1 and being saved for its qualities of character, it would have still been *Mannix* if Joe had gone off to pursue another profession, so long as Joe stayed Joe, whatever that meant. We tuned in each week to discover what that meant.

Viewers tuned in to see that dignified, tough individual. The coupling of the decency and dignity to the toughness was the core attraction, whether we realized it or not at the time. A singular distinguishing quality of *Mannix* that causes the series to be associated with oft repeated words like "classic" and "iconic" is that singular portrayal of decent, dignified toughness. And so, while *Mannix* is considered to be a part of, or even to have spawned an entire genre of personalized crime fighters, the thematic roots of the series and its main character have far more in common with characters from different genres than the one it is most commonly associated with.

In terms of character, *Mannix* stands apart from its lesser crime drama offspring, who seemed by contrast designed to affirm a sense of entitlement, more than to convey the core values that enabled that sense of entitlement to happen in the first place. Confirmation of entitlement tends to be desired by generations raised during times of prosperity. But in terms of character, Joe Mannix has more in common with Will Kane from *High Noon*, who leaves his bride to go back to the small town and fight the bad guys all alone…or even Frodo Baggins from *The Lord of the Rings*, who goes through so much because he is the one who does not let The Ring, which represents Power, itself, affect him. While Frodo Baggins was created by an Englishman, its themes are consistent with the tough, heroic, everyman (or every Hobbit).

But while *High Noon* is a movie set in an old Western town, and *The Lord of the Rings* is a fantasy series (of both books and movies), *Mannix* was produced in a modern-day setting and needed to tell a different story about its main character week after week. Those two properties make it that much more difficult, that much tougher, for classically tough heroes like Joe Mannix to be believable. Settings in the past, future, or some other place entirely (such as in fantasy) tend to cause an audience to lessen their implicit tests of credulity, and thus enable broader, more easily attainable, dramatic elements to fill in gaps of plausibility. Furthermore, the telling of any single story, even if over a series of three books or movies, further lessens tests of credibility since once-in-a-lifetime stories may well happen to singular individuals.

But, incredibly, *Mannix's* themes of dignified, tough individuality are explored in each and every episode of the series, making it impossible to find even one episode that does not have all three of those displayed to some degree, and with some episodes exploring those themes in the classical extremes.

Tuning in to *Mannix* once a week, year after year, was almost like getting a fix of those themes. They were explored to such a degree that critics of the series focus on the way so many things would happen to the main characters over the number of episodes that it was beyond implausible, including the number of times Joe was shot, knocked unconscious, beaten, in a fistfight, did not get paid, or had to rescue Peggy from being kidnapped. But of course, all drama suspends belief about something and this is especially true of series television, even situation comedies, or else the main characters lead boring lives that are not worth watching on a weekly basis. Since *Mannix* was about a tough individual, the elements that conveyed properties of toughness had to be believably repeatable.

One metric of the singularity of *Mannix* is the way viewers happily suspended disbelief that Joe could survive all he encountered unscathed, coupled with the fact that all of this was supposed to be happening right in L.A., right in the present day, right in a place they could visit if they so desired. Viewers watched anyway because they so wanted the core elements of the character to be true. Great characters can be measured by the extent to which they make us *want* to believe in them, in their timeless properties, more than we want to criticize the obvious implausibility in the way those properties are conveyed in time and place. In turn, when those core properties are conveyed in such a way that rings so true to us that we project beyond the time and place in which they are told to us, we can then take those core properties and project them into our own time and place.

When I was a kid, I had no way of knowing *Mannix* held those properties, any more than I knew that there would never be another show quite like it. As a kid I barely had the sophistication to articulate any kind of differentiation between the shows I liked. I only knew that I liked some series more than others, and *Mannix* above all others, but I did not know why. Still, a specific subset of episodes wound up being so committed to my memory, facilitated by nearly constant recall over the years, that they left an imprint. They, somehow, conveyed to me the inherent logic and beauty of what it means to be a dignified, tough individual. Never having understood the attraction of things like piercings or tattoos, those episodes are a kind of mental tattoo to which I'm happy to admit.

While some episodes of *Mannix* were more concerned with plot than others, and the main character was, at times, more incidental to the drama surrounding him, the series has a singular collection of episodes so much about the core properties of its main character that they can be considered to be the signature episodes of the series. Those are the ones that became imprinted on my mind, so much so that I actually enjoyed recalling them over the years, often in specific situations, even though I did not have access to re-viewing them. Those are the ones where the main character seemed to be doing things that were inconsistent with what others were telling me were important in life, reflected in the shifting cultural norms. I could never get those things out of my mind.

Over the eight-year run of *Mannix* so many candidates for signature episodes exist that *Mannix* fans will undoubtedly argue with any list any one fan might create. And that is as it should be. My own informal list of signature episodes is at least a dozen long, with personal definition of signature episodes as those that can be watched over and over again, as a great piece of music can be listened to over and over again, and each time you do you can learn something more about yourself, or about life, if you can give yourself over enough to what you are watching to let that happen. Given that definition, virtually all episodes of *Mannix* could be considered signature. Some stand out more than others.

Those episodes are driven by plot, but are not about plot. They are about character. Because of this, and because they are so well done, the more one has lived, the more one can find in them—even as they made complete sense to a kid. How many things appeal to the kid version of ourselves and wind up speaking truth to us as adults?

There was nothing—nothing—like looking forward to one of these signature episodes airing for the first time, with some of their scenes revealed in the "Next, on *Mannix*" pre-views attached to the end of the previous episode. I can still hear the network announcer's voice telling me to pay attention to the next few seconds of clips, designed to make me want to watch—such an easy task. Other than that, all one had in those days were incredibly brief descriptions in *TV Guide* and other similar publications which seemed to prize being cryptic. Two of these I remember to this very day. For season 5's "Death is the Fifth Gear," one description went, "Mannix is in a race car accident and suffers serious head injuries." For season 7's "The Dark Hours," one description went, "Barely alive after being shot with his own gun, Mannix tries to piece together what happened during the previous twenty-four hours." Those descriptions say very little, indeed practically nothing, about what these shows were really all about. They do, however, point to something significant having happened to Joe, to his very person, something in the extreme. You came to know that when that happened, what you were going to see when you watched those episodes was dignified toughness, personified.

Those episodes made you want to be tough first, and powerful second.

I took for granted then, but am amazed now, that those episodes never failed to deliver on their promise, not once, in the eight-year run of the series. It's still possible to put myself back in that week that preceded one of those episodes and, even though I did not have the words for it at the time, think that the kinds of things that I was about to experience were somehow more real than the things I was being told in school, somehow more life affirming than the platitudes that were a part of education. What I was being taught in school made sense on one level. But what I was watching in those episodes made sense at an entirely different level.

We are ultimately attracted and sharpened by the things that make the most sense to us in the big scheme of things, and indifferent and dulled by things we somehow know cannot stand to the deeper truths of our own existence. Even kids know full well they are going to get hurt, all the more as life goes on and in direct proportion to how engaged they are in it. They also know that the way they respond to adversity will define who they are and, ultimately, enable them to do more. Of course, adults sometimes come to forget that, even as I did during those times I was less connected to those episodes.

All of the signature episodes are about the toughness of Joe Mannix. They are also about how that toughness was not so easy for him, at times. Prior to this, most hero types on TV and in the movies who embodied toughness made it all seem too easy, that doing hard things was just an innate part of their nature, or else they made it seem as if being that way was not the least bit desirable because the end result was a kind of wooden, mechanistic or hardened individual. But in *Mannix*, most especially through these signature episodes, you felt for this man, found yourself relating to his struggle, because he seemed to have that next level of toughness—that next level of character that let you in on the secret that what he was doing wasn't so easy, but he did it anyway.

The key word in that previous sentence is *struggle*. There used to be an automobile ad that ran in the U.S. which contained the phrase, "Half the fun in life is getting there." If character is a destination, then a better line might be, "Half the value of a life is in its struggles." No one can explain that to you. If they try, then you are most likely to resist, especially if you have a tough core to begin with. The expression "life is tough" is tantamount to putting someone in their place, not something used to convey appreciation for properties of existence. Only when we can reconcile "life is tough" with "life is beautiful" can we move from cynical observer to engaged doer.

It took the adult in me to realize that most of the signature episodes of *Mannix* have at least one scene that actually makes me feel uncomfortable, a scene where Joe seems to lose his cool or act in a way that is not normally associated with heroism. Here is this show where the hero is commonly described as "Joe cool" and who seems to personify coolness. He drives a cool car, wears the cool sport coats, is desired by women, takes beatings with wry comments, and seems to be able to jump over obstacles, both physically and metaphorically, as if they are welcome.

Then there are those signature episodes. In those, Joe is taken right up to his limits of toughness—and just a little bit beyond. You get to see that his response to his struggles takes him to the point where he loses his cool, and has to gain it back again. That, when it comes right down to it, is beyond cool—and ultimately useful. *Mannix* has a foundation of energy, lots of action is conveyed starting in the opening credits—both visuals and music are famously energetic, with multi-dimensional imagery and rapid-paced theme music. Then there is the tight-paced editing of the show, the physical stunts, the car chases, the fights and the way crime was used to convey big, consequential outcomes to the stories. But nothing is a better source of energy, in the long run, than the way its leading character gave you the sense that it was okay to get out there and get involved in life in ways that were likely to result in your getting hurt, because if you did, and you went right up against the brink so that you even lost your cool, you could get it back again, and just a little more besides. The truly tough are not afraid of their limits and, instead, view tests of them as opportunities for growth.

One thing that seems inarguable is that the first of the signature episodes of *Mannix* is "The Sound of Darkness," an episode layered with toughness and sweetness and what many consider to be the signature episode of the entire series. The claim is rightly made in the sense that the episode is transformational, since it is the first of its kind in the series, the first in which Joe encounters serious physical adversity that he, as well as those around him, takes seriously enough so that his response to his dilemma is explored.

Joe is shot so that a bullet grazes his temple, resulting in psychosomatic blindness. Okay, that said, many savvy TV viewers may feel they do not need to watch this episode, that they already know what it is about because they have seen the same story countless times before. Hero goes blind. Hero deals with it, heroically. Hero gets his sight back at the end. The basic elements of fear being what they are, and the number of episodes of TV series being what they are, lots of elements of story are repeated across multiple series, out of necessity. But thinking that "The Sound of Darkness" is trite because it can be classified on the basis of broad story elements is similar to saying that the Beatles' "Yesterday" is one of many solo, lightly instrumented love-lost ballads and if you've heard one of those you've heard them all. "Yesterday" is really quite different, but it takes some thinking about it to realize why.

So much of "The Sound of Darkness" is not about its plot, but about exploring and defining those characters. There is yet another thing about *Mannix* that makes it groundbreaking. The attention paid to qualities of character allowed the viewer to have a relationship to those characters that made it possible to tell a more significant, more intense story than the one ostensibly being told in any given week.

Put another way, *Mannix* had character context, in contrast to overarching plot context. Series like *The Fugitive* and even *Hawaii Five-O* (CBS-TV 1968-1980) had an overarching story being told around the main characters. For example, Kimball (*The Fugitive*) was on the run from his constant pursuer and McGarrett (*Hawaii Five-O*) had an archenemy, Wo Fat. These global plot contexts gave shortcuts to individual stories that allowed more to be accomplished in a fifty-minute episode than would be possible in, for example, a completely self-contained fifty-minute movie. So much of series TV is like that. Even series like *Mission: Impossible*, which had no back story, had structure which enabled all sorts of plot elements to be accepted before the opening scene. Still, those episodes were not exploring character. They were all about plot, one plot at a time.

But *Mannix* is a show about character with no overarching story, no serialization, no global plot context other than that Joe Mannix was a PI based in L.A. Despite having a collection of nutty Korean War buddies, even none of those recurred. Not one single villain recurred over the 194 episodes of the series (with the exception of three two-part episodes). Each episode stood on its own, with qualities of character the only real premise or basis for continuity. Everything possible in the signature episodes came from expectations that the viewer knew who Joe Mannix was. They recognized him, even if they could not put what that meant precisely into words. Their ongoing relationship was with his qualities of character. And so, the signature episodes in *Mannix* are not about some development in the back story of the hero, or when plot is extremely intricate, but when Joe's character is stretched to the limit, to the limits of his toughness.

Because that relationship between character and viewers was developed over weeks, years for loyal viewers, the signature episodes wound up being so much more powerful than any movie could be. A movie might make you wonder how you would respond in a similar situation or feel for the plight of those in the kind of situation established by the plot. But when you see stuff happen to Joe Mannix, you are seeing stuff happen to someone who is in your life on a weekly basis. Seeing him in extreme kinds of situations, such as facing the possibility of permanent blindness that is the result of his own psychological doing, but still something he can't control, puts you right in the middle, with only a few minutes of plot premise required to connect with years of established character relationship. The possibility to feel this event is right there—if the main character has the guts to let you into his experience of this dilemma.

"The Sound of Darkness" has Robert Reed, who first guest starred in *Mannix* in season 2's "The Girl Who Came in With the Tide," in his recurring role as Lt. Adam Tobias. Reed was initially only to appear in that one episode, filling one of the many cop buddy roles that rotated through the series. But Connors had chemistry with Reed and is quoted as saying, "I loved working with him. He'd say, 'I'm available next week; if you've got something, I'd love to do it.' We had a great rapport. We had a sympatico or something. Everything worked, the timing and all, and we had a lot of fun working together."[6.2]

Adam and Joe are presumed to already be friends when Adam first appears in *Mannix*. This is the way *Mannix* did things—the regular characters just appear as if they had already been there, with some prior history you never do get to see. This even includes the way Peggy appeared. But the presumption of prior friendship, and thus the chemistry that supported it, was important to Tobias' very first appearance, something quickly built upon and which leads directly to "The Sound of Darkness."

In "The Girl Who Came In With the Tide," Adam uses the pre-existing friendship and rapport to challenge Joe when Joe gets too personally involved with a pretty client, which seems to get in the way of his trapping a killer. Adam Tobias challenges Joe's judgment to the point of Joe blowing up at him and Adam leaving Joe's office with a sort of part hurt, part disappointed, and part disgusted look on his face, yet another complex *Mannix* visual expression.

Connors was always willing to take that hero, that larger-than-life Joe Cool and let him be wrong, even to the point of disappointing us, if only for the moment. Right there, right in that episode, you are disappointed in Joe. He loses his cool. He's letting something get to him. He blows up at someone who is clearly his friend. In that exchange, Joe accuses Adam of thinking that he is seeking revenge and trying to set someone up. Joe is angry when he says this line—he is not cool. Adam, coolly, much more coolly than Joe in this moment, says, "I know you better than that." It is a single line, well delivered, that affirms Tobias' character—right in a moment when we need that kind of affirmation, because our hero is not acting all that heroic at the moment. Connors gives the cool over, in that moment, to another character. And how cool is that?

Unlike so many other PI or cop-centric crime dramas that came before or after, this is not a playful kind of giving over of "the cool" to some other character. So many series simply make the leading character shrug off so much, often in a good ole boy or super-cool manner. By contrast, this seems like the real deal. If cool is what you like, in that scene, you identify with Adam more than Joe. Even Peggy has the cool over Joe in that scene. That, of course, is the paradox that makes Joe Mannix the bigger hero in the bigger scheme of things. Joe is beyond cool, because he reaches those limits where he is not so cool, and he has to work to get it back, for both himself and those around him. He also has the courage to let himself get to that point in the first place.

It is probably no accident that Reed's Adam Tobias, the first cop-buddy in *Mannix* with which Connors had real chemistry and the one who lasted longer in the series than any other, save Ward Wood's Art Malcolm, was also in "The Sound of Darkness." Reed played an important role in that signature episode. Curiously, Reed was only in two episodes of season 2, and "To Catch a Rabbit" was one in which he appeared very little, really incidental to the story. Thus, it may also be no accident that he appeared in two episodes of season 3 prior to "The Sound of Darkness," including the opening episode of the third season. In those early season 3 episodes a warmer kind of relationship is established between Adam and Joe. Those episodes also give more substance to Gail Fisher's Peggy. By the time "The Sound of Darkness" is filmed and aired, there is enough behind Peggy and Adam, as well as their relationships with Joe, that the scenes in "The Sound of Darkness" have that much more intensity and meaning.

If "The Sound of Darkness" is the only, or even the first, episode of *Mannix* that you watch, it is still good, but it has so much less impact than if you already know those characters. Because Joe is one heroic type, one dignified tough individual, his friends do not want to see him diminished. Viewers already know he represents something more to them than just his friendship. Because he has that larger-than-life quality, they do not want his qualities of character to disappoint them either. Beyond this, Joe is aware of his own larger-than-life properties. He is a hero type who owns who he is, and does not shrug his deeds off. Because Joe owns that, is aware of who he is, he also owns it when he does not live up to his own expectations for himself. By owning it, he ultimately overcomes. And so he becomes a bigger hero.

So much happens in the fifty minutes of this episode because you know these things, and none of them is about plot premise; they are all about character premise.

In the first few minutes of "The Sound of Darkness," a story is established where Joe is almost hired by a car salesman who wants to find out who is trying to kill him. Someone is shooting at this guy, but not to kill him, because he could have easily been killed if the potential killer had wanted that. When Joe starts to ask questions, the guy tells him to forget about it. But, Joe being Joe, he does not forget, is intrigued now, wants to know what is going on and does not let it go. The next scene has him in his office, discussing the situation with Adam and Peggy. At this point, Adam is now established as Joe's primary cop buddy. Joe reasons that his almost-client has a secret of some kind, and is being scared *towards* something—something that a hired killer is also pursuing.

Joe follows his almost-client and winds up in a deserted building, one condemned and even in the process of being torn down. The killer is there as well. Joe sees his almost-client shot dead by the killer. Joe goes after the killer, and is shot across the temple. A creative scene follows as Joe slowly loses his sight (using a colorful film technique of the day), after which Joe continues to pursue the killer even as he is having trouble seeing. We follow Joe as he, symbolically, climbs down a ladder to continue to pursue the guy who just killed someone else and who just shot him across the temple. Joe is having difficulty though, and this is the very first time in the series you start to see him really struggle in a physical way. This scene establishes that Joe is a guy tough enough to continue to pursue a killer even when he realizes something is very wrong with him. The scene is that much more impactful because this is the guy we are used to seeing relatively easily overcome everything he encounters, shrugging off injuries the way so many hero types did before him. When Joe does lose his sight, the last thing he sees is a bunch of boxes falling onto him, with the boxes changing color in a way that indicates something is very wrong. That vision then goes to black, with the fact that his sight is gone confirmed by his inability to see his own gun waved right in front of his eyes. We feel the terror he shows on his face. We thought we knew who Joe was. He overcame everything, right? He's Joe Cool. We aren't used to seeing him terrified, which is exactly the way he looks.

The next scene cuts to a bright, pointed light in the darkness. The darkness is Joe's iris and the beam comes from an ophthalmologist's light as he examines Joe. The camera pulls back.

In this scene, Joe Mannix fully departs from James Bond and Sam Spade. He becomes that rare thing, the larger-than-life heroic type who has that non-frivolous, human side—one you can relate to week after week. He has some special skills and is willing to risk himself, when necessary, in using those skills for good purposes. He already had a pretty heroic foundation. But now he can be hurt—really hurt, not just in the many ways heroes often shrug things off. Viewers now know it. His friends know it.

Joe is informed by the doctor that he has psychosomatic blindness, and Connors is, in one of those classic visual expressions that contain a variety of emotions, simultaneously incredulous, scared and disgusted. The doctor goes on to explain that he lives a life of danger, risking his life constantly in his profession as an "occupational hazard." The doctor also goes on to say, "But you're a man, and mortal."

In this moment, Peggy responds, completely non-verbally, again with one of those great, complex expressions—one of simultaneous recognition, empathy and a kind of "well this makes some sort of sense, since I didn't think all of that stuff he did could be quite that real without it getting to him." In that moment, almost in that single moment, Peggy sees that there is a vulnerable human behind the heroic deeds she had been witnessing and Joe goes up a rung or two on the ladder of heroic qualities—paradoxically, since Joe had descended down a ladder into darkness. That is only the beginning of the symbolism in this episode, well worth paying attention to, along with the many complex expressions on faces.

Take away that reaction shot of Peggy and you change a lot of the richness and meaning of the scene, of the episode, and even of the series. But Peggy sees Joe's humanity. And through her, *you* see his humanity. This is one of many such reaction shots like that to come, not only in this episode but in the series. "The Sound of Darkness" is an episode I could barely stand to watch in syndication. In *Mannix* so much of the richness of character was conveyed in incredibly brief moments just like this one that were, sadly, removed in syndication runs over the years. They were cut in favor of plot and action, or effectively ruined by being sped up so that they could hardly been seen. Most series in syndication are run slightly faster than they were first aired, so that a fifty-minute episode of *Mannix* might air in forty-seven minutes, even if no scenes were cut. Typically both cutting and speeding up would happen, making the episodes practically unwatchable for true fans who saw character revealed through nuance during the first run. Character is so often revealed, in real life as well as dramatically, through nuance.

Joe is told that his sight could come back in "six months, six days, or six hours." Joe goes on to say, "Or never." The doctor confirms, "Or never."

Now we are hooked. Joe is not only human, but he is so human that he is doing this to himself—and he could wind up permanently disabled out of his own fear, disabled in a way that would be, for him, potentially a fate worse than death. Peggy has to drive him home—utterly symbolic for an icon known for driving a convertible around L.A. He is instructed to take her arm. We see, for the first time in the series, but not the last (not even in this episode), tears streaming down Peggy's face, tears Joe cannot see as he awkwardly takes her arm and tries to look like Joe Cool. As he does so, he says to the doctor, in typical Joe Cool fashion, but looking so painfully awkward now, "I'll be seeing ya."

The next scene has Joe, Peggy and Adam in Joe's apartment. This scene is so classic that some of its dialogue can be found on the Web to this day. But, in typical *Mannix* fashion, the dialogue is nothing compared to the emotion behind the way it was delivered.

The scene establishes that Joe is feeling sorry for himself. The look on his face is complex, including fear, anger, confusion, self-disgust, and self-pity. In real life, emotions are rarely one thing only, and in this case the situation lends itself to a variety of emotions. But that emotion is not at all what anyone expected to see from a combination of James Bond and Sam Spade. That emotion is also nothing we ever saw on Joe Mannix's face before, in the little more than two years the series previously aired. The first time you saw it, when you didn't know it was coming, it was a bit unnerving.

Adam is talking with Joe, and Joe's responses indicate that he is not taking his predicament so very well. Peggy brings him a drink. He gets up to take it, and accidentally hits it with his arm, spilling it. Apologizing, he rather childishly refuses another one, saying he really didn't want one anyway. If there was any doubt that Joe is not taking this so well, and that his behavior is uncharacteristic, that doubt is removed by the looks on his friend's faces. Their complex emotions convey a combination of empathy, shock and disappointment.

Joe goes on to light a cigarette. The lighter misses, and Adam offers to light it. Joe angrily throws the cigarette down. What comes next is classic dialogue.

Joe: "What time is it?"

Peggy (looking at her watch): "7:30."

Joe: "Look, why don't you go home before you make your babysitter rich?"

Peggy: "I haven't finished that Javis report."

Joe: "Forget it. We're out of business."

There are more complex emotions on the part of Adam and Peggy—surprise, even a bit of disgust for our hero, with a bit of pity mixed in there. No words convey what is going on here. It's all, ironically, what Joe can't see at this point. That awareness works on you too, somehow.

Adam: "Joe, listen, I've got this friend, uh, ex-Marine. He's a great guy. He works with the blind."

Adam sort of checks himself on those last two words, sensing he just labeled Joe as one of "the blind," something that is not lost on Joe.

Joe: "You mean, he sells them those white canes?"

At this point the complex emotions on the part of Adam and Peggy have pretty much all transitioned to disgust. The first time I saw the episode—watching it with others—I shrunk into the couch and hoped some miracle would happen and no one would remember I am a big fan of this series. Based on this scene, I was fully prepared to deny my affinity for this guy. I've now seen this segment countless numbers of times, and have yet to view it even once without some amount of cringing.

Peggy: "Let's face it, Joe, it's a brand new ballgame."

Joe: "Ballgame called because of darkness."

Peggy: "You're feeling sorry for yourself, right?"

Joe: "Can't you get it through your thick head? I don't need a secretary. What I need is a seeing-eye dog. Now, can you bark?"

Peggy: "Yes, I can bark. And I can bite, too. I thought I was working for a guy who could take anything that was handed out to him.

But maybe I was wrong. Maybe I ought to rent you a corner and give you a tin cup with six pencils!"

Peggy lets him have it—intensely. All of the chemistry those characters built up in the previous episodes comes into that exchange. Even if you don't know those characters, that moment is still good. But it is most effective when viewed in the context of those prior relationships—both the characters with each other, and you with those characters. Then again, if you don't know those characters so well, you might not be trying to hide under the pillows on the couch at that moment.

But if you do know those characters, what you just saw was Joe being anything—*anything*—other than that which is normally associated with a hero. And his secretary just let him have it—intensely. This is not Joe being Joe. Or is it?

Peggy, with almost immediate regret and newfound empathy for Joe, mixed in with her own version of self-disgust for letting Joe have it when he is at his very worst, all simultaneously conveyed on her face, simply says, "I'm sorry, Joe."

And Joe, with his own complex expression, including hurt, shame, and then self-awareness, simply takes it from her. He not only takes it, but it turns out to be the trigger that makes him face his predicament. He gets something he needs, right from her, someone who works for him, by letting himself be humiliated by her and accepting what she had to say. The trigger is effective because Joe is aware of his own image, not only to himself, but that he portrays a certain kind of image to others. We also know Peggy is right—we buy into her blow-up, because we know Joe. She wants Joe back. And so do we.

Joe wasn't being Joe in that moment. But Peggy knew it. And she let him know who he was by expressing our own frustration with him, just out of raw emotion borne out of wanting him back.

Joe being Joe again, and just a little bit more now, is tough enough to take it, even at his worst. And then use it.

How tough is that?

Connors was able to pull off being a heroic type who looks downright cringe-worthy and, at the same time, let the power in the scene go over to his secretary—a female and a minority to boot—and ultimately wind up looking that much larger for it. And it gets better.

The story goes on to have Joe learn how to survive while blind, including training from a black man, played by James Edwards. That is one of many times in *Mannix* where a black actor was inserted in a role which was both unusual and significant. This results in a scene where Joe is in his own apartment, virtually helpless in dealing with his own blindness. Notice how the power in this scene is given over to a black man and a black woman (the only other two people in the apartment), since Peggy is in the room as well. This is another one of those times where you don't realize this unless you pay attention—it's a misdirection. You were paying attention to Joe's plight, which is probably why you missed it. But the scene was not merely unusual: I cannot think of one example in any other series—prior to this episode—where the power in a scene was given over to two minorities like that.

After Edward's character leaves, a great scene happens where Joe is alone in his apartment with Peggy, but he can't see her and has no idea where she is. She is, for the second time in the episode and the series, crying over Joe's predicament, with tears running down her face. He can't see this. Instead, he has yet another one of those great looks where you realize he has no idea where she is, and asks her to at least be decent and make a sound. The scene ends with him up against a wall, literally, and sliding down it with yet another great, complex set of emotions on his face. Sadly, the ending of this scene is often cut out of the syndicated runs of the series.

After a classic Malibu beach scene that is simply beautifully done—one that includes Peggy handing Joe a volleyball that has gone away from a group of beach volleyball players so that he can toss it back to them with one of those classic Connors smiles—the episode goes to its closing act.

The act opens with discussion of "the money" which Joe reasons has to be what the killer, now his hunter, had to have been looking for in the building where he was shot and his almost-client was killed. The previous scene had Peggy actually driving a dual-control equipped car to the point of the killer going off a cliff—a standard *Mannix* device—and not the first time she was placed in harm's way for the sake of Joe. Adam comes in to say that not only has the killer not been found, he somehow got away from the car that went over the cliff. But the pile of money the killer was not only after, but already killed for, has not been found in the building either. Joe proclaims he knows that the money is in there, and from everything we know about the story until then, it makes complete logical sense to us as well.

Joe now wants to bring the killer—who knows Joe saw him and therefore wants to kill Joe—out of hiding, out into the open. He wants to do so by facing the killer on his own, while blind. In order to accomplish this, Joe has to convince Adam to remove the police guards from his apartment. The killer does not know Joe is blind, and does not know Joe is such an easy target for that reason. Joe wants the police guards to be removed for a single day. Adam refuses, of course, and makes a good case that without eyes, Joe is not really the professional he thinks he is; he is, rather, a "sitting duck." Joe says, "I've worked harder for this than anything in my life." He asks for "one day."

Here, the complex expressions on the part of Adam and Peggy convey the appreciation for the toughness that is personified in the character of Joe Mannix.

Earlier in the episode, they both witness Joe when he was at his very worst, when he was anything but Joe, when he was drowning in self-pity and feeling helpless, when he was anything but tough. It was painful for them to witness, painful for the loyal *Mannix* viewer to see.

Now, the looks on their faces are complex: recognition that what he is saying is true, resignation that they have to let him do this, and utter admiration for his tough qualities—that he wants so badly to face the killer on his own like that, with seemingly impossible odds against him. Notice Peggy, in particular, who has a great expression on her face that lasts only a brief moment, so brief the DVD has to be frozen in order to fully appreciate it. Notice how that still moment conveys all of this in one singular expression on her face. At the end of this shot, she slowly puts her head down. You wonder if she even feels responsible that Joe now feels he needs to face this killer on his own—putting himself in jeopardy by so doing—because she is the one who shamed him by saying she thought she was working for a guy who could take anything that was handed out to him.

Joe goes on to face the killer on his own, in total darkness. He, of course prevails, falling down in the process, actually tripping right over the killer's body. The closing scene has Adam coming into the room, knocking the door down and entering with a flashlight in hand. Joe, still on the floor, discovers his sight is back when Adam shines the light into his eyes.

Joe faces his inner demon, his own fear, by facing his external threat while handicapped, and all alone. As a result, he became whole again—and that much more besides.

This closing scene has almost no words. It is almost entirely visual.

Joe walks over to turn the master light switch back on, the switch he had turned off when he sensed the killer at the window of his apartment. Joe spends some time visually taking in the apartment that was his virtual prison, now that he can actually see what he worked so hard to visualize while he was blind. The look on Adam's face when he is wordlessly watching Joe conveys utter admiration for the qualities of toughness Joe just displayed. Actor Robert Reed's performance in that one scene is so effective that it still winds up on some Web pages that cover Reed's career.

When Peggy comes into Joe's apartment—because she can no longer wait to see what happened to her larger-than-life boss, and now friend—the looks between those two are transcendent. They now have heartfelt appreciation and deep admiration for each other—so much that a nine-year-old kid could swear, on the basis of seeing that one scene alone, that such platonic love was greater than any other kind. That nine-year-old would never forget that, and, a lifetime later, never have that notion refuted either.

Peggy does not initially realize Joe has regained his sight.

With incredibly few words, a bridge is made back to the airport scene in the late season 2 episode "Last Rites for Miss Emma," because Joe reveals to Peggy that he has regained his sight by asking if she is wearing a new dress. Bridges like that are always being made in *Mannix*.

No writing describes the looks on the faces of these two during this final scene.

The true reward for facing and overcoming adversity is right on those faces, revealed as self-knowledge that one has done so, with even just one or two credible witnesses of how such a struggle was faced, alone. No other story ever conveyed to me, quite so well, why toughness is simply beautiful—and whatever power has to offer cannot compare.

We never do find out what happened to the money—and it does not matter.

Promotional photo for the September 16, 1967 premiere of Mannix. *Mike Connors is in the foreground, with Joseph Campanella (who played Lew Wickersham) in the background. Behind them are Intertect's room-sized computers. (Copyright Paramount Pictures Corporation.)*

Photo taken during filming of the second episode to air, "Skid Marks on a Dry Run." The script was re-used in season 6's "Search for a Whisper," so you get to see Connors play the pool scene again. (Copyright Paramount Pictures Corporation.)

An iconic photo, taken during the filming of the season 1 two-part episode, "Deadfall." Joe's left hand (or arm) would be bandaged many more times to come. (Copyright Paramount Pictures Corporation.)

At the start of season 2, Joe Campanella was replaced by Gail Fisher, who played Peggy Fair, Joe's "Girl Friday" for the next seven seasons. (Copyright Paramount Pictures Corporation.)

Also at the start of season 2, the computers, high-rise office building and corporate climate of Intertect were replaced by Joe's Spanish-Mediterranean office with upstairs apartment, at 17 Paseo Verde. Here, Connors is reading a script at Joe Mannix's desk. The accompanying release from Paramount, dated April 15, 1969, says that Mannix will go into its third year of production on May 12. (Copyright Paramount Pictures Corporation.)

Joe was perhaps the best-dressed Private Eye in history. Here, Connors serves as a model for Botany 500, the tailor that is mentioned in the closing credits of episodes. Notice the "Mannix" label on the equipment in the background. (Copyright Botany 500.)

Promotional photo for season 3's "A Penny for the Peep Show": We never do see Joe in a pose like this in the episode. Joe would gracefully leap over such a banister in season 4's "The Lost Art of Dying." (Copyright Paramount Pictures Corporation.)

From season 3's "Who Killed Me?", Connors is pictured with Susan Howard. Joe championed both women and men, and sometimes became involved with his female clients. But no villain, nor love interest, ever recurred in Mannix. (Copyright Paramount Pictures Corporation.)

Peggy's last name, "Fair," brings a knight's "Lady Fair" to mind. (Copyright Paramount Pictures Corporation.)

This great publicity photo has Joe standing with the creepy people he hallucinated in season 4's classic, "The Mouse That Died." In the actual episode, Joe never did stand like this with these creeps. (Copyright Paramount Pictures Corporation.)

This extremely curious publicity photo could have been taken in conjunction with the filming of "Deja Vu" where Joe is referred to by his client as a knight. But we never see Joe dressed like this in an episode. (Copyright Paramount Pictures Corporation.)

Season 4's "A Day Filled with Shadows" has Connors going one-on-one with Gail Goodrich. Both played basketball for John Wooden, the legendary UCLA coach. In the background is Kareem Abdul-Jabbar (then Lew Alcindor) waiting for his scene. (Copyright Paramount Pictures Corporation.)

PR firm McFadden, Strauss & Irwin released this fun publicity sketch with accompanying text: "Sight-in on action with Mike Connors starring as private investigator Joe Mannix in Paramount Television's popular 'Mannix' series, now airing in its fifth season, Wednesday nights over CBS-TV. Gail Fisher co-stars as Peggy Fair and 'Brady Bunch' star Robert Reed returns in the recurring role of police lieutenant Adam Tobias in the hour-long crime drama." (Copyright Paramount Pictures Corporation.)

Taken during the filming of season 5's "Lifeline," Connors seems thoroughly engaged in what is going on, even though he is not part of the scene—just like Joe Mannix might be. A longer shot reveals he is wearing a parka over his Joe Mannix attire. It must have been cold, since Joe never wore a parka in the episode. (Copyright Paramount Pictures Corporation.)

The season 6 premiere, "The Open Web," features former NYPD police officer Eddie Egan, the real-life, tough hero of The French Connection. One of Egan's first acting roles was in this episode of Mannix. Connors and Egan never do smile like this in the actual episode. (Copyright Paramount Pictures Corporation.)

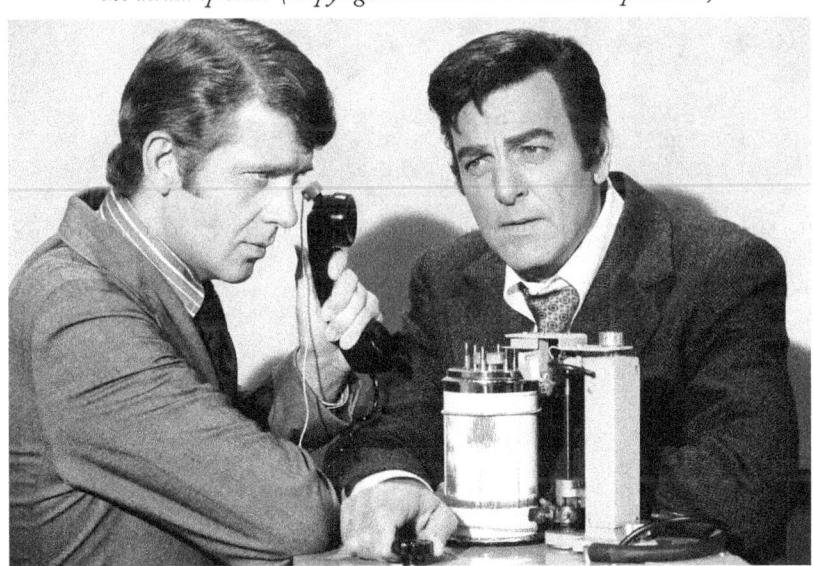

Connors and Robert Reed on the set of season 6's "The Inside Man," even though they never appear in the episode together in front of the electromechanical recording equipment. (Copyright Paramount Pictures Corporation.)

This fun photo suggests that Mannix is moving! In January 1973, Mannix did move its timeslot, while staying on Sunday nights—a move important enough that Connors made his first appearance on The Tonight Show Starring Johnny Carson on January 5, 1973 in order to let viewers know. Judging by the wardrobe, this photo was taken during the filming of season 6's "To Quote a Dead Man," likely filmed in December 1972 since the episode showed some holiday garland in the then-Hollywood-Burbank Airport. (Copyright Paramount Pictures Corporation.)

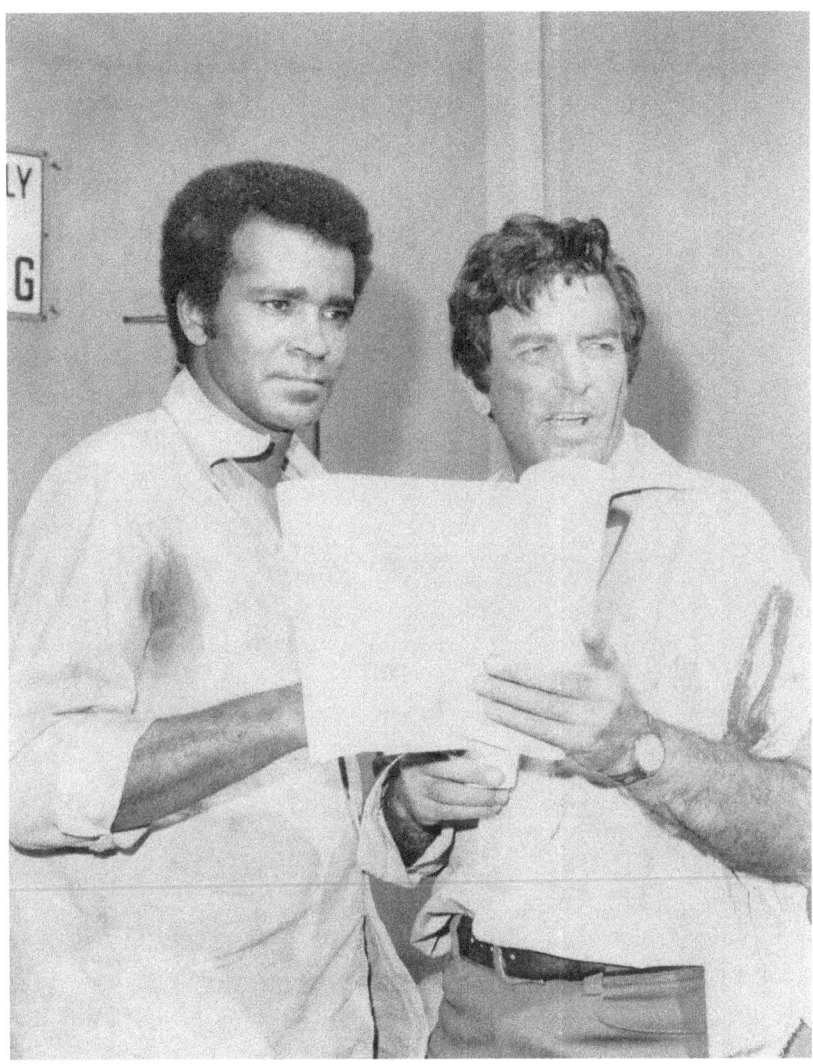

The press release for this photo describes a friendly rivalry with Greg Morris, shown here with Connors during the filming of season 7's "Climb a Deadly Mountain." The gag-filled "feud" was all about ratings supremacy, especially during the 1971-1972 season. Mannix and Mission Impossible were "sister series," each produced by Paramount, filmed on the Paramount lot and executive produced by Bruce Geller. (Copyright Paramount Pictures Corporation.)

In season 7's "Silent Target," Barbara Luna (pictured with Connors) plays Elena, who winds up taking a bullet for Joe. Making a woman such a heroine in 1973 was very unusual, to say the least, but just one of many stereotypes Mannix was not afraid to break. (Copyright Paramount Pictures Corporation.)

Connors and Fisher are each dressed as they were in season 8's "Picture of a Shadow." Joe and Peggy are in Joe's classic 17 Paseo Verde office for the last season. Mannix was canceled in April 1975 despite climbing back into the Top 20 for its eighth season. Fans would not get to see season 8 again until the DVDs were finally released on December 4, 2012. (Copyright Paramount Pictures Corporation.)

and now, back to mannix

Chapter 7
It's About the Mouse

We are all alone, in the middle of a mystery, one where we know the ultimate outcome, and yet one that is so confusing, terrifying and downright unfair that the wonder is how we find ways to keep moving at all, to do what needs to be done, when we have no idea what that really even is.

That's life. And that's what two of the signature episodes of *Mannix* are all about.

After establishing core qualities of character via more than three season's worth of episodes, seasons 4 and 5 each have a signature episode that puts us, along with Joe, in the middle of a confusing and completely threatening dilemma, including extreme mental and physical peril. In each case Joe is hospitalized early on, but he chooses to be out and about, helping himself, even though he can't even completely trust himself, mentally or physically. "The Mouse that Died" (or "Mouse" for *Mannix* fans) aired early in season 4 and "Death is the Fifth Gear" (or "Gear") was the last episode aired in season 5. Both of these episodes were written by Chester Krumholz, which probably explains some of their structural similarities. Don't drink the coffee. Just trust me on this.

The Internet Movie Database (IMDb)[7.1] reveals that Krumholz wrote eleven episodes of *Mannix*, more than for any other series, despite his writing episodes for more than twenty-five other TV series. Similarly, "Mouse" was directed by Sutton Roley, for whom the IMDb lists sixteen *Mannix* directing credits, more than for any other series, despite his directing episodes for over fifty TV series. Roley has something of a following, and he brought a style to *Mannix* that helped it feel different from other series, especially his penchant for extreme close-ups on faces when characters were in the most peril. In "Mouse" the tops and bottoms of faces were sometimes cut off, amplifying the way the situation was really getting to those characters. The extremity of the circumstances was also revealed in powerful ways because the characters did not over-express themselves. Roley seemed to leverage the often subtle realism in the acting. Roley also supposedly had a reputation for being difficult, to the point that some would not work with him.[7.2] But he was welcome on *Mannix*, whose main character was all about not letting much of anything intimidate him, thus lending more authenticity to the series.

In "Mouse," plot does not matter as much as the way qualities of character are revealed as befits a *Mannix* signature episode. *Mannix* included a wide variety of episode types, unlike many series for which you see the same basic formula from week to week. In this type of episode you know the outcome in advance. Joe is going to survive. How he responds to his dilemma is what matters. The episode is re-watchable for the same reason. Intricate plot is tantamount to cleverness, which impresses us exactly once, if at all, the first time we see it. The second time around cleverness seems like so much less, much like listening to the same joke the second time around. Seen several times, cleverness becomes boring, or even worse. But stories that reveal qualities of character seem capable of holding our interest long after they have exhausted the "wow" effect the first time we see them. They seem to hold things for us that we see differently in the context of the life we have lived in the meantime, where even just a single day can make a difference to what we see in those stories, depending upon what happened to us in that day.

In "Mouse," Joe is seemingly okay at the beginning of the episode, which is important to establish. We need to refresh ourselves with who Joe is, since we (in the first run) could not have seen him for at least a week prior to the start of the episode. The teaser shows Joe in a physics professor's office, where he takes a call from his client, the sister of a missing college student. Joe learns that the missing student has been found. But the camera pulls back from the sister, on the other end of the phone call, to reveal the student telling his sister that if Joe had stayed involved, he could have been killed. So far, nothing about this kind of situation is new to Joe or to viewers.

Joe moves on to his next case, but is ultimately called back to his office while on his way to St. Louis. The student is, once again, missing. Joe goes back to the same professor's office. While there, Joe feels something that seems, to him, like an earthquake. Since the professor did not feel it, Joe concludes he has some sort of bug. The fun begins.

We next see Joe in an apartment going through a trash can of the missing student, finding letters that have been torn into individual pieces. He sort of loses his balance and falls, looking stunned at his physical condition for the second time in the episode. This is unusual. We've not seen Joe like this. On the way out of the apartment Joe encounters some robed, extremely creepy people, carrying candles and chanting as Joe slowly descends a staircase to discover himself at the bottom, a hallucination that is projecting his death since that is what is happening inside of him. He screams.

Yep, Joe Cool *screams*—and he is clearly scared to death! As in "The Sound of Darkness" we have Joe Cool losing his cool, and it is not the only time that will happen in this episode. The camera is close in on his face, and we see that he is restrained, strapped down—another recurring theme of these two episodes (and really the entire series), so much so that it became one of the elements that was included in the *Diagnosis: Murder* reprise. The symbolism could not be clearer. Strength and energy are threatening, to ourselves as well as to others, when they are unbridled or malevolent. We normally never want to see a hero so restrained, because heroes combine strength and energy with self-discipline and benevolence. How Joe deals with possessing strength and energy is one of those matters of character that we find appealing, and ultimately heroic. Normally, the last thing you want is to see Joe restrained. But something is very wrong with Joe now.

This is one of the few, and may be the only, times in the series we hear Joe actually say "Where am I?" as opposed to conveying it using his facial expressions, alone. We quickly discover that he is in the hospital, strapped down with the consent of his friends, who appear only in extreme close-ups, faces around the examining table, interleaved, each with intense, complex, understated emotion. You know that Joe is not quite right. If you didn't know that from the hallucination that resulted in his screaming, you can see it on those faces, the faces of Peggy and Art, who know something Joe does not yet know.

They know Joe is dying. He has been poisoned. The doctor rather abruptly tells this to Joe when his friends cannot seem to. In what is yet another powerful expression of emotion, Joe's friends can't face what is happening to him enough to even be able to bring themselves to tell him. Both Peggy and Art convey difficulty even processing the news. This is particularly true of Peggy, who wasn't a big fan of the doctor telling Joe in the way he did and who knows, after Joe is told, that Joe is going to look right at her to confirm if what he was told is true or not.

When this completely visual exchange happens, using no words at all, it solidifies just how good those characters, the acting and this series are. Extremes on either side of pretty much anything tend to appear in similar forms. For example, we are similarly bored when something is too trite for us to follow as when something is so complex that it is over our heads. In each case we do not connect and do not engage, but for completely opposite reasons. This is the most fundamental of lessons teachers must learn when trying to calibrate their material to their class. Emotion is also like this. We seem as cold when we do not care as when we are overwhelmed because we can't handle how much we care. In each case, genuine expression is not something we have to give. But notice how so many characters in TV and the movies overact in extreme situations anyway, telling us what we should be feeling rather than pulling us into the situation. But not in *Mannix*. Not on those faces.

When Joe looks back at Peggy to confirm the bad news, she looks, well, downright cold! Yet you sense that she is feeling exactly the opposite, not only in the context of the characters that *Mannix* gives you credit for knowing by now, but also in other subtle ways. Because you *infer* this on her face as opposed to it being expressed to you in a way that is more "*in* your face," it has that much more impact.

We see Peggy look at Joe after he has been told the bad news and before he looks over at her, and we see the set-up for what is coming next. She knows he is going to look right at her as the final word on this bad news, to find out if it is real. That, in turn, tells us how close they've become, and in a completely wordless way. She is steeling herself for this.

When we get back to Peggy's face, right after Joe looks to her to confirm the bad news, she looks at him only briefly before giving a look that could almost be termed extreme disappointment. It's almost as if she's disappointed Joe managed to get himself poisoned—portraying another real emotion when people are close. Then she just turns away from his gaze. The powerful moment of this scene is when she can't hold his gaze. She can't process Joe's impending death and so she can't even look at him, knowing that he is basically hoping for a reprieve from her, one she does not have to give. Peggy also seems to convey the knowledge that she may only be able to look at him, while he is looking back at her, for a short time in the coming hours, since his time is now limited. Her look conveys that what is happening is so big she is having a hard time processing it, even as she is trying to hold herself together for his sake. So very sweet.

We discover Joe was poisoned "sometime in the past twenty-four hours" and "in any number of ways." Joe does not know who. He does not know how. And while there may be an antidote out there, perhaps in the possession of the person who poisoned him, the doctors do not have one. The doctors may or may not discover one in time, however much time Joe has left. Even the doctors do not know how long he has to live. All they know is that Joe has been poisoned with a nerve drug affecting his muscles, and that at the end he will experience increasing weakness, hallucinations and blurred vision.

In order to try to establish a baseline or reference for what is going to happen to Joe, as well as establish how much time he has left, they have injected a mouse with Joe's blood. We're told the mouse will anticipate what will happen to Joe because the mouse's body is smaller and more fragile. After the mouse dies, Joe is not going to have much time left. And so, when Joe leaves the hospital, against the strong objections of the doctor and his own friends, his closing line on the way out the door is, "Besides, you want to save that mouse, don't ya?"

Joe is used to having a client, someone for whom he can be a champion. Working on behalf of someone else brings out the best in him and is a core part of his character. This news that he has been poisoned, with a projected steady downhill slide, mentally and physically, is, well, perhaps a bit on the large side in terms of something to deal with. Time being what it is, he needs to find ways to keep moving before he completely processes the meaning behind his now compact life's dilemma. His response is to invent a symbolic client. He and the mouse are now in this together.

The next scenes follow Joe as he tries to investigate this case, and we see some physical problems start to creep in as he can't read Peggy's notes and even has difficulty putting his jacket on. Peggy gets in front of him and insists upon driving. Joe can't drive his own car—and he can't even easily put on his own "*Mannix* jacket?" This is deeply, symbolically serious stuff now.

But Joe is trying to deal with it by being Joe, as best he can. When Peggy asks him if he is okay, after having trouble putting that jacket on, he says he is fine—and wonders how the mouse is doing.

Think that mouse might come up again in this episode?

Beyond those physical problems, Joe is hallucinating, starting right in the next scene, wherein he is not even sure what happened during his visit to a dry cleaner to try to obtain some information about the missing student, a likely key to his dilemma. We next see Joe in Art Malcolm's office, where Art is also trying to find out what happened by calling the dry cleaner, since he can't trust Joe's take on the visit. It would seem that not everything we saw at that dry cleaner was real, because a broken window is all of a sudden fixed the next time we see it. So, now even *we* aren't quite sure what is going on. When Art suggests that Joe should go back to the hospital instead of running around, that seems like a pretty reasonable request. Joe stops him by saying, "There is a very sick mouse depending on me."

This line, this episode, had so much opportunity to be delivered in a frivolous way, poking fun at itself, just as so many other series might handle such a script. But it was done with just enough awareness of the darkness of the situation to make you realize that humor, at its very best, enables you to deal with, rather than distance yourself, from struggle—a subtle and yet important differentiator of fictional characters, as well as of character, itself.

That same scene in Art's office begins with a close-up on Joe's hands, and since the previous scene left us with a close-up on those hands shaking, Joe's now examining them as if he can't trust them anymore—symbolic of his not being able to trust himself just when he needs himself the most, and coming to realize that. Also symbolic is a bracelet Joe is wearing on his left wrist, given to Peggy to put there, at the doctor's request. It has an emergency number on it. It is symbolic for the viewer that, even if Joe appears okay at times, something is not quite right with him. No words are required when we see him with that bracelet on, because he would not normally wear that. The bracelet labels him in this episode, just as symbols are used to label things from the arts to mathematics to the sciences.

That *Mannix* was a show about character—working on us at a symbolic level, deeper than the more transparent level of plot-driven story—is evident in the very way the show was put together. The signature episodes make this clearer still, drawing upon our foundational knowledge of the series and character, building upon that knowledge in order to take short-cuts that make the signature episodes that much more powerful. Symbols are powerful short-cuts we use so that we do not have to deal with repetitious detail time and again, detail that slows us down, can become mindlessly boring and, even worse, meaningless. Unless we can deal with things symbolically, with reality in a representational way, we can't see the big picture. We infer symbolic images from what are really only patterns of light on a screen, images that have meaning to us, potentially to the core of our very being. The same is true of the way we infer meaning from the words on this page, and the letters that form them—but more on letters, and that mouse, later.

We can't fully exercise our minds unless we properly deal with assignment and inference of meaning and its symbolic representations. Because they mask detail, symbols allow us to project what is not always really there, or perhaps only partially really there, ultimately allowing us to manipulate a representation of reality instead of reality, itself. The meaning behind that symbolic representation is something we explicitly assign and manipulate as engineers, or implicitly discover and interpret as artists, of the world around us. Both cases involve symbols and their relationship to meaning. The assignment and inference of meaning is something we do all of the time, without realizing it. Because they allow us to process real things more effectively, to think at a higher level, symbols have the power to affect our personal reality in ways we often do not realize. Some symbols we assign ourselves, while others we take for granted, collectively processing them without thinking about their meaning. We do this when we see others process symbols in ways we merely mimic. The process of assignment and inference of meaning is central to what it means to be human, providing layers of depth we, implicitly and symbolically, associate with human intelligence. When we find it pleasurable, even fun, to understand and manipulate things symbolically, we find the energy to do more with our lives. Now, back to those letters, and that mouse.

The story progresses as Joe needs to find the missing student, Geoffrey Parradine, who is the only real lead. Those letters, found in the student's garbage can, are Joe's only clue. But he can't put them in proper order, so he has no idea what they mean. We next see Joe working on trying to piece the letters together, working at his desk in his apartment. He looks something up in a dictionary. He finds it is not a word either. Frustrated, Joe angrily throws the dictionary down.

You get the sense that he's just as frustrated that he might die soon as he is that he might die without understanding the meaning behind this situation. Peggy, who has presumably been downstairs, kind of just hanging out waiting to see what is going to happen next with Joe, comes up with a book in her hand. Was she just down there, reading? She takes in what happened, and goes to pick up the dictionary. He, again angrily, tells her to "leave it alone."

But this is the same guy who is commonly advertised as "taking bullet wounds in stride!" You can still find that description, to this day, out there on the Web, supposedly summarizing the main character of this series. But Joe is not taking this in stride—at all. Similar to his behavior in "The Sound of Darkness," he is angry, disgusted with his situation, and even scared. It gets worse—or better, depending upon your point of view.

The scene between Joe and Peggy conveys deep, raw affection, especially on the part of Peggy for Joe, conveying, like so many other scenes in *Mannix*, so much more in the context of those characters. She, of course, wants him to go back to the hospital. But that is just what Peggy *would* want. She is his right hand for a reason—she is capable, highly reliable, and quite rational.

But wait a minute. Isn't she *right*?

Gee, the man was hallucinating, and so could not even trust himself mentally, let alone physically, and was clearly a strong enough person to do all sorts of harm. Also, practicality would dictate that the best course of action is to be in a hospital where doctors might be able to give you medical aid that would prolong your life long enough for them to find the antidote. C'mon Joe. What are you *thinking*?

It was a revelation to me just how much I had changed over the years when I watched "Mouse" again, on those DVDs in January 2011, with so many years lived in-between. Those years were lived in concert with a society oriented around all sorts of details, cleverness and rationale, a society that even likes to absurdly and very inappropriately insert the word "literally" into sentences as if to make them sound more important, when it really means "symbolically." I discovered myself thinking—really thinking—Peggy was right and that Joe was acting irresponsibly. After a few minutes of contemplating this—coupled with an incredibly strong imprint of who I was when I first watched the series, precisely because I connected with it and loved it so much way back then—was a moment of awareness where I swear I felt concrete break inside my head. If you think I should have inserted the word "literally" after the word "concrete" in the previous sentence, you are in worse shape than Joe is in this episode.

Joe is in the middle of a life-and-death mystery with him at the center, and his choice is to face it on his own terms, bringing his own skills to bear with whatever he's got left of them and with whatever time he's got left. This choice may not hold up to rational scrutiny, especially in a society that seems more focused on collective safety than personal dignity. But it makes all sorts of sense for this man, so much so that you don't question his choice when you know him deeply, which is to say, symbolically. He represents a kind of dignity to which we wish to aspire, an example we'd like to leave behind that others may find inspiring. By contrast, rationality or normality, the status quo, is utterly un-memorable.

Not only don't you even really question this behavior, you *want* Joe out there, most especially under those circumstances. You want there to be no circumstances under which Joe will not be Joe, and all the more so, as the situation demands. And what that means is that when he is up against it, he is going to presume that he may well be the only one who can help himself. If other help comes in, that's fine. He is willing to accept it, even appreciate it. But he isn't going to count on help from anyone else. And he can't stand the thought of inaction with so much on the line—that mouse, for example.

As the scene continues we are, once again, treated to seeing Peggy unable to hold back tears in Joe's apartment (the previous time was in "The Sound of Darkness"), with her boss once again in all sorts of physical peril. But, of course, she does not just break down and cry. She continues to communicate just as if she is not crying, her tone of voice almost unaffected, with the tears seemingly incidental. How great is that? In this same scene, which includes a reference to *Citizen Kane*, Joe, once again blows up at Peggy. This comes right after Peggy suggests that, perhaps, Joe should go back to the hospital. In response Joe says "And do what? Lie around while someone else tries to save my life?" He tells her to forget it. She says, "I was only trying to help, Joe." He responds by turning towards her and yelling "Then *help*!"

He just blew up at Peggy—*Peggy*—when she can barely hold herself together watching her boss fight for his life? Here is yet another cringe-worthy moment in a signature episode of a series that so many think is only about this Joe Cool character. He quickly—quickly—apologizes.

Peggy, in yet more realistic fashion, does not say, "Oh, that's okay, I accept your apology, seeing as how you've just been poisoned and don't have long to live and all." She actually looks a little hurt, despite his apology, combined with even deeper feelings as she is seeing how this is all getting to her normally cool boss. Her emotions are, once again, in true *Mannix* fashion, complex, making them all the more real.

After his apology Joe says, "You have to understand. It's my life. Nobody is going to fight for it harder than me. *Nobody*."

In a situation where a lot of people, most especially of the Baby Boomer generation, would rather be surrounded by friends and people who want to help, Joe chooses to acknowledge that, when it comes to certain things, we are essentially all alone, with no one to rely upon more than ourselves. Someone is trying to kill him and may succeed. But, if they do, they are not going to diminish who he is in the process. Thus, we feel, all the more, the enormity of the potential loss of this character, of the loss of his particular brand of character, of his particular form of dignity.

Things quickly get even worse for Joe when Geoffrey Parradine appears at Joe's office door, dead. Peggy opens the door in response to a knock, the student's last door knock. When Joe sees that the student, his one lead, is now dead, he declares, "That mouse is not going to like this, one bit." Right there is yet another great close-up on Peggy as she, again, turns away, unable to face the situation. Fans of Peggy, don't be concerned. She more than redeems herself in the next signature episode, "Death is the Fifth Gear," discussed next.

"Mouse" continues with several plot developments. Microfilm is discovered on the student's arm. In the process of discussing that, and the potential meaning behind the letters, with Art Malcolm, we see Joe getting worse. Art tells Joe that they need time, something Joe clearly has in short supply now. Joe says, in response to Art telling him what they are up against: "Tell it to the mouse."

Joe keeps getting out there, with the sister of the now dead student driving Joe's car, because Peggy has been benched in this one. Joe actually snapped at her a second time, even after she tries to offer help—a bit painful to watch, actually. After a long hallucination, and after the meaning behind the letters is revealed, Joe calls Art. Joe has found a potential suspect and is trying to convey that to Art, even as Art is trying to tell him something, getting annoyed at his friend even though he knows his friend is near the end. He knows this fact better than Joe. Art tells Joe, "It's about the mouse."

Well, we knew what was going to happen to the mouse. It was right in the title of the episode, after all.

Next is a classic scene where Connors' face is really kind of white and cold-looking along with some red eyes. We no longer need to see that bracelet to know that something is terribly wrong with Joe. A suspect is being questioned by Art, who does a lot of yelling at the guy in order to try to get information out of him. When the guy resists, Art pronounces it a "dead end." Joe, clearly on his last legs now, gets up to use decidedly different tactics to question the guy, calmly and logically scaring him into believing that what is happening to Joe is going to happen to him. And so you see more of Joe still being Joe, even in his worst moment. So does Art, who has increased appreciation for Joe right before he is, apparently, going to succumb to the poison. This is more great character, revealed.

Joe figures out it was the physics professor he had visited days earlier, with the poison given to him right in the faculty office coffee, the professor having killed the student as well. A technology professor is a killer, motivated by money. Why didn't I watch this episode more closely as a kid?

Joe makes it, of course, and in the closing scene, when Joe wakes up, this time with clear vision, in a hospital bed and not strapped down, we get not one, but two great concluding lines. But notice the eyes. They had to have been nearly impossible to see on standard TV when the series first aired, but just follow those eyes, on both Joe and Peggy. She waits for his eyes to meet hers before delivering her set-up line, "Next time, stick to my coffee, huh?" To which Joe responds, "I'd rather be dead."

Sounds like a great concluding line. But then Joe sort of groans, feeling bad about something, causing Peggy to ask him what is wrong. He replies, with perfect sweetness, "I just thought about the mouse."

The kid version of me never did quite get that line. The adult, after having lived a little, does.

The next signature episode, "Death is the Fifth Gear," or "Gear," is the last episode to air in season 5. Like "Mouse," drugged coffee and hallucinations are involved, making me wish I was a fly on the wall at one of Chester Krumholz's parties during those days. This time though, not only do we not know who is doing bad things to Joe, we don't even particularly know what is happening to Joe at all, for a long time.

In the teaser we have Joe and three other race car drivers getting ready for a race. They drink coffee that is passed out incorrectly—Joe gets the wrong cup of coffee. When he then goes out to race, he sees a fireball coming right at him, and he crashes his race car. We then go into the *Mannix* opening title sequence, the very last episode in which the teaser leads into the titles (the format was changed for seasons 6-8, so that the titles came first).

The scene right after the opening credits has Joe definitely not being Joe. He is terrified, screaming, literally backing himself into a corner as he has just seen his race car driving buddies talking about killing him as if he wasn't even there to hear it. We know Joe so well we know that, if he was himself, even in that kind of situation he would not respond that way, would never be quite so terrified. Two orderlies try to keep him down as he is given an injection by a nurse. We see the tranquilizer work on him as he slowly passes out to a calm, drugged oblivion.

March 8, 1972, just after 10:00 p.m., after a week of anticipating this episode based upon the "next on *Mannix*" previews the previous week, the rest of the episode unfolds, one of the very few things I've ever anticipated with such great expectation that turned out as good, or even better, than I hoped.

The very next scene quickly cuts to a doctor's office with Peggy and Art there, and Peggy insisting she wants to know what is wrong with Joe. The doctor can't tell them; all he knows is that it has something to do with "the brain," and that means finding out will be "difficult," even dangerous, as Joe will have to undergo a series of tests. We discover Peggy has Joe's power of attorney when the doctor needs some forms signed. This is quite cool! Joe gave his medical power of attorney over to Peggy in 1972, or even earlier? Really? Imagine that!

That fact also has a purpose in this story. After a few scenes where we see some great acting, especially on the part of Connors, it becomes clear that Joe is not quite Joe; yet Joe is still somehow in there, somewhere, only affected by something. Savvy viewers might have suspected that coffee from the get-go, but they can't be quite sure. They also saw that crash. Viewers who take savvy to the next level want to go along with this ride.

Peggy insists upon seeing her boss before she signs anything, like commitment papers, or her consent for "dangerous" tests. When Peggy and Art first see Joe in this condition, he is sitting in a wheelchair and tosses a tray of food, thinking the food has been poisoned. He grabs Art by the lapel, and asks to be let out because he thinks people are trying to kill him. Fat chance! After saying this, Joe almost immediately hallucinates, this time thinking both Art and Peggy are out to get him, cashing him in for money. In the process he grabs Peggy's wrist, or does he? We don't really know if he is imagining it or if it is real.

Significantly, many of the things Joe is imagining turn out to happen, for real, later on in the episode. His hallucinations take on symbolic form. He thinks people are trying to kill him, that he's being given poison (or a drug), that Art and Peggy might be out to get him, and that he grabbed Peggy hard enough to actually hurt her. Deep down in his psyche, Joe seems to know what is going on and is even prescient—and yet his friends are not listening to him. Clearly paranoid now, he runs up a staircase and into "Room 207" which holds an old lady, played by Elsa Lanchester. Ultimately trapped, Joe jumps out the window and hallucinates into the next scene, all the while screaming, "Leave me alone."

The next scene has Joe waking up again—that's a number that really needs to be counted, just how many times he did that in the series. This time he is regaining consciousness after a hallucination. He does so uniquely, as fits the situation. Again, it's all about the eyes. This time they open up fast, with a scream, and they look really quite stunned as he discovers where he is. This time the wordless expression on his face is more like "Where the %@&* am I?"

The camera pans out to reveal Peggy, Art, and the doctor talking about Joe as if he isn't there, as if he did not just wake up, even though it has to be obvious to them that he just did so. They are fulfilling a nightmare, a reality even worse than the hallucinations. They are talking about him as if he isn't there, because they consider him to not be all there. We also discover that Joe is in a straightjacket as well as a tub filled with ice cubes, presumably as a way of controlling him by cooling him down. Being strong when you are not in control of yourself is not such a great thing, since it means you'll be bound up and controlled all the more.

Peggy agrees to sign the commitment forms, something the viewer can't very well object to at this point, in the process giving us yet more complex expressions, unique to the situation. She hates doing this, hates being the one to have to do it, and hate is really not a strong enough word for this. But this time she is at least able to look at Joe, actually has to look at Joe in order to evaluate him, even though she does not like what she sees. She is in considerable pain, well expressed, understated, as always. Regardless of the situations Peggy was in over all of the years of the series, she seemed to reserve certain expressions for Joe and Joe alone—and that worked to convey a special affection between them.

When Joe responds to her signing the form with an almost whimper—"Oh, no Peggy. Don't sign. No."—sort of repeating these words in a decidedly pathetic way, she takes her expression to the next level. Seeing Joe like this is beyond awful. Then she signs. Joe is aware he is being committed, aware Peggy has this power, can do this to him, and is doing it to him. Right after she signs, Joe gives us another complex expression, one combining resignation, exhaustion, and utter confusion.

The amazing thing about this episode, and one that makes it so unique to *Mannix*, is the way this incredible situation seems almost plausible. This episode was described as "wild" when it first aired, something of an understatement. The reason it not only works, but is believable in a deeper sense, is because the actors, especially Connors, were able to retain the essence of their characters in such extraordinary circumstances. Here we have Joe not being Joe, and yet still being Joe, deep down. That comes across and that gets to you—it is ultimately what makes the episode so powerful and even touching. This was not because Connors could not play someone other than Joe. The episode that aired the previous week, "Scapegoat," was one of those oft-used stories where the hero has an exact double. Not one of my favorite episodes, it clearly showed how Connors could play someone that was completely *not* Joe Mannix, even though he was wearing the same clothes and was supposed to behave with the same mannerisms as a double would. In "Gear" you have Joe who is not quite Joe, yet somehow still Joe. Because of that, the episode is classic—and so unique.

Back to the plot—no one seems to know what is going on at this point. All we know is that we have this person that everyone can realize is Joe, but who is not quite himself. And, as a strong man, clearly capable of doing all sorts of stuff, perhaps he shouldn't be out on the street.

But *Mannix* isn't a show about "should." In fact, it symbolizes the dignity of the individual and even the basis for a kind of psychic energy that helps us to get out of bed every day, where we tell ourselves that we can face whatever happens to come our way, and even welcome it.

You know Joe is going to get out on the street in this condition—and you, deep down, *want* to see that. Joe represents that part of you that nothing can get to, certainly not organizational power, and not even the insidious and paradoxical way common sense can serve to diminish, and even work against, the common good. Joe is the uncommon, common man precisely because of his dignity. Anyway, that part of you that wants to see Joe out and about like that is, well, just a little on the wild side, after all. It does not always follow rational thinking. It might even have its dark side, that side where all sorts of energy happens to reside in all of us as some sort of primal will. The trick is to find how to harness that energy in ways that seem good to you, without destroying it by always bowing to others or staying some sort of juvenile imp. That is why we find Joe Mannix intriguing, because how we resolve that says a lot about the kind of character for which we will wind up being remembered as well. And so we want to see Joe get the heck out of that hospital, and see what he does this time, see his character in action.

Joe's nurse helps him get out of the hospital, telling Joe that his doctor, who was also in the car race, is trying to kill him. At this point Joe looks a little better, a little less wild, and even he is wondering aloud what is going on, clearly starting to try to process things. Once he gets out, he looks just a little more recognizable, especially in that *Mannix* jacket, but he also looks slightly off—a combination of confused and something else that we can't quite put our finger on.

This sets up a scene in Joe's office where Peggy is about to leave for the day, dutifully still working for Joe even though common sense would dictate she might think about working on her résumé instead. She's been working for Joe too long to let common sense dominate her. Art comes in as Peggy is about to leave and she announces she is on her way to the hospital—to see Joe, of course. Art looks worried. Peggy notices this, and asks what is wrong. Art announces that Joe isn't there, "He's gone."

Peggy: "*Gone?*"

Art (in full recognition of what this means): "He got out, somehow."

Peggy: "Do you have any idea where he is?"

Art: "No."

Peggy: "Oh, Art. In his condition, he could hurt himself, or..."

Art: "I know. We have an APB out on him. Maybe we'll get lucky."

Peggy: "The question is, *will he?*"

Now, this scene is brief, and does not establish plot any further—we already know that Joe got out and is capable of pretty much anything. Thus, it was always the first to be cut from the syndicated versions of this episode. But I remembered it all those years, knew it was there, and it was the very first thing I looked for when the season 5 DVDs arrived on my doorstep, more than forty-one years after the episode first ran, a scene that reveals why *Mannix* is so good.

In this brief exchange, Joe is there, right in that room, even though he is not there at all. His essence, his character, is really quite strongly there, even though he is not physically there. Peggy and Art care about him, but so much of that is because they *know who he is* and value that enormously, even though some of those qualities might very well be harmful under these circumstances, and even though the last time they saw him he was barely recognizable as the person they remembered. He is the strongest presence in that room because their knowledge of his character and the way they value that is right on their faces, surrounding that simple dialogue. This is not the only episode where Peggy and Art wonder where the heck Joe is, and Joe is out there, somewhere, doing his thing. But it is the only episode where Joe is out there and they realize Joe can't even trust himself. So you get a double down on thinking about who Joe is, implicitly reflecting on his particular set of qualities, what they are as well as why they are so valued in the first place, even though he isn't even in the room.

Again, this scene is typically cut for syndication because it does not further the plot. But it illustrates how qualities of character can infuse us. If the definition of spirit is when someone or something is there even when they are not physically there, then this scene is all about spirit. Few stories can convey that quite like strong, well-done characters in series TV, because we know TV characters so well. We know Joe so well that he is in that scene, even though he is not in that scene at all. And we become a bit more spiritual ourselves when we realize that what we ultimately leave behind is character, itself—how our character affects people when we are not in the room.

Joe runs around and, of course, gets into trouble, ultimately framed for not one, but two murders. When Joe discovers, through a dream that isn't quite a hallucination, that he got the wrong cup of coffee, he is true to his nature and goes off to warn his doctor, despite having been committed at that point. The doctor is already dead though. Joe is framed.

Joe sets up a meeting with Art that takes place in one of those dark, industrial type areas, where Connors plays a not-quite-right Joe who is clearly having some difficulty thinking, but also re-emerging as the character we have come to know so well. Joe is in there, somewhere—even as he is not quite himself. Joe trusts Art, explains how he came to discover that he got the wrong coffee, that someone else was supposed to die in the race, and says the whole thing was "a mistake." Art, evaluating Joe as still sick, feigns belief.

Watching this scene is another one of those litmus tests for the ability to connect with the symbolic, like the scene in "Mouse," where you might think it would be a good idea for Joe to go back to the hospital. If you believe Art is right and Joe should go back to the hospital, go off and buy yourself some Play-Doh. Come back to this episode only after having worn it out.

This scene between Joe and Art is yet another that was butchered for syndication, since a key—key—reaction shot, brief but significant, was cut out. It is where Joe realizes he can't trust Art. The look on Connors' face is just great—combined shock, disbelief, hurt. It makes such a difference that the entire scene, even the entire episode, seems different when it is back in there. This is just a single look on a face, taking only seconds, maybe less, of airtime. But it explains his behavior later on, and actually makes his predicament that much stronger, especially in the great office scene with Peggy, yet to come.

Joe has a gun at this point, the one planted on the now dead doctor, and it is his own. He uses it to get away from Art. Back to the nurse, who is the next one to bite the dust. Towards the end of this scene, which takes place in her apartment, we realize, for the first time, what has been going on. Joe's coffee has been drugged by the nurse all along and, while we don't quite know yet who else is involved, a man pushes the nurse out the window when he realizes she has gotten too close to Joe. (Earlier, after helping Joe escape, the nurse had asked Joe how he could manage on his own. Joe was particularly endearing in his response: "Whatever it is, I gotta do it." Sweet.) Come the commercial break, the viewer is left with the police arriving, Joe leaving the nurse's apartment and no place to go. Wait a minute. What about Peggy? Oh, this is going to be so good—get those commercials over with!

The next scene opens with Peggy in her office, over by the coffee—watch out for that stuff—and we hear Joe say "Peggy" before we see him in his office. The door to his office is closed, and she runs to open it, saying probably her best "Joe" of the entire series. This scene is so rich. Peggy's visually conveyed, complex emotions change from one extreme to another within fractions of seconds. Joe is, incredibly, coming across as someone you know you can still believe in, but also someone who Peggy, at this point, can simultaneously care about and yet actually fear. What? Peggy is afraid of *Joe*?

Joe admits staying with the nurse. Peggy says that she heard on the radio that the nurse was dead. Joe responds, part strangely excited, confused, and innocent. "I know," he says. "I was there when it happened." This does not look so good to Peggy, who is now alone with Joe in the office. Joe is a strong man, and is quite capable of killing her with his bare hands. Normal Joe would not let such a thing happen to that nurse while he was there. Joe notices her reaction and says, "I couldn't stop it." This sounds even worse. Couldn't stop *what*?

Joe looks confused, but actually he's sort of thinking things through now. Still, confusion makes Joe still look sick. Peggy says, so compassionately, and as if it matters to her desperately, "Joe, you're ill. And you won't get better without help." Take any scene where two people are in bed with each other, any hot sex scene. I'll take this one over any of those, any day, to this very day. This is emotion, affection, concern, with underpinnings of value and respect for qualities of character.

The camera now cuts to them both, and she is holding his hand. He moves away, really thinking things through and talking them out. He remembers the old woman in "Room 207." Peggy is processing all of this, starting to see Joe in there, somewhere. Is he making sense? There is a knock on the door. It is Art Malcolm. Joe grabs Peggy—in such a way that it actually hurts her! The look on Peggy's face is one of being both scared and beyond disbelief. Is Joe going to kill her now, too? *Joe?*

He manages to convince her that he can't prove he is innocent unless she helps transport him back to the hospital to check that old woman out. Or does he? We aren't quite sure, since he still looks like he isn't quite Joe and Peggy seems to be placating him just enough to get away from him. When he cautiously lets her go to answer the door, we see a tear roll down his face. So *very* sweet.

When Peggy answers the door, we aren't quite sure what she is going to do. She is initially calm, hiding Joe right behind his own office door. Art informs Peggy that Joe is the likely killer of both the doctor and the nurse, and Peggy, in yet another way that drives the essence of character home, "Oh Art, you know Joe couldn't do anything like that." This line, as so many others, is all about the delivery. Peggy still believes in Joe, deep down, even though she was just afraid of him seconds earlier. But she is struggling with how best to help him and that is not clear to her, at all.

Art wants Peggy to not hold out on him, in case Joe should call. He is managing to convince Peggy—almost—that Joe is sick, is not himself, can't be held responsible, and needs help. There is this moment, just a moment, where Peggy hesitates—and then agrees with Art just enough to send him on his way. She is, for loyal viewers, and in this instant, different. She is no longer primarily loyal to the police, despite her background of having a dead cop-hero husband and lots of ties to the police force. She is now more loyal to Joe—even under these extreme circumstances. Joe's character has won her over—to the point of aiding and abetting—in the process also redeeming herself for her inability to face the situation in "Mouse."

Joe opens his office door—cautiously—and thanks Peggy. Something in the way he does that tells her that the Joe we know is in there, still. The look on her face reveals this knowledge—in the split second before cutting to the next scene.

Peggy drives Joe to the hospital so that he can break in and see what is in "Room 207." He tells her to "Go back to the office. If I'm not there in an hour, call Lt. Malcolm." Now Peggy really knows Joe is still Joe. He's indicating that he isn't entirely sure he can even trust himself. Peggy starts to warn Joe to "be careful"—an ongoing means in the series of expressing concern—and he realizes this and acknowledges it. At this point, the two of them could not be closer, even as they are about to part and she is about to let him go try to help himself, despite his condition. We see her watch him as he climbs over the iron fence, and she slowly puts her head down on the steering wheel and sighs, wordlessly conveying the enormity of the situation and her love for Joe—a strong candidate for the single sweetest moment of a series that held so many.

Joe finds out that another race car driver, a lawyer, is involved with extorting money from the old woman, and goes off to confront the guy on his own. In the process, he misses the meeting time back at his office, causing Peggy and Art to come after him at the lawyer's house, with Art laying a subtle guilt trip on Peggy during this scene. The ending of the episode, involving a race car crashing through a garage door, with Joe in the car, is classic *Mannix*. So is the scene where Peggy races to the car first, before Art Malcolm, opens the car door, and sort of tries to protect Joe from actually falling out of the car, since he's almost been asphyxiated and is having some trouble breathing. But the outcome, the plot, is not the point.

Qualities of character are the whole point, symbolic qualities with which we would like to identify, and from which we can infer our own instance, our own version, of reality. Because we and Joe's friends know those qualities, know Joe's character, so very well, he is the strongest presence in the room even when he is not physically there. He is there in a spiritual, symbolic and thus powerful way.

Joe has his mouse.

And we have Joe.

Chapter 8
The Private Kind

We struggle to accomplish two things in life: to survive and to succeed. Survival is objective, defined and measured by whether we continue to live or not. But success is subjective, largely defined in terms of societal norms and using conventional metrics of money, status and power. While survival seems to be of paramount importance, especially on an instinctual level, we often place success ahead of survival. Life spent merely surviving seems meaningless. At the same time, there are many things most of us would never do in order to obtain conventional metrics of success, things that would render such rewards meaningless to us. This creates a paradox, since success is somehow more important than our very lives, even as we value something more than the rewards we tend to associate with achieving it.

The foundation of this dilemma lies in the very origins of success, as a concept. The bulk of our lives are not spent struggling to survive, but rather struggling to succeed. The reason this is possible in the first place is due to original individuals from amongst our primitive ancestors who were able to look beyond the immediate circumstances of their lives, making it possible to transcend the limitations imposed by the need to pay constant attention to survival. These individuals thought for themselves, beyond the norm, about what life could be like, thereby making life efficient enough for mankind to orient itself around a myriad of metrics of success. The modern-day equivalent of those visionary individuals who were once able to transcend a life defined by mere survival are those individuals who are now able to transcend a life defined by conventional societal metrics of success. Those individuals show us that true success is that which we define for ourselves, in an original way, measured against our own, private metrics.

Accordingly, the impetus to think in a truly original way cannot be taught, nor facilitated through any system of rewards. Mankind seems to evolve more via the inspiration story provides than through any other means. For example, myths that once caused mankind to place a higher value on romantic love helped to evolve us into a modern society, with implications that reach well beyond what we normally associate with romantic love. Romantic heroes helped to move us from the dark ages into enlightenment, enabling us to consider our heart's desire more important than mere survival. But foundational stories must also evolve as mankind evolves.[0.4] And no story serves modern-day mankind better than that of the hero who chooses to live life as an engaged and yet original individual, at all costs. These highly individualistic heroes inspire us to address the problems created by modern society by placing values into proper perspective, by showing us how to live lives that are both engaged and enlightened.

Heroic characters that provide the inspiration for us to have the courage to be original individuals must resolve another paradox. They must, simultaneously, be compelling enough to inspire us to find our own, personal, original answer to what our own successful life might be, but not in such a way that we desire only to merely mimic them. Because if we do merely mimic them, or anyone else, then the originality, the whole point of why they were compelling to us in the first place, is lost. The paradox lies in the dilemma that people tend to be attracted to those with the courage to be original, often so much so that they try to mimic them in superficial ways, seemingly hoping something will rub off in the process of so doing, without understanding why they were attracted to them in the first place. This superficial mimicry, of course, ultimately defeats the point.

Inspiration for us to have the courage and desire to be original individuals must come from a deeper, more symbolic place, ultimately a kind of spiritual place, and yet an utterly human place, similar to the way we do not consider ourselves intelligent unless we understand the difference between the spirit of the law and the letter of the law. Story succeeds when it inspires us to visit our own, private place within ourselves, a place we might otherwise be afraid to go, or even feel is a selfish place to go, unless we understand it better. Great characters in story give us the desire and the courage to be consistent with them in our behavior in the real world, achieving this once again via paradox, by allowing us to be more comfortable with ourselves when we are the most alone. When we understand why we find some kinds of symbolism in story so appealing, and why we wish to be in concert with it, we seem to become more than we were before, even though nothing else changed.

If anyone who watches and enjoys *Mannix* wants to become a private investigator, or drive around L.A. in a convertible, or carry a gun, or wear a *Mannix* jacket, they are missing why this guy, Joe Mannix, appealed to them in the first place. None of that was the point of the show, or the character. Those things were signposts, and thus symbols, enabling you to identify Joe as Joe pretty quickly from week to week, and so to keep him in mind as well, but also identifying him as original precisely because those things were original to his character. Joe was cool enough to drive around L.A. in a convertible and confident enough to wear some pretty loud jackets, at times. He carried and used a gun because, as art so often needs to do, *Mannix* equates something subjective with something objective, in this case, success and survival. In so doing it conveys how we feel utterly and completely threatened when our success is threatened. It also conveys how we feel devastated, in the real world, when we are mistreated in our evaluation by others, ultimately even worse than if our lives were threatened, because the very meaning of our lives seems threatened when we are rejected by others, and especially when we are wrongly rejected by others. Accordingly, it conveys how much we put ourselves on the line when we risk our self-image, our self-concept, our external valuation of success, when we attempt to transcend norms, in an individualistic attempt to push the world forward.

And so, Joe's life was in danger pretty much each and every week, symbolic of the way we feel when we struggle to succeed on a daily basis and seem to be constantly threatened in that struggle. The violence in *Mannix* is similarly symbolic of the way it feels to us when we willingly put ourselves into situations where we become targets and where we need to learn to fight for ourselves, or more precisely for what we believe in, or still more precisely for our personal, even private, definition of success.

In yet another paradox, it can help us to be more peaceful individuals and cultures when we have more violence in our arts, because art gives us a place to work out the way we feel about our struggles in life.[0.4] If success matters more to us than our very survival, and yet is very personal to us, then a symbolic way to reveal this importance is by portraying it as a matter of life and death. The struggle to live instead of die symbolizes the struggle to achieve personal success, or meaning for our being here in the first place, for we feel on some deep level that if we do not do this, who we are will surely die. When we can work these issues out in our arts, and so symbolically, we can work them out in our minds without living them out in the real world when we are more likely to cause pain to others. Through violent struggles portrayed in our arts we can become more comfortable with our own struggles and our own resultant pain—which is always a by-product of true, heroic struggles—instead of causing others pain in the outside world, as many do and in so many ways for which they often excuse themselves as just trying to survive. Given this, it helps us when our heroes show us how necessary it is to accept the pain involved with being true individuals, and it hurts us when mythical heroes simply overcome the bad guys out there without having to endure this pain.

Of all of the things that made *Mannix* unique, perhaps the single biggest thing, artistically, was the way Joe Mannix was willing to endure all sorts of physical punishment and make himself into a target as a part of doing what needed to be done. Not only was he willing to do these things, he seemed to understand that doing these things was a necessary part of being a true individual.

Joe Mannix was also a private investigator, or "PI." In season 1's "The Girl in the Frame," the last episode of *Mannix* in which Joe still works for Intertect before going out on his own in season 2, Joe reveals to a suspect—who is actually suspicious of him at the time (and with good reason since Joe is holding her as kind of hostage in his house)—that he is "some kind of cop." The woman asks which kind, challenging him by saying, "There are only four kinds—federal, state, county and city." Joe replies, "The fifth kind—private."

As a matter of convenience, Joe introduces himself as either a private kind of cop or no kind of cop at all, depending upon the circumstances. He is not hung up on labels. Nor is he beyond doing a bit of play-acting and stretching the truth in order to get in the front door, among other things. And this never seems the least bit wrong. He is what he needs to be, one unique situation at a time.

Even the word "private" has certain connotations, with inescapable ties to valuation of success. A PI is largely the product of western society (America and Western Europe), someone who can be hired to work for you in private, an agent who will find out just about anything on your behalf, the results of which—whether the outcome is successful or not—are entirely private. But the Joe Mannix version of a PI was also very physical, very action-oriented and very engaged in the outside world.

We have romanticized our PIs going as deep and far as they need to go, solving problems and finding the truth on behalf of their clients, putting themselves in peril in so doing, mostly because of Joe Mannix. He became a kind of modern-day knight in shining armor, openly hinted at in season 4's "Deja Vu." That Joe Mannix chooses to live from case to case—acting on behalf of clients with identities he often cannot even reveal to the police, with successful outcomes kept confidential and private, and willing to pay the ultimate price to be an agent for those private concerns—is what makes his character so compelling and so valuable.

Since the pursuit of success is enabled by not always having to be pre-occupied with our own survival in the first place, success is really lived in the excesses of life. Those excesses are enabled because humans live in a highly cooperative society with plenty of time left over to live for things other than to ensure the survival of either themselves or the species. By the same token, that same cooperation leads only to the continued survival of society, and is not a part of its advancement. That is one reason why when we let our success be defined by others it seems somehow empty and meaningless, resulting in a chronic kind of pain often difficult to identify or diagnose, and which is often discovered when we can't go on any longer, or only later in life, when it is too late. Despite a myriad of societal and family cues for what a successful life might mean, deviations of which are designed to get to us via our instinct for survival, only we can define our own success. Realization of this gives us a tremendous burden of responsibility to define success, even as it has the potential to take away the emptiness by leading us to a place that is lonely, but also, paradoxically, to a home where heroes dwell—and so one where we ultimately come to find we are the least alone. Through heroes, we come to find we are the least alone when we have the courage to be the most alone.

With still more paradox at work, we find ways to contribute the most to society when we find ways to go beyond its conventional metrics of success. In many ways, western society cannot survive without certain kinds of hero motifs around, and we are less when our heroes become watered down versions of those original, tough individuals, with successful outcomes ultimately evaluated in private.

Heroes that enable us to find the beauty in living this way are necessary precisely because mankind has yet to, and probably never will, form a true meritocracy. There is no currency with which we can place a proper value on the contribution of one life compared to another, and there probably never will be. Those who contribute the most find deep desirability, even longing, in settling for the possibility of having relatively lesser conventional societal rewards than those who fit norms and expectations, and are handsomely rewarded for so doing.

Curiously, Ayn Rand, arguably the largest advocate that a meritocracy could be formed around the currency of an economic system, tried to use an engineering example to make her case.[8.1] Her example was a scientific breakthrough with clear economic benefits. In so doing, her assumption, which many fail to consider, is that others would be able to both recognize and properly value the breakthrough she described. But that is not the way things are in the real world of science or engineering, which, because they seek physical precision, are presumably among the most objective professions we have yet to conceive. Thomas Kuhn makes a clear and compelling case for why this is so.[3.2] He goes further to imply that the more something is a true breakthrough the less likely someone is to be rewarded for discovering it, and the more likely, by contrast, true discoverers will be considered outsiders and even ostracized in their lifetimes, with their contributions discovered only later, if they are even ever directly credited to them at all. These individuals, original thinkers, those whom we rely upon to push the world forward, must do so largely because they are capable of defining their own success and because they are inspired to think that way, to be that way, come what may. Something tough, even painful, ultimately always comes their way—the price one pays for thinking for oneself.

The real key to the success of western society is not in its fabric of economic success, but in its ability to cultivate heroic individuals through story. On some level we know this, despite having gotten away from it in recent years, with emphasis placed these past decades more on pleasing others in an almost institutionalized way, and the immediate, material kinds of rewards that go with that. We seem to place less emphasis on the more spiritual valuation of individuals with guts and true originality because there are so many other kinds of cooperatively enabled rewards to reap. And yet, social status, organizational rank, even inter-personal relationships are all types of rewards granted to us by others. Like monetary rewards, they are conventional hallmarks of success, even as there are always some things we will not do for those types of rewards.

Those things we will or will not do for societal rewards are those things we tend to equate with matters of character, that point at which our self-identity, our very individuality, implicitly assigns personal meaning to life by virtue of transcendence of the status quo, of the norm. Character is the point at which we make our lives our own, the point at which we do not seek affirmation from others so much as from ourselves via leading self-examined lives. We become individuals, true heroes, when we realize that life is so constructed and have the courage to live it accordingly, come what may, and in full knowledge that we are likely to open ourselves up to risk and pain along the way. But risk and pain go with responsibility of choice, originality of thought. Even just a few more people around who understand this, in the right places and at the right times, can make an enormous difference.

One of season 6's best episodes in *Mannix* is "The Faces of Murder." In this episode Joe's client is trying to get convicted of murder in order to save her brother. It's actually an interesting story. But in typical *Mannix* fashion the best thing about the episode is not the main plot, but something that happens in the context of the main plot, and so in the process you might not initially even notice it. This is yet another example of the kind of misdirection and layering that was part of the brilliance of *Mannix*, where it diverted your attention with what seemed like first-order plot developments, when far more was going on under that surface. This type of layering is also an artistic parallel for real life, in which we strive to achieve superficial things that really only matter for the way in which we achieve them, similar to the way outcomes in sport only have meaning because we attach meaning to the outcome of the games that otherwise do not mean much.

In this episode Joe Mannix, our hero, openly and brazenly breaks the law. And we, the viewer, are entirely okay with that, because it is clear, quite clear, that Joe is, overall, highly moral, and a hero to boot. We quickly conclude that Joe isn't exactly outside the law, but beyond it, transcending it. If he is going to break the law, we simply accept that he is going to do that for a greater good, in this case try to make sure that someone who is innocent does not go to jail, since the police have completely given up on investigating alternatives to the murder, which is the plot's focal point. Joe puts pursuit of the truth, and therefore justice, ahead of the law, since the law was getting in the way of its own intended purpose.

Not only does Joe break the law, but the way he does so is quite elaborate, even fun, with an intricate scheme set-up for the viewer when Joe visits a fellow PI. The scene where Joe breaks the law takes many minutes so that you can't miss it, nor can you miss that he is putting himself at risk to do it. The next scene drives home even further the risk that Joe took and is one of the best of the entire series, reflecting a maturity of series regulars and semi-regulars in their roles, including Joe, Peggy and Art Malcolm. It takes place in Joe's office the next morning. Notice the look on Peggy's face right after she hands Joe his customary morning cup of coffee. Joe is, well, in the process of misleading Art, and Peggy looks upon this with one of those signature, complex expressions—a mix of admonishment, amusement, affection and admiration. Sadly, her expression is nearly cut off as she leaves the room, not the only time great in-character expressions are treated that way, making a person so grateful to finally see the series on DVDs so that scenes can be frozen and such facial expressions fully appreciated.

Joe isn't an outlaw. He does not rob banks, is not the least bit the anti-hero. He is a pure hero, almost as pure as it gets. And that is precisely why he needs to break the law, but not on a whim or for personal gain. He does so in order to transcend the limitations of the law, as true heroes must.

I re-watched this episode, coincidentally, after spending several days dealing with a very small-minded individual in a committee setting. This small-minded individual was able to dominate precisely because he was able to leverage a kind of righteousness that has permeated our culture these past decades, so much so that others were more inclined to be run over by that bandwagon than to search their souls for what was really right and to find the courage to stand up for it. The power this person had in this situation came from an ability to leverage groupthink, to make people feel smaller than the stand-in for "the law," which, in this case, was "the rules." If anyone really cared to pay attention they could see how this person was manipulating the rules in order to obtain the outcome they *personally* wanted. Perhaps not surprisingly, this person who invoked the rules as sacrosanct is not known for creativity. Artistically, creativity is tantamount to breaking the rules, transcending them where they are incomplete, limiting and even damaging. Creative people often need to pay a price for so doing, the price of pushback from the status quo, in order to move a new idea forward.

Yet creativity is the very foundation of that which helps us not to survive, but to succeed. If Thomas Friedman is right and the single biggest differentiator of the U.S. with respect to the rest of the world is its culture of creativity,[8.2] then creative people must be inspired. They cannot be educated. Both innovative thinkers and those who stand up to injustice transcend identification as a "good boy" or "good girl" in any system, and must be tough enough to fight for something that has never been done before, in concert with the spirit of the law, as opposed to the letter of the law. In order to be in concert with "the spirit" of the intent behind anything, we need to be more in concert with matters of the spirit to begin with, in full awareness of how those matters impact the world we live in.

On the surface the law is right. If you stop there, however, you realize that the law, itself, has contradictions. It is impossible to write any kind of language, agreement, constitution or other body of rules that (a) cover all situations and (b) completely prescribe the meaning behind the original intent. That is why law, itself, is subject to all kinds of interpretation, even political ones, especially at the constitutional level. In computers the law is analogous to the creation of a rule base that covers all situations, including those which are not anticipated, and that is impossible in computers in part because mankind cannot achieve it either.[8.3] Outside of the rules lies the judgment of tough individuals who trust their intelligence, over and above intellect, enough to fill in the gaps, to live in the spiritual realm. These individuals that we implicitly rely upon to be there in critical, often private, moments must have sufficient (a) intelligence, (b) will, (c) morals and (d) independence. We ultimately rely upon them to be there for us in the many places we cannot understand, let alone police, let alone legislate, in a highly specialized and cooperative society. If we are lucky, we hope to be like them as well, in those moments where we can make such a difference. Even just a few such individuals can make an enormous difference, and whether those few individuals are enabled to act or not when the time comes, and whether we choose to act or not when our time comes, is affected by exposure to myths and heroes in story that enable us to do better.

Joe Mannix is one such enabling hero motif, perhaps even uniquely constructed as such, because he lives a character-driven, largely self-defined life, one where he manages to resolve individuality with engagement in society, engagement that consistently causes him pain. We come to see that the pain he endures as a result of being so engaged is ultimately far less than the kind of pain he would endure if he was not so involved, the pain of being so much less. He is, once again, paradoxically, highly individualistic precisely because he does not hide in the boondocks, does not turn his back on society by tuning out or acting as if he is somehow above the fray. He is both grown up and involved. At the same time, he does not fill a position within an organization or have any real societal status of any kind.

A PI is considered, by admission in the series, a seamy kind of profession, a fact brought up in season after season. Joe transcends this by virtue of his deeds and those deeds do not distill to items on a résumé. His character is completely defined not by association with organizationally sanctioned goodness but because of what you see him do from week to week, with that evolving over the years, as a kind of shadow résumé of good deeds, the kind that can't be put down on paper in a job résumé, but the only kind that really matters. Joe's shadow résumé, his character, is his real résumé. The convertible, gun, jacket and job became cool only because of the things you see Joe do, and so those things became associated with him, with his character. His character became defined so well that in those signature episodes where you thought something might really happen to Joe, you let yourself believe it, let yourself play with it some, even though you knew that would never happen in series TV. But you wanted to try his potential loss on for size, because that became symbolic of the loss of someone like that to western society. And that made you see him better, made you value matters of character more.

Joe does not hold any office, or have any protection of any kind from any group. This is a hero without position, without any real qualifications of any kind, and without the need even for education, although he did go to college for a degree that is never named. But he did not require education for his job, nor did he have to pass some rigorous test in order to display those enviable qualities of character. The toughest training in the world, after all, has to be achievable by some people. Some people always graduate from Harvard or become Navy SEALs. We always have one President of the United States. Someone always wins in sport, at least at the end of a season. None of those accomplishments, however prestigious, are unique. Whatever success they hold is defined by others, defined implicitly as a line of succession by comparison to others who previously held those same positions of status.

When we start to define heroes as those who fill pre-existing positions well, we get into all kinds of trouble. If, for example, we believed that a life could be considered good only if it was lived on the beach, then limited resources would quickly degrade the quality of our lives. Only so much beachfront property exists. If a good life meant living there, everyone would head for the beach, causing overcrowding, and those who could not make it there would consider their lives worthless. We might have constant war, with everyone fighting for beachfront property. But with an impetus to think that life can be pretty good, maybe even better, if we choose to not live on the beach, we can transcend the limitation of the physical resource, living more spiritually by finding a new, original way that might be better. Well-constructed heroes somehow convey the courage and beauty of thinking and acting originally, creatively, without telling us to do so, or even how to do so.

Without understanding it very well as a kid, Joe's status as a PI worked on a symbolic level that never made me want to consider ever being a PI, but still made me want to be like him at some deeper level that also made me understand that there were symbolic physical beatings as well as symbolic professions. He also made me understand and appreciate that risk and pain were not incidental, but somehow important to qualities of character. He endured so much, but always for a good cause, always because he was out there, all alone, so clearly reaching places others could not. What his profession as a PI did do was enable the visualization, the deep consideration, of the need to resolve the dilemma of true originality, of separation from conventional standards of societal success, while still being very engaged in society—so engaged that Joe was completely willing to accept all sorts of physical punishment as part of his job, as part of leading what seemed to be not "the good life" but rather "a good life."

Joe was, again paradoxically, completely engaged and yet completely apart. The police and his friends were always telling him not to do something that he would do anyway, things that made sense to a kid, do not make sense to an "educated" adult, but make perfect sense to a more enlightened human being.

Not only did Joe's status as a PI mean little to me as a kid, I might have even wondered if Joe wasn't good enough to be a cop. Gee, it seemed, to me at least, that everything I was being taught had to do with meeting expectations of some organization, from school on out. We were not instructed, and indeed not encouraged, to find ways to be better individuals—even hinting at such a thing was tantamount to the possibility of us sort of running amok, thereby making us more difficult to control. We were constantly gauged for our levels of conformity and obedience. So while it made no sense to me on one level that Joe was not a cop, on some other level Joe was so clearly the hero, the good guy of the series. I should have had a hard time reconciling why he was always being hassled by the police, and why he was out there all alone getting beaten up, and comfortable with the police just laughing at those beatings. Why would he do that if he could just get hired by the police? Cops didn't get beaten up like that. Was he getting beaten up like that because he wasn't as good as them? If so, why did I consider him the hero, and, more than that, my all-time favorite hero?

Yet another thing that hit me in the face when I re-connected with the series is that I never resolved this dilemma before, and yet just kept on loving the show anyway. Joe was clearly doing good, difficult things, and even managing to do things the cops could not seem to do. If he was doing them despite his inability to be a cop, then so be it. I did not consider this further. Or so I thought.

It was enlightening to discover, when re-connecting with the series as an adult, that it was central to Joe's character that he actually chose to be a PI in fighting the good fight instead of being a cop; that he actually chose to live a life that was, for him, harder than that of the police precisely because of the way he wanted to bring the gifts he was given to bear. He clearly seemed capable of doing all sorts of other things in life, but would never have chosen to be a cop, because of the restrictions of having to work within that organization. Cops were more powerful because of that organizational backing, and thus more protected from random beatings. By contrast, Joe Mannix had hardly any power at all, save that of his own gun, fists, and wit. When he would to go the police, he would often have to beg for information. Even though he had compiled quite a track record of doing good deeds, he was still resented by many of the police, year after year. His private successes, one client at a time, did buy him some note from the public. But that did not make his life any easier. After all, the public quickly moves on, but organizations never forget. His life was always about the next opportunity to engage, the next case, when he'd seem to get beaten up again. That he actually chose to live that way—let himself get hurt and be that vulnerable—and that it was so appealing to me, all of a sudden made perfect sense.

Central to the character of Joe Mannix is his tough, maverick-like independence, but not just for the sake of independence. Implicit was the assumption that organizations were going to get in his way, to limit him, somehow, in pursuit of what he wanted to accomplish. But what did he want to accomplish? It seems somehow vague to the point of drifting to say "to do good deeds." That seems entirely too easy to say. Most people have more than a handful of examples of others who have told them that, but when tested they were far more concerned with career advancement than doing any real kind of good. Too many people equate "good" with "others consider me good" in terms of filling some role or set of expectations.

We also saw how Joe was able to do, at times, what the police could not—and we saw that this made perfect sense. Organizations limit what people can do precisely because they are designed to outlive people, and therefore minimize the impact of any individual, one way or the other. Characters in story show us the value of transcending the limitations of systems; they give us the reason to find the beauty in trusting ourselves, so long as we are able to endure the personal cost, the sacrifice, which is always—always—involved with so doing. Character takes over where systems fail, as they always do, to cover all the cases life presents to us. Organizations are powerful. Individuals are tough.

As an independent advocate for the truth, enabled by pursuing it one client, one case, at a time, Joe's character type is the foundation of all great research, writing, leadership, and ideas, for those things are only great when they are pursued by true original, tough individuals with guts. All of those things are ultimately done outside of accepted norms of approval, often going against the wishes of the powers that be. We only write stories of inspiration around people who transcend, not adhere to, organizational norms. We rely upon people who find that inspiration from somewhere, even as we never teach it, and really cannot teach it, instead implicitly hoping that key individuals in the proper, often quiet, largely private places find the impetus to be original, tough individuals, comfortable being apart, with full knowledge of how that ultimately makes us feel the least alone.

In season 4 is an episode of *Mannix* that I was almost completely unable to appreciate as a kid. I distinctly remember being disappointed when it re-ran during the summer of 1971, because I did not connect with the episode when I first saw it. It was, in fact, one of my least favorite episodes of the series when I was young. This child's-eye memory of this particular episode was so strong that I actually delayed watching it, so it wound up being one of the last ones I viewed from the season 4 DVDs. But when I watched it, all these many years later, it had the kind of impact that left me slumped in my chair, just staring in thought, realizing just how much useful content was in the show I loved all along without my even fully realizing it.

In season 4's "A Gathering of Ghosts," we see Joe driving into the desert as the episode begins. He is looking at a map. Everything about the map, and the setting, leads us to believe he is driving to the middle of nowhere, to a place called "Silver Town." The map shows the roads around the L.A. environs to include labels of interstate highways that we never once see Joe drive on. "Silver Town" is in the desert, mostly east and a bit north of San Clemente, and does not even seem to have a road that leads to it. Indeed, when we see Joe drive, he is on a dirt road that one might think is not labeled on a map at all. He drives to the town. The opening scene has him trying to find his client, a "Mr. Webster." Joe is shot at, hides behind his green 'cuda convertible, and we go into the classic season 4 opening grid.

We quickly discover that Joe has been lured to "Silver Town," which is an old western ghost town, because he once played football for the "Silver Ghosts" when he was in college. A football is thrown from the top of a building and Joe catches it with one hand, on the run. He discovers that this is a reunion that his ex-teammates felt they could not hold without him since he was both the team captain and "a legend." Assuming he would not come to a reunion, they lure him there with the fake client, which happens to be the name of the college Joe helped defeat with a legendary run on the last play of the last game of the season. We see, in one of those subtle facial expressions, that Joe is not entirely crazy about having been lured here like this, but he goes along with it, at least initially.

Joe's ex-teammates include a doctor, a lawyer, an engineer and an advertising man, thus a well-represented subset of conventionally successful society. Joe is, easily, in the least reputable profession of that bunch. That bunch has also remained friends all these years, and continues to have professional involvement with each other, fifteen years after Joe was the big hero in the final game of the season where he ran for the winning touchdown, with time expiring on the clock, to enable an undefeated season. A giant poster is even revealed of this play, and we even hear an audio recording of the play being announced. Even Joe seems nostalgic for this moment, saying "I'll never forget that play."

We quickly discover that Joe's professional, well-educated, successful ex-teammates are not the sort we'd want to hang out with much. This gets dramatically worse when they play a prank on Joe. One of them fakes having been shot with an arrow, and the doctor pronounces him dead. Joe, being Joe, starts to behave as a PI, and tries to figure out who did it, someone who may still be after them. He spreads the group out, taking one of them with him, the only "outsider" of the group, a woman who did not attend the college but who married one of the ex-teammates. Another woman, "Diana," is in the group, but she is not an outsider, having hung around the team during its school days. The outsider, "Leslie," played by Diana Muldaur, is a lush, presumably for not being able to stand the bunch she married into, and so Joe sort of takes her under his wing. When he does, the following dialogue is exchanged between them:

Leslie: "They hate you too, Joe, the team."

Joe: "Why is that?"

Leslie: "Because you go your own way, do your own thing."

Okay, so "do your own thing" might be one of the few times dated dialogue makes it into the series that seemed to always have a sense of its potential to be a classic and so avoided popular parlance. But they got the sentiment right. During those days, it was supposed to be the younger generation, even the hippies, who did their own thing. Joe is, by contrast to that, establishment, even as he embodies more of what a true individual is all about. He works for a living, is very responsible to his clients, and does his own thing to the point he gets beaten up, shot and generally abused for so doing. But, compared to this bunch of his ex-college chums, Joe is not only the outsider, he is the only one you want to identify with. He is an individual, and not by accident, but by design.

This episode, brilliantly constructed, has Joe in the middle of nowhere, a deserted ghost town without even proper roads leading to it. The place has no electricity and no running water. It is many miles from any kind of major road. And yet, after only a few minutes, you get the sense that Joe, who is surrounded by college chums, really would be better off if he was all alone in that town, without the people there, than he is being around those he is supposed to consider friends. You feel it. And so you get it.

There are many ways we find ourselves alone in life. The most obvious is when we are in the middle of the desert or the woods, without any kind of human presence. Another is when we are in the middle of a large city where we are surrounded by people but where we cannot speak the language or read the signs, as once happened to me in Kyoto, Japan when I ventured too far from my hotel. We are alone when we stand up to injustice, and no one else has the courage to do so. But perhaps the time we feel the most alone is when we are surrounded by friends or even loved ones, and we feel we do not belong to the way they think, as a group.

Mannix is characterized by having a wide variety of episode types, with recurring themes in some of those types. One of the recurring themes in *Mannix* is "Joe alone in a small town." The very first of this type of episode is the excellent "Huntdown" from season 1, an episode which has Connors in a boot-cast and hobbling around so much that viewers openly wondered if he actually needed to be in the cast while the episode was shot. That episode is the first of many where we see Joe all alone and he does not want to be there, he wants out, and even has his chance to leave. But something always compels him to stay or, in this case, go back and find out why people were after him in the first place, to discover and expose the injustice. Normally in this type of episode Joe is surrounded by people he does not know. But in "A Gathering of Ghosts," he is surrounded by supposed friends. Only, Joe has somehow found a way to live his own life in a way they have not. They never really separated from the team, from their college days. By virtue of being his own person, and testing himself in the process, which is a required part of being one's own person, he has grown up in a way they have not. He gives every impression of truly being less alone when he is by himself, being true to himself, than when he is surrounded by people he was once thrown together with while he was ostensibly pursuing something else—in this case his education.

After Joe tries to find out who is killing people in their group, he is made fun of when it is revealed that the whole thing was a prank. Joe, understandably angry, starts to leave the "party" and asks to be removed from the mailing list. Joe is told to be a better sport, and that he used to be a better sport. Diana tells him that he can't leave, that the party is just beginning.

Leslie: "Your party, Diana. In the real world, Joe has work to do."
Joe: "Thanks, outsider."

But Joe discovers he can't leave, that his gas tank has been ruptured and his car phone has been sabotaged as well, along with the only other means of transportation out of the isolated town. These things were not part of the prank, and we discover that the doctor is murdered, for real this time. After a sort of *And Then There Were None* kind of story ensues, where members of the party are murdered one by one, with secrets being revealed the whole time, we get to the end of the episode to discover who among the bunch was responsible. Joe is then left, in the dark, in the small town, with Leslie, Diana, and a customary bullet wound in the arm. He sits there and says, to no one in particular, with irony, "A reunion."

As a kid, the whole episode just seemed so dark. It was even filmed in the dark, one of the few episodes of *Mannix* that did not use day-for-night shooting. The ghost town was on the Paramount lot and used in numerous *Mannix* episodes. *Mannix* was perhaps the only Desilu-Paramount series to use so much of the Paramount lot, including the Paseo, the New York Streets, the Chicago streets, the warehouse area, and even the those western streets several times. As a result, numerous settings recognizable from movies appear in *Mannix*, along with the many locations around L.A. where *Mannix* filmed. Often, even though the setting was right on the Paramount lot, the show would be filmed using day-for-night, presuming that the audience would buy into one incredibly bright moonlit night after another. But in this episode the night scenes were actually filmed at night, adding to the feelings of isolation and darkness.

Because there were so many things contributing to the sense of isolation and darkness—the isolated town, the night, the threat of a killer, and the group of friends who did not quite grow up—the viewer is left to sort out which of the causes of isolation and darkness are the worst. The group of friends wins that contest, in such a way that you just get it and in such a way that it makes perfect sense, if you bother to pay attention.

Joe seemed less alone, at the end, in the dark and in the isolated town, by choosing to be his own man, and by surviving this particular test of just that, than when he was in the midst of supposed friends. We want Joe to make that choice and are proud he is our hero because he consistently does so. We want to be like him so much more than any of the more conventionally successful types in his cohort of college chums, and for very good reasons that are exposed to us, by direct comparison to things that are very easily recognizable to the adult who has lived some. Because we want him to make that choice to be his own man we are forced to at least consider his choice when we need to make our own choices, in the many such opportunities we have in life. Joe is right there with us when we make those choices to be our own person, to define our own success.

And that, too, is evidence of the way heroes work on a spiritual level.

The key to being a heroic, original individual, one that finds ways to contribute the most to society, is the ability to feel the least spiritually alone when we are the most physically alone, in the middle of the desert, in a crowd, or amidst a group of family or friends.

Through heroes, we come to find that we are the least alone when we are the most alone. Heroes help us to resolve that paradox by substituting the spiritual for the physical, ultimately enabling us to define successful lives on our own terms, the only kind of terms for which success is more real than illusion—the private kind.

Chapter 9
The Art in the Background

Mannix was known for sneaking nude art past the censors. Apparently, in those days, network censors used to monitor scripts for things like profanity and potential nudity in the scene descriptions, but not bother to visit sets when shows were actually being filmed. I'm not sure what this says about me, but I watched nearly every episode during the series' first run, generally twice, including the summer reruns, and quite a few episodes on the DVDs, without noticing this on my own. I'll never know if that art wasn't quite visible enough on the standard TV sets I watched when *Mannix* first ran, but since I missed it on those sharp DVDs as well I will always wonder if it was there for me to see all along. Alas, I had to be told, and only found out when searching for information on the show in early 2011 that this was something of a unique reputation for the series. Closer inspection of the DVDs confirms that *Mannix* succeeded in sneaking quite a few pieces of nude art into its episodes, in each and every season.

Chronologically, the first nude art that that appears in *Mannix*, that I am aware of, sort of made sense in the context of the episode, "The Girl in the Frame," which was about art. Some curious sketches of the male form appear in the background of an art studio Joe visits, another thing that makes it worth pausing the DVD playback for closer examination. Since this was the last episode of season 1 to be produced as well as to air, maybe they thought they were going to have some fun. But, despite nearly being canceled after the first season and still being stuck in a Saturday 10:00 p.m. timeslot, they didn't stop. Season 2 has "Merry Go Round for Murder," with a quite large nude female painting in a scene where a Las Vegas casino boss is getting a rubdown. My favorite nude art scene is in season 5's "The Glass Trap," which was the very first episode produced (but not aired) in that highest-rated season. Very early in the episode, Joe and Peggy enter a bar to sit down together at a table and listen to Peggy's jazz musician boyfriend play some music. They walk right in front of a giant nude painting of a female, sit down, and order drinks. The camera angle is specifically oriented to showcase the painting that is right behind Connors and Fisher, who act as if there is nothing the least bit unusual behind them.

Most of the nude art in *Mannix* was of females, but a few male nudes surface as well, especially behind Joe in a scene in the final episode to air in season 6, "The Danford File." That painting has a collection of nearly nude males that appear to have been re-touched, perhaps just for the DVDs, looking quite out of place in what is supposed to be a talent agent's office. Male nudes were often "covered up," as in the opening episode of season 3's "Sometimes Eagles Can't Fly," which has a giant painting of a semi-nude male in the background of the climax of the episode. The nude art never appeared in Joe or Peggy's offices or living quarters, tending to show up in bars and some of the higher-priced clientele's homes or places of business. Sculpture even gets into the act, so to speak, as late as the final episode of season 7 to air, "The Ragged Edge," in which an outstanding performance by Connors as Joe addicted to heroin is decorated by a not quite nude, but very highly suggestive, female art form behind him in a bar scene. A similarly suggestive, decidedly male sculpture graces season 8's "Edge of the Web."

Since the nude art kept appearing, and can still be spotted in each season, I don't know if the censors got lazy, just gave up, or actually started to enjoy it. But since it pertained directly to censorship, which was a big and serious issue in those days, the whole nude art thing didn't seem to be just for fun. Nor did it seem to be a petulant statement about either the show's success or its mistreatment. The nude art occurred when the series was award-winning, highly rated, and in its best timeslot, in season 5, as well as when it was on the ropes and thrown into nasty timeslots, including seasons 1 and 7. It occurred under multiple producers. It wasn't practical in those days to change the background after the scenes were filmed, and so it had to be right there on the set, for everyone to see. When I found out about this nude art thing, it exposed, so to speak, how something behind the fantasy I so loved was based in reality. It was just so interesting to discover this stubborn act of defiance, part fun and part serious, was really happening in the show I loved. But try not to think about that nude art, for now.

We can't have everything we want in life, but we can choose to manage fear and anxiety well. How we deal with these psychological elements may have more to do with how we ultimately affect others deep down—the real mark we leave on the world—than anything else we do. Life seems built around intimidation, if not from other humans, then from nature. In contrast to any artifact or object we produce, or any kind of status we achieve, the real contribution of a life well lived may be in the attitude we adopt towards fear and anxiety, in the way we do not deny their existence, do not avoid them, and do not let them dominate us. We profess to want our loved ones, and even ourselves, to be happy, achieve some ends, or make specific contributions. But we seldom, if ever, desire that they learn how to effectively manage those psychological elements that can make the biggest difference between our lives being miserable and ineffective, ultimately doing real damage to ourselves and others, or enjoyable and effective. That is where heroes come in. Real heroes are not about giving us ends. They are about giving us means. Behind them, in the background of their character but for all to see, is the means to manage fear and anxiety well.

Everything that exists can be feared, for fear amounts to a projection of loss—and everything that exists, including that which we value the most, can be lost. We fear the loss of that which we love dearly, including ourselves, loved ones, even our expectations and hopes. We fear the loss of our physical bodies as well as our more spiritual self-image, with each of those put more at risk the more we do in life, the more obstacles we encounter, threatening situations we survive, and oppression we endure. We also fear that life is unfair, so much so that we give that concept a name of its own and call it simply, "evil." Nothing seems worse to us than the thought that bad things can happen to us with no meaning, no connection to something larger than ourselves, and that pain is arbitrary. Even worse than fear, we become anxious, in a more perpetual state of fear, the less we can seem to identify the root cause of our fear. Anxiousness, which is chronic fear coupled with a sense of arbitrariness, may be the worst state in which man can live.[4.4]

Perhaps for this reason, our very self-image is somehow intertwined with the way we cope with life being unfair, to include unfairness that happens to us as well as to others. If good is that which is most desirable, and evil is that which is most undesirable, then we consider people good in proportion to the way they seem able to transform that which is undesirable into that which is desirable. That being the case, good people are not good because they accept evil as good, creating some sort of muted equivalency between desirable and undesirable states of being, because that can really only wind up producing a sense of anxiety-provoking arbitrariness. Good people manage to find the means, the energy, to transform evil into good. Given this, the first thing good people must do is adopt an attitude towards the fear that evil arouses. Denying fear tends to not work to great effect for very long, not only because it does not work to trick ourselves for more than short periods of time, but because it denies the energy fear includes. Energy cannot be denied, since matter and energy are the foundation of all that exists, and even these two can be thought of as transmutable. Emotion is, if nothing else, a state of aroused energy. Energy must go somewhere.

Accordingly, true heroes not only have emotion, they teach us how to deal with at least one emotion in particular, that of fear. They go beyond FDR when he said that the only thing we have to fear was fear, itself. FDR only pointed to the problem, not how to solve it. Mythical heroes help us to solve it.

In the PBS Special, *Pioneers of Television: Crime Dramas*, Mike Connors said very little about what distinguished Joe Mannix from crime fighting heroes that came before him.[1.7] He talked about the fast-paced, tight editing of the show, and how Bruce Geller gave it an energetic feeling as a result. When he talked about his character, the primary distinguishing feature he gave about Joe Mannix was that Joe Mannix had emotion. But while some more recent heroic types might also be considered to have emotion, they do not necessarily show us how to deal with it well.

The way Joe Mannix did this was subtle, but so effective, especially for a very young person who had a lot to fear and to face in the outside world. The way he did so was, in retrospect, so clear, right there in the background, just like that nude art, really there all the time, making a statement all its own. Joe Mannix taught us that it was okay, and even good, to get just a little angry at the causes of fear.

Let me go back to this one sentence again: Joe Mannix taught us that it was okay, and even good, to get just a little angry at the causes of fear. That sentence deserves more scrutiny. It says that fear has causes, real things that can be identified, if we have the courage to so identify them. Because the first problem we have in dealing with fear is identifying what can actually happen to us, preferring instead to deny or exaggerate, seemingly providing some false sense of control. The sentence says that it is okay to be angry at those causes, and perhaps even unavoidably so. Because the next problem we have in dealing with fear is trying to remove the energy behind the emotion, thereby avoiding the unpleasantness we normally associate with anger by ultimately forcing it underground into an amorphous pool of anxiety. The sentence also describes an ability to transform the energy behind the fear into something else, into anger. Fear can so often be immobilizing, especially the more we are exposed to fearful situations that we do not deal with, but anger can mobilize us into action. The sentence also suggests transformation into just a little anger—not too much, because too much would ultimately get in the way of being effective in dealing with the root causes of the fear. Proper proportioning and direction of anger also work to allow it to not grow over time into something larger than we can manage. After all, if evil is so bad, so undesirable, then isn't a wise hero going to get just a little angry at it?

Joe Mannix did show fear, at times. But he never seemed to show anxiety. There seemed to be a connection there. Because he wasn't afraid of his own fear, and he didn't deny it either, he seemed to live most of his life pretty calm, when there was nothing in particular to fear. Because he dealt with fear pretty much in the moment, he seemed to live without what is perhaps the number one problem we face as a society these days—anxiety. He would face the situation that caused him fear when the situation arose, and, because he did that, he was not filled with anxiety the rest of the time. He simply got appropriately angry when someone tried to do something to hurt either him or people he cared about, or cause injustice right in front of him, on his watch. That anger subtly shifted fear into something useful, letting the energy out in proportion to its cause, not over the top, and not denying the way he felt either. This was a key part of what mobilized him to turn the energy of fear into something useful, burning it off so that it did not build up into something pathological. Chronic anxiety saps energy, even as it seems to need to maintain itself with its own, often dysfunctional, energy level. Acute fear can burn off that undesirable energy in the moment, thus not letting it build up inside of us and either destroy us through anxiety or eventually come out in undesirable ways.

It didn't take much for a young girl with a lot of stuff happening in the outside world to be drawn to a hero who seemed to be so anxiety-free most of the time, but who was also clearly more than capable of dealing with things that happened around him. By subtle manipulation of fear and anger he showed how fear was not only real, but okay, and thus not to be feared. In an era where most heroes were either wooden or perpetual frat boys, effectively making a mockery of fear, this was amazing, so different—and utterly enabling. Joe Mannix got a little angry—but just a little, just enough. The rest of the time he seemed like a pretty calm character, really calmer than those around him, not anxious at all. This meant that he trusted himself enough to not be afraid of the next thing he was going to encounter, because he did not seem afraid of himself, afraid of his own emotional responses. Genuine confidence is, after all, trust in ourselves, amounting to trust in our ability to be able to handle the next unknown situation, the one we have yet to encounter, yet to imagine, if we can imagine it at all. Since the unknown tends to provoke fear, genuine confidence is rooted in trust that we can handle fear well.

The first time I saw this kind of response in *Mannix* in a way that stuck in my memory, and, in retrospect, stayed with me all of these years, was in the season 1 episode, "Huntdown." This is one of a category of episodes of *Mannix* that might be called "Joe Goes to a Small Town."

Mannix is not about some super-hero out to "save the world," which is really kind of an ego-enterprise designed to appeal to people who like to think that if they only had those special abilities the hero has, and were asked to help with such an obvious outcome on the line, they would rise to the occasion. Alas, the world is not normally threatened and they don't have those abilities anyway, so might as well just keep eating the popcorn. Sure, the world is generally not threatened on our watch, at least in an obvious way. If it does get to that point, then all sorts of individuals failed along the way, and probably in all sorts of isolated, even esoteric local ways. That sort of thing happens all of the time on our watch, and right in front of us, inching the world closer to being threatened the more individuals fail to act privately. Global interests are affected by the behavior of individuals in very private, sometimes even esoteric, situations.

Mannix is about a hero who stood up to things symbolic of the kinds of things we all encounter, and if we think we are someone left off the hook of having to stand up to them, we aren't really paying attention. For example, like a lot of people I know, I assumed that as long as I was essentially good hearted, people would treat me that way in return. My ambitions, such as they were, mostly centered on doing something interesting and somewhat challenging for a living and reaping whatever rewards hopefully went with that. My philosophy was to focus on what I was doing, and not pay a whole lot of attention to what motivated others. This turned out to be incredibly naive, and thus probably even a bit arrogant. Was I so good that my perpetual state of innocence was powerful enough to counteract evil around me?

Over the course of 194 episodes, spanning eight years, probably the single evil portrayed the most in *Mannix* was that of the syndicate. The notion of gangs, mobs, and mafia was not new to *Mannix*, which was one of a broad and varied collection of TV shows to incorporate such concepts over the years, including *The Sopranos* (HBO 1999-2007). Prior to *Mannix*, another Desilu production, *The Untouchables* (ABC-TV 1959-1963) was almost exclusively about the concept of "organized crime"—emphasis on the "organization" for which syndicate is really just a label. The syndicate in *Mannix* was often portrayed as ethnic characters, perhaps somewhat forgivable given the immense popularity of *The Godfather*,[9.1] which would also seem to have been responsible for the use of the term *Cosa Nostra* in the season 3 episode "Who is Sylvia?" Perhaps not coincidentally, *The Godfather* movies were also produced by Paramount, filmed on the same lot as *Mannix*, with the two even sharing some of the same sound stages, at least according to the plaques Paramount had on those stages in 2011.

Syndicates and gangs are a symbolic way of describing organized and powerful groups of people without publicly sanctioned rules. If there is an informal purpose for the group's existence, it is trumped by the need to maintain the privileges its members enjoy at the expense of pretty much everyone else on the outside, individuals as well as other groups.

As a kid, I never could relate to those stories about the syndicate. I was quite certain I would never run into one in my real life, once I grew up and got out of grade school, anyway. Years passed. I went to work, ultimately entering academia, surfacing in a department where another faculty member used to refer to a certain sub-group of colleagues, other professors who worked in his same academic discipline, as the "X Mafia." When he would make this joke, people laughed—very nervously. "X" could be filled in with a lot of very serious topics. Academics live and die by acceptance of proposals for money to fund their research and papers about subject matter so esoteric that only a small subset of people, generally other academics organized into informal groups, are even capable of beginning to evaluate the value of any given piece of work. This creates all sorts of unsanctioned power structures.[3.2] You might think that the more intelligent and educated groups of people are, the less inclined they are to fall prey to the kinds of insecurities that can lead them to identify with a group more than the topics they are supposed to be pushing forward. If so, I suggest you think again. Just like Joe Mannix, those who have the courage to identify as individuals are all too rare, but what a difference they could make if more of them felt enabled.

Yet another type of evil symbolized well in *Mannix* is the evil of the misdirected wrath of the nut case. Over the years, Joe Mannix had quite a few ex-Korean War buddies go bad, with their rather extreme, highly intelligent, even intricate, behavior manifest as over-the-top-wrath towards Joe. Just killing Joe wasn't nearly enough for them. These nut jobs didn't just want to do Joe in, they wanted to see him suffer and to know that he was suffering at their hands, clearly implying that Joe represented far more to these nut jobs than just himself, or anything he ever did. The first of these episodes is the excellent "End Game" from season 2, which has the very first appearance of Joe's longest-lasting police buddy and ex-war pal, Art Malcolm, then still a sergeant. In this story, Art is held hostage in a building booby-trapped with bombs and mines. This is extremely symbolic stuff and it results in a riveting episode that can be watched over and over again. The subject matter was so well done that different nutty ex-war buddies appear with elaborate schemes at least four more times, including twice in season 8, creating yet another collection of episodes I enjoyed, but which I never thought would have applicability to me.

These nut jobs symbolize people who wind up in positions of power precisely because they are intensely drawn to seek valuation from society as a substitute for not quite being able to find it in themselves. Despite kudos that follow from a never-ending quest to please the powers that be, these people need to vilify others, even using those kudos as a means of justifying their ability to pick and choose who they can vilify. Their attitude and actions towards a select few under their power is way out of proportion to whatever provoked them, if anything real provoked them in the first place. Anyone who has been on the receiving end of this type of evil knows that it is coming from some "other place," some place outside of the bounds of the way we interacted with such people, if we ever even interacted with them before. When we encounter this, it can help to have a model that gives you the guts to identify that their behavior is their problem—not yours. This is not such an easy thing when they are in positions of power over you. Simply and naively assuming they are good not only gets you nowhere, it can get you and others badly hurt. Instead of assuming that life will be Nirvana if we simply ignore such evil behavior, how much better off would we be with more individuals around who find it important to stand up to such power, especially on the behalf of those being hurt?

A third category of evils portrayed in *Mannix* is that of small-town thinking. Like the syndicate, this is also about self-protective group-think. Unlike the syndicate, which is predicated around organizational structure, small-town thinking tends to include a secret that the group is protecting, a secret enabled by their isolation. The small-town thinking is all about borders of the evil, tantamount to the right to keep the secret inside the borders. Our hero is the outsider to this isolated group, and he tends to stumble onto the secret, threatening to expose it. At that point he is attacked and he often does not even know why. Because he is all alone in a small town, he does not know who to trust. Those in the small town want our hero out of town, so that they can keep their secret safe. In this type of episode, our hero always has the opportunity to leave town and simply let them be, let the secret fester. There is always some decision point in these episodes where he decides not to run away, where it matters more to him to expose the secret than to go back to what is really a pretty good life, back there in L.A. This type of story is pursuit of the truth at a visceral level, one where the truth is being systematically obscured, thus creating harm to innocents. Our hero would rather be hurt than to walk away from something for which he does not even know the real problem—what it is or how much it might even matter to make it right. His only metric for his decision to decide to risk everything is the degree of defensiveness of the group, and he can see this defensiveness because they are trying to hurt him without just cause.

Here, again, is a recurring episode type I never thought I would relate to in real life. But small-town thinking is symbolic for any isolated group, whether that group is physically isolated in a small town, or logically isolated because outsiders cannot understand its metrics of evaluation, even its very purpose for being. One example that was enabled by both logical and physical isolation is the Penn State football scandal, where a child sex predator was not only allowed to remain in a small-town campus setting, but was employed while knowledge of his activity went up the organized hierarchy of the school. The more specialized professions become, to include sub-specializations within professions, the more isolated groups of people become. Americans tend to change jobs and even careers many times over the course of a lifetime, and in some ways this freedom is built into the fabric of our success as a society. Each time we enter a new profession is like entering a new logical small town, one that does not welcome outsiders, generally because it has secrets to protect. Supposed outsiders may even be harmed as the group tries to protect the status quo. Examples for this abound. One I am most familiar with is in my own profession where women, especially women born in the U.S., still comprise an eye-opening small fraction. The small numbers, combined with metrics that show a high attrition rate among women as they try to advance their careers, strongly suggest the presence of highly effective, insidious exclusionary practices. Because my profession includes technological invention, something that directly impacts our economy as well as quality of life, potential discoveries and associated impacts of countless individuals are lost as a result of these exclusionary practices. Ultimately, such practices are enabled because of isolated metrics of evaluation, ones outsiders supposedly cannot understand. Heroes who can stand up to this kind of evil are rare these past forty years, as the record shows. Even just a few could make an enormous difference.

Back to "Huntdown" and that scene that stuck with me. The small town has a secret, and they wind up being so self-protective about it that they start to come after Joe in some pretty creative ways. Because season 1 was not shown in syndication in the U.S. market, with only a handful of episodes from that season making it into VHS release (Desilu, for some reason, failed to copyright some of them), most of the episodes from season 1, like "Huntdown," remained unseen until the DVD release. But when I watched the episode in early 2011, it was clear I had seen it before. It permeated me in the same way so many episodes of *Mannix* did over the years, not for plot, but because of specific scenes. One such scene in "Huntdown" seems kind of simple on the surface; it is where Joe is trying to get out of town and steal a jeep in the process. Joe gets a gas pump in his hand after igniting the contents of one of those steel barrels that used to serve as garbage cans. Joe points the gas pump at the barrel. If he sprays gas on the barrel the whole place is going to go up in flames. Since he has no gun, and no other weapon, this is his line of defense. The gas station owner, upon discovering this, points a gun at Joe.

Gas Station Owner: "One move, you're dead."

Joe: "Shoot, friend, and there'll be two of us. Now put the gun down on that Jeep."

Gas Station Owner: "You won't. You'll be dead, too!"

Joe: "That's right, friend. But as long as you're holding that gun I got nothing to lose. Now put that gun down."

Okay, as of now, we have some fairly ordinary dialogue. But it is delivered with a fair amount of intensity. Then, in delivering the next line, Joe takes it to the next level.

Joe (*intensely, with clear anger*): "Shoot or put it down!"

When Joe says this last line, he is a combination of scared and angry, in pitch perfect tone. You can read the amazing look on his face, one that says that it's not only okay to get angry at these people who seem to want to kill him for no reason, it actually makes a whole lot of sense. He could be killed by this guy with a gun, and has all sorts of reasons to be angry enough to begin with, considering what's happened to him so far at the hands of the people in this small town. But the way he delivers the line indicates that he is just angry enough to do what he says he will. The anger seems to be enabling him to deal with this situation, in proper proportion to the situation. As a result, he gets his point across and the gas station guy puts his gun down.

This line has so much more impact on the viewer because Joe is normally this calm, anxiety-free, even confident guy—except when provoked. He is consistently labeled for "taking bullet wounds in stride." Not so fast. He does seem like that most of the time. But that is enabled by what he does when he needs to deal with fear.

After seeing what was happening to him during the previous minutes of the episode, it was pretty easy to conclude Joe was probably afraid—or a little off his rocker if he wasn't. But that's just the thing. Some heroes are off their rocker, just like that. They do the right things, and they deserve to be commended for that. But we wind up watching their deeds and not learning anything from them, at least anything terribly useful. Actions tend to not be transmutable from one individual to another, from one situation to another. What is transmutable is that which is behind the actions, something in the background.

When heroes show no fear in fearful situations, there isn't a whole lot to take away from their deeds. You are glad people might be out there who can get the job done in the absence of fear. But you know you can't be one of them. Other heroes seem angry all of the time, which seems more real but in an unattractive way because it seems too righteous—not in measure to what is happening, and coming from some place you don't understand and therefore can't relate to. They come across as not having dealt with anger properly in the past. True heroes put us right in their place, one to which we can emotionally relate. They do so in a way that is also appealing, one that seems like it might work in real life. In more recent times we seem so much more focused on plot and outcomes, which seems consistent with the way we have become more enamored with results and status than matters of character. I watched *Mannix* for those scenes that seemed to hold much more wisdom than plot ever could—scenes that almost seemed to be in the background.

One such scene is in season 5's "The Man Outside." In this episode, Andrew Duggan plays a retired U.S. Army general, a friend of Joe Mannix when both served in the Korean War. The general hires Joe to find some missing film, with all sorts of plot misdirection that was the hallmark of virtually every episode of season 5. But, of course, I tuned in to see Joe being Joe. What that meant, in this episode, is sweetly captured in a scene that takes place in Joe's office, when he comes back after having been dumped down yet another hillside and spending the night in the hospital. Well, to be precise, he jumped out of a moving car and consequently rolled down the hillside on purpose.

Joe comes into his office to find the phone ringing. Peggy, in those pre-answering machine days, is not there to answer it. He yells for her, wondering where she is. She opens his office door, and he sort of admonishes her, "Why didn't you answer the phone?" This is a big mistake. She is being held at gunpoint by two "thugs."

The scene quickly cuts to seeing Peggy seated on the burnt orange couch beside Joe's desk. (*Set decoration note:* This couch graced Joe's office during seasons 2-6 before it went through a slight re-modeling for season 7. That happened because *Mission: Impossible* ended its run the previous season, so Joe's office was no longer used as a set foundation for offices in various third world countries. The set-sharing is presumably the reason the pictures on the walls of Joe's office moved around from episode to episode during seasons 2-6). Back to the scene: Peggy is on the couch, while one thug is seated behind Joe's desk and another is standing beside him. Joe is told to put his hands on the desk, which means he has to lean forward and face the thugs, one in particular.

The thugs want a roll of film. At this point, even we do not know what is on that film roll, nor does Joe, who does not have the film the thugs want. He was tricked by a photographer, Carol Barr, who gave him a counterfeit roll that one the thugs stole from Joe the night before, which resulted in his winding up at the bottom of the hillside. If Joe had the film, he could produce it and give it to them. He's done this sort of thing in episode after episode, making the reasonable trade of giving up some prized evidence because someone just threatened his or someone else's life. But he can't do that this time.

One of the thugs points a gun at Joe. The gun is one of those relatively tame revolvers used in those days, in contrast to the semi-automatic weapons that are a part of popular culture these days, but it is still lethal enough to kill Joe, especially at close range. This was an era when pistols were wielded and used more like sharp knives or even medieval swords. They could kill, but not via mass slaughter. Heroes used them in story the way we think of knights using swords, with appeal to fair play.

In this case, Joe does not have a gun. He can't even use his hands, which are affixed to the top of the desk. He can't move. All he has at his disposal is his face. And with that face, he has to manage to convince these thugs that he does not have what they want, so killing him would not be fair play. He does so in a way that is fun to think about in some of those moments that arise when unnamed anxieties creep into one's life. And he does it right in front of Peggy, with her facial expressions intercut with those of Joe and the two thugs.

Thug 1: "Okay, where is it?"

Joe: "Where's what?"

Thug 1: "The film"

Joe looks annoyed. He is, in effect, being held hostage in his office, which seems like a pretty fearful situation. He's clearly a little angry.

Joe: "What film is it you want *this* time?"

Thug 1: "The film you took from Carol Barr."

Joe: "You took that from me last night, remember? And sold it this morning."

Thug 1: "Don't be funny, Mannix. This is the film we got last night."

The thug proceeds to put a bunch of photographs on Joe's desk, all showing images of a female model.

Thug 1: "The right film, please."

Joe now looks—in the span of only a few seconds—scared, confused, and just angry enough to deal with the situation.

Peggy, being tuned in to both Joe and the situation, responds in a purely visual manner. It's all on her face, no words. She is really scared now, but holding it in because she sees there is nothing Joe can do—at least with his fists or a gun. What Joe does do is answer these guys in an honest a way as possible. And that means he looks just a little more scared now, but he is holding his ground. He reasons that his best course of action is to convince these guys, even if it means that he has to stand there and be shot. He knows he's been had by Carol Barr—just a little bit more of a source of anger.

Joe: "I told you. I haven't got it. Carol Barr must have switched cameras on me."

The thug, at this point, either does not believe Joe or is going to test him. He cocks the revolver at Joe. (Lest we not forget in this era of semi-automatic weapons—symbolic of all sorts of impersonal dismissal of people—there is something noble about giving a person a fair chance and testing their mettle, as well as taking the time to find out where they are coming from. This is where so-called violence in film and TV does have purpose. Weapons symbolize power, and chivalry in story shows us how to nobly deal with power, both our own and that which others try to wield against us.)

Thug 1: "You got approximately ten seconds to come up with that film."

Joe: "I can't give you what I never had."

Now, with this line, Joe's tone and facial expression are pitch perfect, identical in impact to a classic piece of music that can be listened to over and over again. His eyes dart around, conveying a multitude of things—his mind rapidly thinking, taking in the situation, along with a combination of fear and anger. He clearly realizes what could happen to him during the next few seconds, and that there is little he can do about it—except convince these guys.

At this point, Thug 1 points the gun at Joe. He slowly pulls the trigger. While he pulls on it, we get to see both Joe's and Peggy's facial expressions. Again, sweet perfection happens. She knows that her beloved boss and friend could be killed right in front of her, knows he is nearly helpless to prevent that from happening. She looks completely scared, practically paralyzed with fear. Curiously though, she does not shut her eyes. She has the guts to keep looking. *Mannix* isn't cheap with its characters. It never had to cheapen the supporting cast to make its hero look better, thereby making the whole show that much better.

Joe also has the guts to keep looking directly at the gun that is pointed at him. He looks from the face of the thug to his gun, then back to his face again. He does not stand there like some sort of stupid, wooden statue, trying to convey an absence of fear, or extreme coolness. He does not make jokes about it. He is absolutely tough. But he is not entirely cool. He shows some fear. And that sweet amount of just a little anger, mixed in there.

Then the thug actually pulls the trigger.

Of course, it was an empty chamber. This was the series' highest-rated season, after all.

This results in a look on Peggy's face that is realistic and packed with emotion, all the more so for her trying to hold it all in. She does not scream. She does not look away. She simply looks incredibly relieved. She has some guts, too. All that does is add credibility to the way she views the situation.

Joe also appears relieved, but less so. He still has that gun pointed at him, and knows this is not over yet. All of this is so subtle, which is where real emotion lives and ultimately affects and moves us.

Thug 1: "What do you know? An empty chamber."

The thug then goes to pull the trigger again. We see it slowly come around, as Joe and Peggy's facial expressions continue to be tightly intercut. Joe got a reprieve. But this is not over, and we are getting a second chance to see the response of these two main characters that we have come to know and love.

It also gives us just a little more time to consider what we might do in that kind of situation. Some of our options might be to try to hide under the desk, scream, or cry. Heroes don't tend to do that, but people do not always act like heroes. Scenes like this simply make us want to be more like them. A famous expression these days, often abused, is "if it saves only one life." We make all sorts of calculations that place the value of one life against another, all of the time and in all sorts of ways, such that this kind of statement is really quite absurd. Life has limited resources that we constantly bring to bear, because we have to. But heroic behavior has no such limitations. It is unbounded, limitless, like real love. Exposure to convincing storied behavior that can allow us to act more nobly in even just one situation can make enormous differences, and not only to the way we think of ourselves, but to the lives we can positively affect. Also like real love, heroic behavior is accessible to all.

Thug 2: "Hold it. He's gotta be telling the truth. He wouldn't die for it."

Thug 1: "Mannix, you'd better be telling the truth."

Joe is, of course, left off the hook. We knew that would happen. But the way he gets off the hook is convincing in a broader sense. He gets off the hook because he puts all of his faith in his emotional veracity, that he can somehow convey the truth right on his face. That truth is conveyed so much more by the emotion in his facial expressions than the words he says. He might have been killed anyway, of course. And he knew that. He even showed that he knew that. But he took his best course of action, given the circumstances. He displayed just enough genuine fear, and did not run from that either. He also conveyed just enough anger to go with that fear, which gave him the resolve to stand up to the unfairness of the situation, which included the threat to him. When we know something is utterly unfair, and acknowledge it with appropriate anger, we might be hurt anyway. But it is our best course of action, even when we can't move, even when they have the power over us, even when we only have our face to show it.

We tend to think of anger as a kind of masculine emotion, because we think of the physical results it tends to produce in men, enabling all sorts of action. But all men have a softer side that we think of as feminine and all women have a tougher side that we think of as masculine. Our discomfort with this "other" piece of our psychological make-up, discomfort often induced by societal norms, can lead to all sorts of problems unless we recognize that this other side of us is there in everyone, to varying degrees. One mistake we can make is thinking that some qualities belong exclusively to one gender and so we should not identify with those qualities when they appear in the opposite gender, something that can practically disable us. For many years, after losing contact with the series, I had come to assume that *Mannix* was quite the sexist show, falling for evolving norms and labels of all sorts, and not just with respect to the series, itself. But, especially compared to the norms of its day, *Mannix* is not sexist, and is even less sexist than many more "modern" shows that followed it, especially those that immediately followed it. Joe Mannix is a pure type of character, a noble heroic type, representing a set of potential attributes and qualities in all of us.

He displayed the ability to stand up to injustice, as an individual that found a way to deal with fear so that he could turn it into a measured, angry, effective response to the evil causing the fear. This allowed him to be free of anxiety in the meantime. He was constantly testing himself, and when those tests were over, he was calm. In turn, he simply appreciated when other people were like that, giving just a hint of disdain when people were not. This included both men and women.

Season 2, in the fall of 1968, has an episode, "Fear I to Fall," in which a female attorney falls into an all too common trap of believing she is actually doing harm to her client because she is not good enough to get him off of a murder charge. Seeing a woman doing that is something I didn't want to see as a seven-year-old girl. She is a "father's daughter," who had a famous attorney father, recently deceased. After she tries to quit the case in court, Joe shows up in her office and gives her a piece of his mind. He does so in a way that perfectly befits the character of Joe Mannix—he'd just been beaten up because he refused to leave town after being told to do so. Thugs in *Mannix* never seemed to learn that beating up Joe like that just made him less inclined to quit, and he wants to share just this kind of attitude with the female attorney. Significantly, he does not flaunt it over her, but actually hopes she will adopt his attitude and be inspired by his example. Later in the same episode, after the attorney does grow a pair, he gives her a respectful, gentle kiss on the cheek—not the romantic kind, the respectful kind. Now he is admiring her character, because he admires toughness in any form it takes, black or white, male or female. This was way ahead of its time and, in so many ways, still is.

We see similar assessments conveyed on Joe's face all throughout the series. In season 3, "Tooth of the Serpent" has a black housewife who tries, for a short period of time, to stand up to her husband. She hired Joe to find her son, and when the husband insists she fire Joe—so that Joe is forced to reveal what he knows to the husband, who is a police officer—the woman refuses. When she later gives in, telling Joe she has to do what her husband demands, Joe responds with a look on his face for which there is no dialogue, but incredible meaning. He is immensely disappointed she gave in, and not only because he was fired when she did that. He is clearly disappointed that this woman was not tough, and did not stand up to her husband. In season 3's "Once Upon a Saturday," Joe helps a female owner of an amusement park, someone who seems to be an old and platonic friend. From the set-up for the rest of the episode, he seems to admire her because she wants to run her own business. There is no sex involved or hinted at in their relationship. Joe admires guts, without qualification to who has guts. Even Peggy displays some guts, and you get the sense Joe would not have any secretary who did not. There was no one woman with whom he was involved, except for Peggy—and that was supposed to be platonic. This was not a show about sex—but, well, it does seem to have been about nudity, after all—that art, right there in the background, all the time.

There was this guy, this character that meant so much to me in my formative years. I knew he wasn't real, that he couldn't possibly be real, especially with all of that stuff that happened to him. Even in my very young mind I was able to separate fantasy from reality, as most kids, and adults, can do better than we give them credit for, especially if we acknowledge the importance—and utter power—of story, in the first place. Yet there was something that seemed so real about him, something more real than reality, itself. But that is just the way story is supposed to work. There isn't anything built into us that instinctively separates good from evil, similar to the way there isn't anything built into us that instinctively rises above our instinct of fear. If good was an instinct, everyone would be good. We seem to need to work it out, think it through, in order to be truly good. For one thing, good can be a complex thing to identify at times; what seems good for one might be terrible for another, unless we really think it through. For example, the good of the group has a tendency to be evil for individuals. Working out a more global kind of good and then living it when the time comes requires not only thought, but projection into circumstances we have yet to live out, ultimately projection into the unknown, a pretty fearful thing. Since this character faced fear so well, I wanted that to be real.

But I knew he wasn't real. He was just a fantasy.

Then again, there is that nude art in the background. It was so interesting. What was it doing there, over all of those years? It seemed somehow quietly defiant, there to make a statement and done in such a way that it, well, was kind of *fun*. It didn't draw attention to itself, unlike our more modern forms of defiance which seem to result only in a cadre of comedians and other forms of attention-seeking. It was in the background, just there, for all to see, all the time, making its statement.

Those illusions we conventionally chase in the foreground, things that belong on résumés, on forms we fill out, or that we openly discuss at parties, have nothing to do with what our lives ultimately come to mean. Nobility is tantamount to understanding that the real meaning of our lives is how our example inspires others to conquer fear, to defiantly think for ourselves, and to stand up for what is right—those things we normally consider to be in the background of our existence. But if nobility is too much for you, just try to be interesting, and maybe something good will happen.

People only interest us when they are interesting. We ultimately only come to value ourselves as noble beings, not needing to seek approval from the outside, when we first find ourselves interesting. We are, by definition, indifferent to people who are not interesting, indifferent to people who are not somehow different, no matter what they seem to have or have accomplished in terms of societal norms.

Interesting people are that way because they have just a little bit of anger, just enough to enable them to think for themselves, and act accordingly. In this way they defiantly overcome fear and anxiety, and so keep putting their art out there, right there in the background all the time, for everyone to see—the reality behind the illusion.

Chapter 10
Asking for Trouble

We are fascinated by energy, almost as if those who possess it along with the courage to display it somehow possess the secret to life. In a way, they do. Those that stay engaged in life regardless of the consequences of the choices they consciously make, how others treat them, what others think of them, or what random fate befalls them, seem to possess a kind of wisdom that defies explanation. Or maybe they are just a little crazy, a secret held in the Paramount vaults for over thirty-eight years.

All twenty-four episodes of season 1, all twenty-four episodes of season 8 and sixteen of the twenty-four episodes of season 7 of *Mannix* were not included in the U.S. syndication packages for the series. Only 130 episodes of the 194 produced, episodes 024 through 152 and 166, were made available for syndication, something that remained true even after the entire series was finally released on DVD.[10.1] As a result, none of those "missing" episodes from seasons 7 or 8 were seen in the U.S.—since their original broadcast by CBS in 1973-1975—until they were released on DVD in 2012. Well, that's close to true. Some desperate fans were able to obtain bootleg copies since they were shown in Australia around 2010 after they were digitally re-mastered. Rumor has it that some *Mannix* fans obtained some of the sixteen "missing" episodes of season 7 on VHS tapes, dubbed in other languages since they were only shown in non-English speaking countries. I've personally never seen one of those, and do not regret it either. While *Mannix* was incredibly visual, meaning was also conveyed from the original actors in tone of voice.

Regardless, the season 8 episodes stayed in the Paramount vaults from the time of their original network airings until they were re-mastered, starting in 2007, and then shown in Australia, with the logo "Fox Classics" in the lower right hand corner. This means that the soonest a *Mannix* fan in the U.S. could have seen those long-lost episodes (unless someone hung around the Paramount vaults in the middle of the night with a projector and a lookout at the door) was when they got their hands on those bootleg Australian versions, or waited for the significantly clearer DVD releases of the re-mastered series from CBS/Paramount on December 4, 2012, the date the entire series was finally—finally—released. It sort of made sense that the first season was not included in the syndication packages, since the format was so different. Well, it only sort of made sense. Credit was not given to viewers to be able to comprehend that the version of Joe Mannix who once worked for Intertect for a season was the same one that was out on his own, with only Peggy working for him. The reason for holding forty other episodes back remains a mystery. Even Connors does not know why.

These days, with instant downloads and DVD or Blu-ray disk releases of TV episodes available for viewing almost as soon as they air for the first time, it's tough for some to imagine what it was like for *Mannix* fans to wait nearly forty years to see, once again, more than an entire season's worth of the series they once loved. The delayed release of *Mannix* to DVD in the first place, and then the long delay between the releases of seasons 3 and 4, long enough to qualify as a "stall," revealed a peculiar kind of pain. The feeling was similar to losing a volume of a book series, actually making it tougher to enjoy the rest of the series. Something was always missing. *Mannix* wasn't a serial, had no concluding episode, and so it is not like there was a missing ending. The feeling was more like immense frustration, because every syndication run ended with an episode in the middle of season 7, and started over again at the first episode of season 2. That fans continued to feel this frustration for nearly forty years is really quite amazing, considering forty years is quite a chunk of a lifetime. But art, unlike perhaps everything else in our lives, is the one thing we have that seems not subject to loss, the one thing we seem to be able to count on to be there for us in pretty much the same form in which we originally experienced it, even as we experience life around it.

When season 8 finally did come back, it did not disappoint, with some scenes that reflect mastery of what the character is all about. In the opening of "Death Has No Face," Joe gets out of his light brown Dodge Challenger and walks into his office from his 17 Paseo Verde car port. Sure, this is actually the exact same opening segment as that used for the season 7 episode, "The Dark Hours," even putting Joe back in his season 7, light brown Challenger instead of his season 8, blue Chevy Camaro. But true fans who are the first to notice this sort of thing are also the first to overlook it.

We never love something so much as when we notice everything about it, including its imperfections, and yet happily forgive those flaws in favor of its reach. These two seem further connected, since reach seems possible because of the courage to overlook perfection to begin with. The need to occasionally re-use footage is rumored to be one of the reasons the green Plymouth 'cuda was kept around, with only minor modifications, for all of seasons 4-6. They even kept the same, custom dark green color for the 'cuda as that used for the Dodge Dart from seasons 2 and 3, just so they could re-use wide shots of Joe's car driving around places like Malibu, shots that actually contained Joe's old vehicle. *Mannix* fans just accept this, because it was clear this sort of thing did was not due to laziness.

If anything, the lack of perfection seemed to lend realism behind the show that was out on the edge to begin with, giving the sense that it was seemingly unable to keep up with its own pace. This makes it all the more significant that *Mannix* not only rebounded to the Top 20 during season 8 (a season which was not known at the time to be the series' swansong), but it stayed fresh. The series seemed to go through subtle re-invention each season, with its overall tone coming across as somehow different, even as the substance of the characters remained the same—an artistic reflection of how our own character is both a part of, and also evolves from, our experiences. For a show with so much energy to begin with, it was amazing that it seemed to increase its action and energy levels in its last two seasons from what was perhaps a low-point in season 6, an otherwise excellent season in its own right. The combination of the increase in energy—along with perfected characters and actors so comfortable in the roles they created that they seemed destined for the ages—made possible something that remains rare in series TV: a second epoch of ratings increase to regain the Top 20, despite viewers not tuning in just to see the last season. The cancellation of *Mannix* was not announced until April 1975, after the last first-run episode aired. How did this series have so much energy in its eighth season?

Possibly no single term is more fundamental to all of science than energy. Physics, the most fundamental of all sciences, is the study of matter and energy, to include how one is understood in terms of the other and how one can be transformed into the other. But while energy is a scientific term primarily used to describe the mechanical behavior of inert objects, it is also commonly used to describe human behavior, so much so that one primary definition of energy[10.2] is

1. The strength and vitality required for sustained physical or mental activity.

2. A feeling of possessing such strength and vitality.

These definitions are not physical, not really even scientific at all, despite the scientific origins of the term *energy*. They are not about the impersonal, material world, not drawn from the mechanistic world of physics. They are about our behavior, and include concepts behind not only how much we do over time but also how much we think over time. The secondary definition actually even defines energy as a feeling of having it—just a feeling, nothing more. These definitions are more about psychic energy,[10.3] something that seems to arise mysteriously, from within us, than physical energy, something that can precisely predict the behavior of matter in a causal way, as one object acts upon another.

It is almost as if we have come to realize that energy, one of the two most fundamental concepts behind the composition of the known world, is also somehow behind the composition of our psyche, or the way we feel about life. But our psychic energy is also somehow very different from physical energy. Significantly, and in stark contrast to physical energy, psychic energy does not seem subject to precise quantification or prediction. Even more significantly, while physical energy is subject to laws of conservation, such that it cannot be created, nor destroyed, the same does not seem to be true about psychic energy. Not only does it not seem as if the low energy state of the psyche of one human being results in higher energy states of the psyche in others, if anything, the opposite seems true. Psychic energy, similar to when we are moved by love and art, does not seem finite, but seems unbounded, limitless.

For example, when we are low, a term which has become synonymous with psychic energy, and are exposed to people with all sorts of positive energy on display, we can often seem to find more energy inside of ourselves, even as nothing is taken away from anyone else. Positive psychic energy seems more contagious than subject to laws of conservation. We seem to want to sing when we hear others sing, however well we sing; dance when we see others dance, however well we dance; run when we see others run, however fast we run; and move when we see others move, however far we go. But, unlike physical energy that obeys strict laws of causality as one object acts upon another, billiard ball-style, the energy we witness has to appeal to us in order for it to move us. In order for it to energize us, we have to want to let it.

Thus, psychic energy, unlike physical energy, is not transmitted in strictly causal ways. This has the secondary property of allowing us to choose to continue to sing long after the song we once listened to has ended, something we tend to do the more the song appealed to us in the first place, like billiard balls that roll farther and faster, exhibiting more energy than that with which they were stricken. This also means that we tend to decline to exhibit energy when our sense of agency is taken away from us, such as when we feel like a cog in a wheel, or when we experience negative energy, including energy that hurts us, such as when we experience abuse. Instead of following negative energy, behavior such as passive resistance, destruction, and depression can result in us. The antidote is to find ways to connect with energy that somehow seems larger, somehow more significant to us that the finite nature of our lives. We claim it as our own and so it moves us.

Perhaps this is why the energetic, independent agent, whether super spy or private investigator, is so appealing. First, there is all that energy right there on the screen, all of that moving around, seeming as if there is so much excess energy to burn, at will. That's pretty appealing, certainly fascinating. But at least as important is the sense of agency, their choice to be that way, come what may. By combining action with choice, always seeming to be able to accept the consequences of their choices, and moving on to the next thing when things do not go their way, they do not seem cowed by anything or anyone else in their quest to move through life and think for themselves. These concepts seem connected, since agents seem to find sustainable energy by giving themselves the freedom to choose in the first place and that freedom of choice seems enabled by the courage to accept the consequences of their own choices. They always get into trouble. And yet, they are not troubled by the trouble their choices get them into. That seems like something of a secret, right there. After all, life is messy, in direct proportion to how deeply we are engaged in it.

Mannix was the first action-oriented PI, where energy that seemed to pop right out of the screen was as much a part of the reason to tune in as story. Since the first season had Joe working for a super-PI agency (Intertect) as sort of a James Bond kind of character—an agent who solved problems on his own, often using his fists instead of a computer (unlike real computer engineers, who use their fists *on* computers)—the show had a lot of action. But when Joe went out to work for himself, on his own, they not only kept the action from season 1, but they emphasized the action—even spelling out m-a-n-n-i-x to the fast-paced, energetic, Lalo Schifrin ¾-time jazz-waltz theme, which they also retained with action shots behind the individual letters as they spelled out the name. They also kept from season 1 the Picasso-like multi-angle scenes of Joe punching out the guy who was bigger than him, as well as that of Joe running across the Commodore Schuyler F. Heim Bridge in San Pedro and the helicopter chase scene from the pilot episode, and even adding a new multi-angle scene of Joe driving a race car. The point was well made—Joe was on his own now, the gun was simpler and the car was closer to stock, but none of the action went away.

Mannix came during an era (1967-1975) for which many feel nostalgia. Both as individuals and societies, we tend to feel more nostalgia for some time periods than others, times of our lives as well as epochs of societies. Sometimes we feel an ineffable sense, almost in the air, that there was once something more.

The space shuttle Discovery landed at Dulles Airport on April 17, 2012, its final flight. While covering the event a CNN reporter asked a former shuttle astronaut to comment on the end of the program. His reply went something like this: "The Space Shuttle was built by people who were nineteen feet tall for people who were nineteen feet tall," metaphorically stating that in the late 1960s and early 1970s, when the shuttle was developed, we had more tolerance for risk, and so we were somehow bigger people then. Those people who were "nineteen feet tall" knew that comfort and security were well worth trading for energy and reach.

We landed on the moon in the summer between *Mannix's* second and third seasons. The Apollo program behind the moon landing actually ended with Apollo-Soyuz, which was a docking between U.S. and Soviet spacecraft.[10.4] This was in July 1975, when *Mannix* aired its last summer reruns on CBS. There are certainly many people in the U.S. who are still nineteen feet tall, who understand that a life is so much more when it has vision and is willing to endure sacrifice and risk as a necessary part of living larger. But the astronaut was right in saying that, in essence, and for all intents and purposes, those nineteen-foot-tall people are not who we are anymore, as a society. Instead, politicians appeal to fear, and the focus on "family values" orients the center of our lives to home—symbolic for safety, security and holding on—instead of to the world. As tends to befall so many societies that lose their sense of purpose, desire for vision, tolerance for risk, contagious forms of energy, and feeling of agency, we fight each other for the decreasing pile of stuff that remains.

Mannix has a tremendous amount of energy right there on the screen, from the car chases to the fist fights, to the cars rolling down the hillside (and then exploding), to the reality behind so many of those stunts, and all of that running around. It seems to capture an era when we actually were physically lighter, even weighing less, and we owned fewer items, because shopping was not the hobby it is now. What we owned didn't seem to be as much a direct reflection of our value as what we did. Doing was not a means to an end, it was the end, even as Joe Mannix seemed suited, and entirely comfortable, living for the next job, his next chance to engage, to do some good. The series also made it very clear, as soon as it had the opportunity, that the energy behind this character came from a sense of agency that went all the way back to the way he not only understood himself, but owned that understanding, owning his choice, accepting whatever trouble came from that action, those choices.

"Return to Summer Grove" aired early in season 3. In the episode, Joe Mannix goes back to his hometown to help an old friend who has been falsely accused of murder and winds up in an iron lung—talk about your bad luck. Joe's old girlfriend, now married to the guy in the iron lung, visits Joe in his office one night. The scene was so sweetly done, with Joe sitting there dictating to Peggy via a tape recorder, clearly working into the night, when this woman appears in his office, a woman who still lights him up. The woman hired another PI before, but of course no other PI is Joe. He is her last resort. Oh how she wasted her time and money before coming to Joe. Of course, Joe helps, and when he arrives in Summer Grove, we see him get out of the van used to transport the man in the iron lung. As he walks over to a lawyer's office an older man stops his truck and gets out, seemingly because he recognizes Joe. We find out, albeit not right away, not even in the first scene with the two of them together, that this is Joe's father, and that Joe is estranged from him.

Later, after Joe wakes up in the hospital after having driven a car over a cliff due to some cut brake lines, we see again him with his father. And in case anyone thinks that some forms of violence on television cause people to act more violently in real life, as if we are billiard balls, no *Mannix* viewer would ever get into a car, let alone drive one, let alone turn the key in the ignition, lest that car's brakes fail, or that car blows up. We are symbolically selective, even about things that energize us.

This hospital scene drives home how Joe's father thinks Joe left home to go serve in the Korean War because his childhood sweetheart married someone else. Joe's father is not the least bit happy Joe is getting beat up and shot all of the time, with stories in the L.A. newspapers, and "with pictures!" In response, Joe says that rejection was only a part of it, and this is significant to the times as well as some of the broader and deeper themes of the series. Joe tells his father that he simply wasn't suited to work in the vineyards, because he needed to work with people. It goes without saying that Joe has proven himself right, that he can help people a lot better as a PI than he can working his father's land; it's just so obvious, so readily apparent to *Mannix* fans. His father does not see this and, gee, this is an only son, destined to inherit and work his father's land. But Joe has a stronger sense of agency in his own life than to buy into that line of thinking.

Joe achieves this because he owns who he is. Unlike plenty of other heroes, he seems to have taken the time to actually think about what that even means, about what moves him, and the series takes the time to let us in on that. Unlike so many modern-day heroes, his life does not seem like an accident of fate, his choices are on purpose, and so his taking those beatings makes him a bigger hero. He is not a "father's son" so much as he is his own man. This makes him so much more powerful a character than one who seems more the product of circumstances or inheritance. Characters created by circumstances have limited potential to inspire us. Far more powerful and universal are characters that make choices and own up to them, seeming to find their purpose and thus so much energy in the process, including a willingness to endure all sorts of messy things, the trouble they encounter along the way.

"Going back home" episodes occurred in other series during those years. Still, this one seems richly symbolic, with the son estranged from his father because the son dares to choose his own lifestyle, very different than the choice his father would make for him. This choice is similar to the one made in romantic love, when the young couple runs away from tyrannical parents who see marriage as an economic institution, because, in each case, a son is getting away from economic tyranny. But it is also very different, because the son chooses to leave not because of another person, but because of his life's work, his vocation. He leaves home not for another being, but for a higher purpose, not as a pair, but as an individual.

This is a post-romantic myth. It was done at time when more people were choosing their careers than ever before, with those choices enabled by an increasingly complex and booming economy as well as a shrinking world. People had a sense of belonging more to the world than to their families, with that kind of thinking enabled by the economy and the opportunity it afforded in the first place. Joe was also a Korean War veteran, and the series made it clear how that was his way out of his origins, similar to the way many WWII veterans, of which Connors is also one, must have felt when they transcended their family and geographical origins and sensed that they belonged more to the world. One has to also wonder if Connors wasn't doing a bit of autobiography in this episode, even beyond that of the portrayal of his Armenian roots. While his own father died when he was only eighteen, Connors was initially destined to follow in his father's footsteps as a lawyer, even studying law at UCLA for a time. He chose to be an actor instead, something that was, at the time, a less reputable profession than that of a lawyer, much like the way a PI is discussed in *Mannix*. But once we are exposed to them, aren't all professions kind of seamy? What they all seem to need are heroes like Joe Mannix that re-define them, transcend them.

Joe Mannix seems to embody the knowledge that we never have so much energy as when we enjoy what we are doing, when we are suited to do it, and when we have the courage to follow our vocational heart's desire, no matter what anyone else thinks of what energizes us, and no matter what the projected reward might be for so doing. Stories abound of people who not only achieved great success for having the courage to follow their vocational heart's desire, but who tell the tale of how they could not imagine having the same levels of energy if they did not have that courage, something that Joseph Campbell would agree with, tying directly into why the hero motif is so important to complex societies. Heroes seem strongly related to the ability to find psychic energy.

In many ways *Mannix* seems a harbinger of a post-romantic era still yet to be fulfilled, one we were evolving towards before we took a step backwards, back to a more feudal kind of system based upon family values that seemed to compensate for an economic system that failed to deliver on the promise of equal opportunity to everyone. *Mannix* is about a hero with all kinds of energy because he has both the courage and opportunity to figure out who he is and to live his life accordingly, despite going against his father's wishes, and despite all those beatings and woundings. He is a hero about the courage to follow what we come to know about ourselves, not just following another human being, winding up in some stable configuration, happily ever after.

Mannix is not happily ever after, but neither is it *un*happily ever after. Nor is it exactly about living in the moment, with that moment the centerpiece of Zen and other forms of Buddhism, which gained popularity in the U.S. in the past forty years or so. Buddhism, in greatly simplified terms, seeks to eliminate all forms of attachment, of desire, with the goal the achievement of a state beyond bliss. *Mannix*, like all art, holds a particular point of view that captured the zeitgeist of an era, one that might be considered more the second derivative of the moment, not a stable state or place, but a feeling of energy, of movement, with symbolism more like that of burning through our lives like a candle.

The phrase, "it is better to light a candle than curse the darkness," the origins of which are in dispute but which seems to be an old Chinese proverb, is attributed to use by President John F. Kennedy, among others. In some ways, it describes the zeitgeist that is *Mannix*, and not only because it is about doing something good (the light) when evil (the darkness) is present. The symbolism goes further. Candles burn, and are symbolic of a unit form of energy, even as individuals represent a single unit of energy, in the form of our person. Candles also burn out, even as we do. The trick to living a good life is to burn ourselves out well, to make the light, the energy, the most useful, to dispel the most darkness. Candles are often held by individuals in religious and other kinds of ceremonies, representing a unit that slowly burns, giving off heat and light, symbolic of life and so life affirming, despite the darkness. Candles that burn in defiance of the darkness are not a state we achieve, some end result; rather they are a way of being, despite not knowing if such an end state even exists. They represent a choice to burn brightly despite the knowledge that our choices are flawed, that we are flawed, that life seems flawed, symbolizing energy that seems to come from some life force that finds a way to burn despite the darkness, symbolizing that we may not have answers, and no one many have answers, but we can still give off light, because that is the best we can do, if we can only figure out how.

After Joe makes it into his office in "Death Has No Face," he answers the phone only to discover that he is getting yet another death threat. This is nothing new for Joe, of course, but it's pretty annoying, nonetheless. He manages to discover one bomb planted under his desk chair, but he was supposed to find that one. Then, when he wearily goes up the stairs to his second-floor apartment, a bomb goes off, right on the stairs. Yep, they actually blow up part of Joe's office, something that was pretty darn tantalizing in the "Next on *Mannix*" previews from the week before! This explosion tosses Joe backwards, but he gets up quickly to put out a few remaining flames.

One thing that *Mannix* was known for was Connors doing a significantly higher percentage of his own stunts than leading men tended to do in other series. He did so specifically because of a desire to lend realism to the show. This is especially true in season 1, where you had Connors' face right there in all sorts of leaps and rolls that you couldn't imagine being allowed by leading men or women today. He seemed to love to run and leap over things. Watch several episodes of *Mannix* in a row and it can be tough to not want to get up and run around. While the percentage of risky stunts done by Connors tended to decline as the seasons went on, something that had to happen if for no other reason than that the tremendous amount of stunts he did in season 1 seems unmatchable; it never quite diminished to the level you see studios enforce today, lest they lose the services of their stars for upcoming episodes. Beyond this, other kinds of safety measures are now enforced by the studios, at the expense of real energy.

I visited the Paramount lot in October 2011, something of a pilgrimage despite both the interior and exterior *Mannix* sets being torn down long ago and even the New York streets, which *Mannix* used so much, burning during the 1980s. The fire was apparently discovered by William Shatner when the sets were not in use for filming purposes. Still, visiting Paramount at that time was worthwhile for a *Mannix* fan, because many exteriors used again and again in *Mannix* were still there, including the exterior of Lucille Ball's office (a sort of townhouse with a red brick façade), which was used in episodes such as "The Man Outside" in which it served as Carol Barr's residence. A small patch of grass in front of that office, a sort of mini-park, was also still there, something that appears in numerous *Mannix* episodes. The fronts of many Paramount buildings, which served as the backdrop for everything from industrial complexes to prisons to, well, television and movie studios, were there as well.

Some *Mannix* fans have compiled lists of the many, many locations in and around the L.A. area where *Mannix* filmed. Visiting even just a few of those is quite a kick, resulting in an instant, broad smile on your face the moment you see them. The very first location I visited was the Shakespeare Bridge, famous to *Mannix* fans for its use in the opening segment of "What Happened to Sunday?", the season 4 episode in which Joe winds up jumping off that bridge to escape some hoods who, chasing him in their cars, were trying to use him as a hockey puck. The opening of that episode is iconic to *Mannix* fans, with Joe taking the only way out, jumping off the bridge no matter the consequence. That consequence was amnesia, meaning this is the "hero gets amnesia" episode in *Mannix*. However, as was always the case in *Mannix*, this type of a stock storyline was done both uniquely and with class. Joe does not lose his memory in such a way that he forgets who is he is, which easily could have set us up for some sappy scene with Peggy. He only forgets a single day. He has to go back and, as a PI, investigate himself, what he did that day, in order to find out who was trying to kill him. I walked around that bridge, taking pictures, for at least a half-hour, possibly longer. The fact that a police car appeared to patrol the area during that time was, I'm sure, only a coincidence.

Mannix was filmed all around L.A., but it even had to move around quite a bit on the Paramount lot. All of that moving around served to make the episodes feel more energetic. So did the use of fire and water—real fire and real water, and not only when cars rolled over hillsides and exploded, but right on the sets. On my tour of Paramount Studios in 2011, when our group stopped at a bathroom set used in the sitcom *Community*, someone asked our very young tour guide if the sinks operated. He replied that, for safety reasons, neither fire nor even running water was permitted on the sets any longer. Having been raised in a safety-first culture, he did not seem inclined to question the wisdom of such restrictions. This stunned me, knowing how much those two elements had been used on the sets of past film and TV productions, *Mannix* included.

Nearly forty years ago, when I watched "Death Has No Face," my myth of choice helped me to not only face trouble and understand it was a necessary part of a full life when it happened to me, but to consider that it might even make good sense to ask for it. And he had real fire and real water to get his point across. I mean, they blew up part of Joe's office, using a stunt man when "Joe" hit the floor, and having Connors, himself, put out the remaining bits of real flame, using a rug and his bare hands for what were probably controlled flames, but real flames nonetheless. Season 7 had even more fire around him, in "The Gang's All Here" as well as "Sing a Song of Murder." The sinks seemed to actually operate as well, with running water apparent in season 6's "A Puzzle for One," one of many episodes where Joe gets a wet towel for yet another bump on the head.

After Joe puts out the fire in his office in "Death Has No Face," the next scene has Art Malcolm visiting, with Joe being examined by a black doctor. (*Mannix* must have set the record for the use of so many different black doctors. They included at least two of Joe's personal physicians who would visit after he was shot or someone tried to blow him up, and other doctors whom he would encounter in various hospital scenes. This seems a subtle way of chipping away at a stereotype, more of that defiant art in the background, since the vast majority of doctors or TV or otherwise were white males during that time.)

After the doc checks Joe out, we discover that Joe is okay, even though he does not know who is trying to kill him. Art Malcolm's investigation reveals that whoever planted the bomb is trying to drag this thing out, placing bombs designed to scare or maim, not kill. Joe reveals he's been getting death threats for twelve days now, without telling his buddy Art. When Art finds this out he is angry, and Joe replies, "C'mon, Art. A private investigator's life is like a public towel, everybody wipes his hands on him."

Hmm ... a candle to curse the darkness or a public towel? Same thing, when you think about it.

The next morning we see Peggy come into the office to discover that part of the stairway has been blown up. She sees Joe sitting at his desk, drinking what appears to be grapefruit juice and calmly doing the newspaper's crossword puzzle. Joe asks for his schedule for the day. Peggy pushes back, saying Joe can't think this is business as usual and that he needs protection. Joe, of course, will have none of that. He informs her that the landlord needs his rent and that life goes on.

Joe: "What's a four letter word for a psychological aberration?"
Peggy: "Crazy."
Joe: "Yeah. It fits!"
Peggy: "That's what you are, you know that? You're crazy."

Joe: "I haven't given it much thought."

This scene is so well done it's almost a crime that it was buried in the vaults for nearly forty years. This is Joe being Joe and Peggy being Peggy at their very finest. And it contains some deeper truths, the philosophy of the times that Joe captured so well. For all intents and purposes, the life he chose to live as a PI was one filled with terrorism, something that, by the way, a lot of people feel in their lives, but for reasons not always directly connected to what we call terrorism. But terrorism was never going to force him to give up his freedom, his liberty, his choice, his energy, his agency. And so he was a little crazy. But isn't Joe the hero of this series, not Peggy? Don't we find him more appealing, for all sorts of reasons that have the ability to energize us? These days, we seem to think that Peggy is right.

The energy that Joe Mannix embodies was exemplified and underscored in many stunts over the years, complex and risky stunts that sometimes take only seconds of airtime. While some of the bigger stunts are from season 1, and include the "*Mannix* roll" from the dune buggy that graced the "m" in the opening for seasons 2-8, you can still see Connors running around and doing graceful leaps over fences and railings as late as season 8. San Francisco, where episodes were filmed in seasons 7 and 8 ("Cry Danger" and "A Small Favor for an Old Friend") seemed a place that prompted Connors to do all sorts of running around, including an impressive run up a rock by the Golden Gate Bridge, lots of running around the Cable Car Museum, and even running around Alcatraz.

Over the whole series, one of my favorite scenes exemplifying the emphasis on graceful movement is one set on the beach in season 2's "The Solid Gold Web," where Connors runs over some pretty big rocks for minutes, searching for someone. That scene is all about movement, almost like a dance, because it only contains that movement, background score, and Connors crying out one word over and over again, "Diana." Connors also seemed to make it into the water at least once a season, starting with the swimming in "Deadfall" that was behind the first "n" in "mannix" for the opener in all of seasons 2-8. The graceful leaps over railings and fences, with just one arm for support, never stopped, starting with "Skid Marks on a Dry Run" from season 1, where just such a leap occurs right before the fight scene that was a part of the opening title sequence. One such leap appears in season 8's "Enter Tami Okada," an episode that, when I first saw it, put the fear in me that they were going to give Joe a Japanese partner. This was the era when *Kung Fu* was a runaway hit. But unlike *Kung Fu*, where the fight scenes were a part of almost every climax and the energetic centerpiece of almost every episode, the energetic movement in *Mannix* was constant. The energy and movement was just a part of getting through his day, thus symbolizing what is behind living a full life, on the edge.

The opening episode, "The Name is Mannix," was partially filmed in Palm Springs, and Connors discusses on the DVDs for that season how he hurt his shoulder rolling on the golf course while being chased by the helicopter, another Picasso-like multi-camera-angle action sequence that made it to the opening for all of the seasons of *Mannix*. Connors also broke his wrist in a fight scene in that same episode where the guy he was fighting was wearing a metal brace that Connors did not know about. He broke his wrist when he hit the brace with his bare hand. Over the eight years of the series, he also endured numerous cuts that required stitches, an elbow that needed to be drained every few days, and even had his back peppered with blanks. Once, a Jeep that was supposed to stop at the bottom of a hill didn't. It would have seriously hurt, if not killed, Connors had he not gotten out of the way at the last minute. *Mannix* was also filmed on the water quite a bit, all sorts of water, including the ocean and lakes. Sometimes the crew and even Connors went into the water when they were not supposed to. Connors cracked some ribs in a fight scene on a boat when he forcefully slammed into a pipe. He is quoted describing the atmosphere on the set: "We had a prop man that we called 'I-Knew-That-Was-Gonna-Happen-Chuck.' When something'd go wrong, an explosion'd go wrong, or the stuff would fly out and hurt somebody, he'd say, 'I knew that was gonna happen.'"[10.5]

Quite a few action and stunt scenes with Connors seem to have a touch more reality than we see these days, like the rooftop hopping in season 6's "See No Evil" that takes only seconds of airtime. One of the larger ones is in season 4's "Bang, Bang, You're Dead," where Joe saves a little girl who is about to be run down by a speeding car. The stunt took place with Joe's 'cuda parked against a concrete wall. The little girl is against one side of the wall, walking towards Joe's 'cuda, when the speeding car, driven by a stunt man, arrives just a bit too early. Connors goes to grab her to get her out of the way, to the safety of the hood of his 'cuda. Not only does the whole thing come across as all too real (especially when slowed down on the DVDs), the actress who played the little girl claims she really *was* saved by Connors and that the series was fined for the stunt that was left in the episode.[10.6]

The 'cudas and Darts are what Connors once referred to as those little green cars that were always breaking down. Other series tended to emphasize car chases more than *Mannix* did, even as *Mannix* was the first to bring elaborate car chases to television. It wasn't that *Mannix* was not loaded with car chases. But Connors' ability to move himself around so gracefully meant that the car chases were somehow less important to conveying energy than in other series. And, really, wouldn't you rather have your hero punch the guy out instead of run him off the road, possessing a force that does not require him to use some external object?

Nonetheless, the cars in *Mannix* have something of a following of their own. The green 'cudas were used for three seasons, 4-6. There were initially three of them, including a ready spare in case the primary broke down while shooting, leading one to wonder how license plates were dealt with in California since the one constant on those *Mannix* cars was that the license plate number would not change in a given season (unless footage of cars from prior seasons was inserted). In season 5 the front of the car actually changed, from episode to episode, but the license plate number did not. One of the 'cudas had four headlights while the others only had two.

After the filming of "Babe in the Woods" in season 5, only two 'cudas were left. That episode includes an elaborate car chase in the hills. While watching "Moving Target," which includes another car chase in the hills, I wondered why the heck they did all that damage to Joe's car. That chase scene ends with Joe crashing his car into the hillside, and showing the 'cuda in a bad way that sure looked extreme, not repairable. It seemed so unnecessary to the story. Since "Moving Target" is the very next production number after "Babe in the Woods" it would seem they decided to use the wrecked footage of the 'cuda for something, placing Mike Connors in the totaled 'cuda for its last scene before being taken off to the junk pile. That 'cuda isn't the only car to be totaled in *Mannix*, which seemed to have a sort of love-hate relationship with the automobile.

Mannix is credited with inventing the "car over the cliff that rolls three times and blows up." So many cars did that in *Mannix* that I used to think the hills around L.A. had to be filled with blown-up, burned out cars. Great time and effort went into the race car that explodes and goes over a cliff in "To the Swiftest, Death," the very first episode filmed in season 2. The sequence takes only a few seconds of airtime but was expensive to produce.[10.7] They got some money's worth out of it though, since it wound up being used for three seasons in the *Mannix* opening, giving those eyes something to look at. One of many cars that blow up when the driver turns the key in the ignition was in "A Way to Dusty Death," in which Joe's rental car explodes when he goes to start it, something they definitely used a stuntman for. But the stunt went out of control, and Dick Ziker, who coordinated and executed so many *Mannix* stunts over the years, considered it the closest he ever came to losing his life, at least at that time.[10.8] Some of that comes across in the footage in the actual episode, where you see him on fire. Another stunt, when the show was filmed in Canada, ended with Ziker caught in the rapids, trapped under some brambles for a long enough period of time that the crew thought the worst. Yet another *Mannix* stunt was discussed in a *TV Guide* article devoted to one of the stunts—the one where the woman falls from the balcony in "What Happened to Sunday?"[10.9] Once again, this is a scene that takes only a few seconds of airtime, but which was complex and expensive to film.

Mannix often conveyed the seemingly paradoxical philosophy that the more energy you burn, the more energy you have to burn. In many ways, this philosophy has been proven to be right. Not only does exercise help depression, hospitals that used to keep people in bed after surgery now routinely do all kinds of surgery on an outpatient, "ambulatory" basis. They also get people out of bed and walking as soon as possible even after major surgery. Due to a recent injury I discovered that even broken bones in some places, such as fingers, are no longer immobilized, because immobilization can quickly lead to atrophy and permanent stiffness. We seem to do better when we move no matter what our condition. Joe was way ahead of that curve.

In season 5's "To Save a Dead Man" is one of many scenes where we have some doctor tell Joe he needs to "take it easy for a few days," only to have Joe ignore the good doctor. This scene takes place in a hospital room, where Peggy comes in to hear the doctor and responds, "He won't listen to you, doctor." She was, of course, right. My all-time favorite of these scenes, and a true classic, is the one that takes place in season 4's "With Intent to Kill," in which Joe is hit by a car, knocked unconscious and left in the parking lot of the oft-used "Holiday House" hotel. After a commercial break, we see Joe being taken to the hospital in an ambulance. Waking up while still being transported and still on the stretcher, he informs the attendant that he is just fine and asks to be let out of the ambulance. When the ambulance attendant says he can't do that because there might be "internal injuries," Joe threatens to sue the ambulance company and the hospital, saying "I know my rights. You can't just pick people up off the streets."

This may be one of the scenes viewers had in mind when they describe Joe as having been hit on the head one too many times. Okay, okay. One case where rest does seem to matter, as we've recently discovered, is for head injuries. And the number of times Joe gets knocked out with possible head injuries would seem to defy reality even more than the number of times he was shot. But, please. This is art. This is about the way life feels to us and, in case you might have observed by monitoring your dreams, we tend to process what we feel the most deeply when we process it symbolically. If you want reality, watch reality TV. But I hope I am never stuck in elevator with only you to talk with.

If you really think about it, really think it all the way through, you would like to find your way to have something in common with this guy. Even as Peggy said in "The Sound of Darkness," he seems to be equipped to take anything that comes his way and just get up and keep going, thereby personifying psychic energy. The tolerance he seems to have for all manner of consequences of his own energy and agency seems not only a part of the mix, it might even be the essential ingredient, the secret behind the secret. In season 5's "Moving Target," Joe visits the home of a guy he is looking for, only to find the housekeeper there, a somewhat older woman. He introduces himself as a PI, which causes her to extract some money from him. She knows he wants information. Joe wants to know if the home owner was around during a certain period of time.

Joe: "What about last March?"

Woman: "I don't know about him. But I know I wasn't."

Joe looks at her, clearly wondering what she means by this.

Woman: "I was in a rest home."

In response to this Joe looks down, sort of says "oh" and seems, well, somewhat sympathetic, but also downright disappointed. The woman notices this reaction.

Woman: "On a forgery rap."

In response, Joe Mannix gives one of his best smiles of the entire series, one of those broad smiles normally held in reserve for special occasions. He is not only smiling broadly, he is smiling approvingly, happily, not just once, but twice. Why? Because he found out that this woman, whom he never even met before, was found guilty of breaking the law and incarcerated rather than in a rest home. That made him happy. Not only that, but she does not hide that fact from him. She just owns up to it by telling him, "You'd have found out anyway." Joe was around a lot of women over the years, beautiful women, and rich, prima donnas. Aside from Peggy, his biggest smile seemed to be for this woman. This sort of love of living at the expense of perfection, of not denying oneself energy, is clearly connected to his energy, his secret. Like a true hero, he wishes the same for everyone.

In season 5's "Murder Times Three" when Joe is leaving his office, Peggy stops him.

Peggy: "Joe, you're asking for trouble."

Joe: "Well, it has been kinda quiet the past couple of hours."

Peggy cautions Joe against putting himself out there like that, risking. His reply confirms that he is what he is by choice, an agent in his own life. Unlike people weighed down with all sorts of stuff to defend, both psychic and material, he does not cause trouble, nor does he hide from it. He asks for it. He is more about movement, about energy, about agency, than about stuff. Candles burn anyway, converting the energy stored within them into heat and light, bringing those to bear on the moment their surroundings dictate. And candles seem to burn brighter when surrounded by the most darkness.

This is simple dialogue. But if you think there's no philosophy there, think again. Similar to the way the music we now consider classical was once mainstream, what we now call philosophy was something people once did in the streets, as an ordinary part of trying to make sense out of life. When we push philosophy into the realm of something that only studied intellectual elites can discuss, it becomes distant from us, less useful and real, and so real philosophy evolves via other means.

So much of our philosophy both evolves and is conveyed to us in our arts, often realized as an amalgam of concepts otherwise academically separate, otherwise seemingly in competition with each other. When those otherwise separate concepts are united they form something new, possibly never more effectively than in TV characters we come to know so well because we come to know their character so well. They seem to capture the essence of an era, the philosophy of an era. Like all philosophy produced in any given era, it tends to not be understood in its own time. It also evolves in fits and starts.

We cannot seem to fully understand what moves us while it is moving us. The best we can seem to do is try to choose well what moves us, then let it move us, and then keep moving forward by understanding that we are so much less when we do not ask for trouble.

Chapter 11
A Pittance

Faith is belief in something that cannot be proved to be true, thus not based upon logical reasoning. We exhibit faith when we believe in something so strongly that we act accordingly. Faith requires both vision, or imagination, and the courage to invest ourselves in that vision. While many have come to associate faith exclusively with conformance to organized systems of belief, even dogma, more fundamentally faith really only describes that humans think, broadly, in two mutually exclusive ways, one based upon logical reason and another based upon something else. The "something else" ranges from personal intuition to subscription to dogmatic deities, and includes everything in-between. All humans think in terms of both reason and faith, and for a simple reason. We have to. We have to be reasonable in order to be a member of the human race, in order to communicate with and be accountable to others, in order to conform. But we also must have faith because we encounter so many situations in our lives when reason fails to provide an answer.

One of these situations is when reason fails to provide an answer in time, before we must act. Because we are alive we must behave, in computer parlance, in "real-time," making decisions in the absence of complete information or without sufficient time to process information even if we had it, or else our very lives might be threatened. We must go with our gut, our intuition, our best guess, having faith that our choice is the correct one. Another of these situations is when we are overwhelmed by circumstances for which there is no answer, and a lifetime of thinking about an answer fails to produce an entirely reasonable one. We must have faith when we take on a job, career path or problem that we seem to be unsuited for, one that seems more than we can reasonably handle but we simply feel we must take on. The best among us do this. But even if we never asked to be overwhelmed, we must exhibit faith as children, because we are born into a world where others seem to agree upon all sorts of reasonable things that we cannot yet understand. A third situation when reason fails us is when we develop the very models upon which we base reasonable answers in the future. We cannot seem to stretch the bounds of knowledge without the kind of insight that allows us to see something that isn't there, and believe in it strongly enough that we ultimately prove it is true. Prior to the proof being accepted by others, it cannot be proven to be true. And yet it is. Finally, even those whose thinking is dominated by reason must acknowledge that life is filled with paradoxes and ambiguities, situations for which two conflicting answers seem to be entirely true. They also must acknowledge that there are times when they went against pure logic or went against the odds, and simply acted on a hunch.

We think in dual realms, one with facets of reason, logic, cooperation, structure, and matter, and the other with facets of faith, imagination, courage, individuality and spirit. The two realms are each a part of us. We must use and develop both in order to be fully human. This presents us with a personal dilemma. When to use one or the other realm has no clear answer. Because it includes individuality as one of its parts, since faith gives us the opportunity to come up with our own answers, the answer to the dilemma must be a uniquely, individual one. But we are also still a part of humankind. Thus, when we become too dominated with one realm or the other we fail to become individuals who are also engaged in the world, allowing it to move us even as we move it.

In order to have faith, we first must have imagination, for imagination is required in order to see something that cannot be proven to exist, and thus is not material. When we act according to what we can only imagine to be true, personal courage is what compels us to go on. This includes those times when we are overwhelmed by our life's circumstances as well as when we have faith in something that only we can see, such as when we have creative insight in the arts or the sciences. Since each of those times occurs when we find ourselves the most alone, when we are forced to feel alone or compelled to think for ourselves, faith is the most individual way we can think. Recently, we have come to associate having faith more with matters of spirit than matters of organized, dogmatic religion. Spirit is a more universal concept, seeming to give us the ability to reclaim faith-based thinking as a necessary and important part of our individuality when religion becomes too structured and dogmatic for us, seeming to defeat its purpose of helping us find our own answers.

Logical thinking is structured and systematic, with origins that date back to the ancient Greeks. Logical reason tells us if, given a set of conditions, events, or inputs that are already known to be true or false, something else—some other condition, event our output—will be true or false. Reason tells us this with complete certainty, so long as the information we have to work with is correct to begin with, and so long as our model of how things relate, how chains of causality are connected, is correct. The systematic reasoning about cause-and-effect relationships is immensely powerful, providing the foundation for not only the kind of deductive reasoning that appeals to courts of law, but also to digital computers. Such technology is built upon the processing of almost incomprehensible amounts of translation of true or false, on or off, 1 or 0, up or down, black or white—in the form of "truth tables" and resulting in answers that link to matters in the world around us. Logical reasoning is also powerful because it is the basis of agreement and cooperation between human beings, and we can feel like utter fools when we do not see the truth when it is right in front of our faces. When we cannot establish for certain whether events are true or false, we often assign probabilities to them, allowing us to reason in terms of the likelihood something will occur instead of its absolute certainty. The probabilities are culled from observations, collections of past events, allowing us to reason about the way a sampling of what happened in the past predicts the likelihood of something occurring in the future, thereby permitting complex, logical, causal models of certainty to be used to process what are really only models of mere chance.

For all of their immense capabilities in facilitating the systematic processing of logic and probability, digital computers are not remotely close to exhibiting intelligence. Precise definitions of intelligence elude us. Even relative levels of intelligence are difficult to pinpoint. But intelligence does seem to require the ability to process the world around us systematically and logically, as well as to imagine things that are not there, and come to act upon them, creatively making them a reality, thereby expressing our personal reality. Computers can systematically establish cause and effect, the truth or falsity of something, when they have information to do so. But when they do not, they cannot imagine, cannot dream, and thus cannot create radically different models that depart from the systematic ones they have been given, which is the reason why we can program computers but they cannot program us. Imagination seems to be the most fundamental of all creative processes, allowing us to create a reality all our own without having to actually live it out, at least just yet. When we do act on our imagination, when we believe in it strongly enough that we have the courage to make our dreams come true, we exhibit faith, thereby changing the world. But in order to communicate our imagination, our personal vision, back to the outside world, we are compelled to at least try to prove its worth. And proof puts us back into the logical realm.

At the top of our intellectual processes seems to be a conflict between when to use reason and when to have faith. That is the process we cannot implement in computers, a process we cannot reach using logical, systematic reasoning alone. Because that conflict includes imagination and fantasy as one of its processes, its resolution seems to require us to work out our individual solution in fantasy, thus in story. Story that compels us enough to project ourselves into it takes on the form of myth.

Fantasy seems to be capable of accommodating the logical realm, but not the other way around. The *Road Runner* cartoons, with Wile E. Coyote, the most prolific engineer ever conceived by mankind, contain a logical foundation, all their own. Their logic does not hold up to scrutiny in the real world, but it is self-consistent, in a contained way. That is the mechanism behind discovery, when a once self-contained vision of something new is found to actually be true. Logic seems incapable of extending itself through its own processes, but fantasy can extend logic, allowing us to create more complete models of reality around us. Fantasy and imagination seem to be at the root of intellectual processes, accommodating both faith and reason as well as helping us to resolve their conflict.

Understanding when to use reason and when to have faith is one of the most difficult challenges we face in life, precisely because there is no single correct answer to be found. Individuals and societies get into the greatest difficulty when they are not comfortable with the duality of the way they must think, including the attendant uncertainty that must be endured as a part of life. When one realm of thinking becomes far more developed and dominates the other, when we become all about one and exclude or suppress the other, we not only fail to grow, we can become defensive, aggressive or both.

Our way out seems to be to connect strongly with certain kinds of story, with myth.

But not all myths have the same ability to help us sort out this fundamental dilemma, nor to allow us to be comfortable with the often painful consequences of individuality. Some myths can even impede growth by keeping us in one realm or the other. Some myths appeal to a sense that prowess of wits or logical reasoning alone can win the day. They belong almost exclusively to the realm of reason. We have recently seen a plethora of these modern-day Sherlock Holmes in the form of the clever cop, PI, or lawyer. The wise guy is a variant on this type. They appeal to the assumption that everyone bows to the power of reason and logic, or that heroes can outsmart people without being so involved that they risk themselves in the process, emotionally or physically, seeming to tell us that courage is not necessary if one has sufficiently developed their capacity for reason. But no one always bows to pure reason and logic, even when the logic seems apparent. Sometimes the greatest courage is required when the logic is the most apparent and others simply refuse to see it, acting badly in the process. Other myths appeal to a sense that righteousness gives some special power that can win the day. They are all about the lone man on a mission and belong almost exclusively to the realm of faith. These *Rambo*-like myths appeal to the sense of empowerment and purpose we feel when survival necessitates thinking in the realm of faith, but do not include the compromises we must make because we are also a part of humankind—individuals, and not lone wolves.

When our myths become less, we become less, as individuals and as societies. We seem less grown up because, in a sense, we are. Myths that help us resolve our personal answer as to when to use reason and when to have faith can help us understand that the struggle exists in the first place. They exhibit personal intuition and have a strong sense of purpose, but are they also reasonable members of society. They willingly, not reluctantly, place themselves into overwhelming situations, and exhibit the capacity to be moved by their experiences. They can reach places in us that others cannot.

Mannix started out with a man vs. machine premise in its very first season, representing the struggle between faith and reason—the faith of a man in himself and his instincts versus systematic, organizational logical thinking, symbolized by not only the organization he worked for, Intertect, but also the computer behind the organization. But Joe Mannix was not an anarchist, did not hide from society, and wasn't the least bit reluctant to engage. He seemed to welcome engagement. He was also about outcomes, and courageous. He was not an antihero, unlike so many protagonists these past decades that seem to point out problems, but do not give us the ability to move forward nobly and with dignity in the absence of complete answers. From its man vs. machine foundation, *Mannix* took on more properties of the classical hero motif, exploring it in many ways over its eight seasons. The result was the portrayal of a classic, heroic struggle between reason and faith on a nearly weekly basis. Joe Mannix is compelling because he chose, on purpose, to invest himself completely in what he believed to be true, and yet he struggled with that, paid a price for that. He also realized that proof was necessary. He is the mythical, heroic version of the adult who has come to face the central dilemma of individuality, when we come to realize that we must face the struggle between reason and faith, that the struggle is costly, that the struggle becomes even harder the more faith we have in ourselves, and that the struggle never ends. He embodies the mythical kind of hero that compels us to think about a place we might reach, one that is clearly not reached by all, perhaps not even by most, because it is not something achievable just by the passage of years, alone.

Since *Mannix* gets so many fundamental constructs right in the struggle between reason and faith, it should have come as no surprise to discover that the series that was unafraid of racism, fire, water, risky stunts or nude art should also be unafraid to explicitly include references to faith in its stories, over virtually all of its tenure. *Mannix* was not a show about religion, and we never did come to know what Joe's religion was, even as it should be. He was far more fundamental than that, designed to not exclude anyone. But because *Mannix* was about the conflict behind the process of individuation, and thinking in the realm of faith is a necessary part of that, references to faith fit right in alongside those law-and-order style, material outcomes.

Some of the references are small. One of these is in one of my favorite episodes of the series, season 5's "Death is the Fifth Gear." The episode, previously discussed, is the one where Joe crashes his race car, is presumed to have head injuries, escapes from a mental hospital, winds up being accused of two murders, and eventually finds out that he was drugged. The actual ending of the episode does not have Joe crashing his car through the garage door, with Peggy asking Joe if he is okay and his nodding that he was. It actually ends with him visiting Mrs. Barrington back at the hospital, the old woman in Room 207 who was the secret to the mystery, who ultimately helped Joe discover what was going on and that he was being drugged instead of going insane.

That episode can be thought of in terms of individuation. When highly creative types go through a process of realizing that they think differently, outside the norm, in a way that is valid but material only to themselves, they can go through a period where they think they are losing their mind. They need to discover that the craziness really only comes from symbolic drugs in the form of systematic thinking ingested from the outside world. By placing his faith in himself alongside his ability to reason about what is going on, Joe finds that his problem is really only due to those drugs. He regains his sanity by using his very individualism to solve his dilemma. So, it should not be a surprise that such a deeply symbolic episode would end with the following lines:

Mrs. Barrington: "Don't ever lose faith, young man."

Joe: "Never, Mrs. Barrington."

Explicit references to faith were only a small part, just a pittance, of the series. Still, small references to God and faith started in the series' first season and continued into its eighth. In the first season, the episode "Eight to Five, It's a Miracle" has Joe, working as an Intertect agent, hired by the Catholic Church. He's investigating the appearance of something that seems to be a miracle. A cross appeared in a pattern of bricks when a building was being torn down, alongside which appeared a stream that was pink and smelled like roses. A young priest wants to find out if a miracle occurred or not, in order to try to save his parish. Notice how the priest is not clinging to the miracle. He wants to know for sure, at the very least to rule out all other possibilities. Reason and faith sit side by side in *Mannix's* portrayal of clergy. The Bishop indulges the priest by hiring Intertect, who assigns its best agent, Joe. (When Joe visits the Bishop's office, by the way, the Bishop is sitting at a desk that looks suspiciously like Joe's future desk in his Paseo Verde office.) Joe finds out that the supposed miracle was really a set-up, a manipulation. The priest says to him, "I'd like to thank you Mr. Mannix." Joe replies, "For destroying a miracle?" The priest replies, "You can't destroy what never was." The priest goes on to claim another miracle instead, since the son of a mob boss risked his life to save Joe's. The priest is not stuck on any one kind of miracle, does not righteously cling to his initial presumption of a miracle. This priest bridges reason and faith, and does not seem to be stuck on one at the exclusion of the other.

This is not the only priest to appear in, let alone hire, *Mannix*. In season 5's "To Save a Dead Man," Joe is hired by a priest, a golfer buddy of Joe's, to help a nun who witnessed a man's death. Joe works to solve a mystery that is supposed to help the dead man get into heaven. In season 6, "Cry Silence" has Anthony Zerbe playing an ex-priest, Jim. Someone is trying to kill Jim, and it would seem to be connected to a man who confessed murder to him when he was still a priest. Jim wants Joe to get the message to this man that his secret is still safe. The episode concludes with Joe and the ex-priest by the side of the man who was trying to kill Jim. The man is dying because Joe just shot him in the process of trying to save Jim's life. Both Joe and Jim offer help. But the man dies first, saying "Skip it Padre. Wherever I'm going I can make it without help." Joe responds, "Everyone can use help." Jim, despite no longer being a priest, gives a blessing. Joe just puts his head down in a reverent kind of way, but does not participate. This is the perfect response for a myth, because he should not be afraid to acknowledge those who have organized forms of faith, not deny them their faith, but also not reveal his affiliation with any organization. All comers to myths must be welcome because they lie in the realm of imagination, not dogma. Joe's last line in this episode is also kind of curious. Joe Mannix is highly individualistic. Yet even he acknowledges the need for help, bridging the individual with society.

The very next episode, "The Crimson Halo," has Joseph Campanella return, but not as Lew Wickersham. Five years after they worked together in the first season of *Mannix*, Connors and Campanella work together on another episode of *Mannix*, only now the show is a very successful hit with Joe (and Connors) on his own, except for Peggy, of course. Since many never saw the first season, or may have forgotten it, the producers seemed to feel comfortable bringing Campanella back as a guest star playing a top brain surgeon, a Dr. Aspinal, whom someone is trying to kill. Introducing himself, Joe says, "Dr. Aspinal. My name is Mannix." Dr. Aspinal replies, "That's supposed to mean something to me?" This would seem to be an inside joke, since that name meant something to Campanella during all of season 1!

But Joe was not hired by Dr. Aspinal. He was hired by a lawyer named Otway, played by Burgess Meredith. The scene where Joe is hired by Otway is a classic, but one that did not seem that way the first time I saw it, when I was only eleven years old. Otway is quite arrogant, and he gives Joe a choice collection of offhand insults, of the kind I can recognize now, a subset of which goes like this:

Joe: "Who is the client?"

Otway: "It's a man you wouldn't normally run into in your circle."

Some other insults follow, then this one:

Otway: "Mr. Mannix, this is not one of your run-of-the-mill keyhole peeping operations. I want a man who will follow orders, to the letter."

Joe gets up, stands beside Otway, and says, softly but firmly, right in his ear, "Then you don't want me."

Otway: "How do you know?"

Joe: "My clients tell me what they want done, not how to get it done."

The whole scene was brilliantly played by Connors with such dignity, the way Joe endured those insults, just calmly answering them, but giving every sense of knowing he was so much more than the stereotypical assessment this man had of him. This is the embodiment of the kind of dignity Connors was referring to when he described Joe Mannix as a "decent, dignified man." Joe Mannix's dignity came from who he was, not from his profession, even despite his profession. Joe did not dismiss this other man's point of view, or get angry. He simply completely stood up to it, without making a fuss, without rejecting it either, finding that sweet spot between showing that, while the words affected him, because you could see that right on his face, he knew they were not true about him. Joe understood a larger truth about himself, and displayed that he had far more grace and class than Otway. The episode is also enjoyable due to Joe's dogged persistence trying to protect Dr. Aspinal, who does not want his protection; it is by far not the only episode in which Joe's persistence is fun to watch and gets to you in subtle ways. Persistence, not reluctance, is yet another requirement of individuality. Reluctant heroes do not help us to reach places that persistent heroes can.

In the end of the episode Joe goes on to prove his worth, putting his life on the line, risking himself when he goes to retrieve some tapes, from a fallout shelter, no less. Otway thinks Joe's retrieval of the tapes could help him get into heaven if he does not survive a dangerous operation, since Otway turned out to be the reason the doctor was being targeted in the first place. Otway does not survive, and Joe expresses to Dr. Aspinal the thought that maybe if he gives those tapes to the police they might just be Otway's ticket to heaven. This sure seems like an act of love that belongs more to the realm of the spiritual than the romantic.

In "The Girl From Nowhere" from season 7, a very young girl is killed in an accident. When no one comes to claim her, Art Malcolm holds a kind of private funeral for her, not wanting to attract the public to such a sad situation. Joe is invited, and Peggy stands alongside him. A minister presides. We hear him read from the Bible, 1 Corinthians. Different versions of the passage go with different versions of the Bible, but it is a passage with which many people are familiar, the one that compares faith, hope and love, making love the greatest of the three. This scene at the funeral has some impact on the story, since Joe discovers a woman who attended the funeral who is a key to the mystery. The reading of the passage was not necessary to the story, nor was showing Joe and Peggy's reaction the reading. It is curious that such a passage would be even read in *Mannix*. But it fits the themes of the series.

Hope that something good will happen stops just short of belief that something more specific will happen, thus making hope less than faith. The passage goes on to say that love is greater than both hope and faith. If we are dominated by faith, and not by love, we can separate ourselves so much from the world so that we fail to love others, can fail to love mankind by positively impacting it—and letting it impact us back. Love can be thought of as a bridge between faith and reason, because it bridges our personal vision, our faith in something that only we can see, with the realization we are in a material world with other human beings with whom we need to communicate and cooperate through reason and matter.

Mannix's comfort in inserting small references to religion continued into season 8 with the episode "Game Plan," in which it is revealed that Joe has a "goddaughter," a pretty unnecessary thing in the context of the story. Late in season 8, and thus one of the last episodes of the entire series, is "A Word Called Courage." This episode involves yet another nutty ex-Korean War buddy, the last of the series, who sets Joe up to be tortured. Joe did not go through enough in the previous seven years by being shot, drugged, poisoned, dumped down hillsides and left for dead, and in both car and airplane crashes. Joe also had to be tortured, or the series would not have been complete. Early in the episode when Joe is trying to convince Art that this nutty guy is after him and dangerous, Joe says to Art, "From your lips to God's ear." The reference, while small, almost seemed to fit this episode, when we actually see Joe endure the torture even after he was warned it was coming and he tried to avoid it. The episode also includes a great scene where Peggy tries to fight off a guy who is trying to hurt Joe while he is strapped down and not in the best of shape, having just been tortured for an unknown period of time. For her part, Peggy shows some chops. She clearly can't overpower this guy, is not acting very logically, but she can't just let this happen to an otherwise helpless Joe. That scene where Peggy displays the courage to try to protect her friend and boss moves us, especially into the seventh year of following these characters, and the eighth year of following Joe. We know why she feels the way she does, why she cannot allow herself to stand by and let someone she has come to admire—precisely because of his individuality and courage—be hurt, even if she logically knows she cannot really help it, even if she gets slammed around in the process. She has to try. If courage is necessary for individuality and love, it may also be the greatest evidence of their presence.

This also explains why viewers never seem to tire of the otherwise unreasonable number of times Peggy was kidnapped in the series, seconds away from certain death, but just kept working for Joe. Perhaps the best "Peggy is kidnapped again" episode, also in season 8, is "Walk on the Blind Side." This is an episode I remember so well from when it first ran, including a specific memory of my reflecting upon it during a boring study hall held in a giant cafeteria during the week after its initial broadcast. One test of a strong myth, one that really captures us, is our desire to play it back in our minds, as well as extend it, fill in missing scenes, consider implications, project the characters into other situations and project ourselves into the characters. When we reflect upon and project into a myth in that way, we are really working out answers to fundamental questions in our minds, using our imagination to solve the deeper questions of our lives, such as sorting out reason and faith. Myth is when story becomes more useful and thus important to us than mere entertainment, when we give consideration to it for a much longer duration than the amount of time it took to experience it in the first place. This is why myths, unlike mere story, don't pass time, but are timeless.

In this episode, Peggy is actually kidnapped as the result of a kind of mistake Joe made. When he sends Peggy to pick a woman up, Peggy is taken by "the syndicate" because she looks too similar to this woman, someone Joe just met and tried to help. Before Joe can do anything about it, he winds up with Peggy's coat with a bullet hole in it. For a short—very short—period of time Joe thinks Peggy might actually be dead. *Mannix* never turned any situation into a sappy melodrama, a soap opera designed to make you feel afraid of the next thing that seems bound to happen. It did just the opposite. All sorts of things happen to Joe and Peggy through the years, and they are simply handled, ready to move onto the next thing. Those things are not, however, handled in a cavalier way. The combination of brevity and depth made Joe and Peggy's reactions to those situations that much more poignant.

Peggy wrote a message, "Playa Del Rey," on the label of her coat, which means she could very well still be alive, and is likely somewhere out by the L.A. International Airport. Joe notices this, giving him enough hope so that he goes out and tries to find her. He winds up visiting the house of the kidnapper, where Peggy is being held hostage, in the basement. The kidnapper, who sort of fell for Peggy (the only reason he did not carry out his instructions to kill her), is a nutcase and used to be imprisoned in that same soundproof basement room by his mother, who is now deceased. Joe winds up finding the house, posing as "Rudy" the real estate agent. It's such a fun scene, Joe being Joe while presuming some fake identity, something Connors did throughout the series. Watching him play Joe playing someone else was sweet, because you could always see Joe in there, distinctly different from the other roles Connors played outside of *Mannix*. Connors showed us Joe inside the other persona, someone Joe had to portray as a part of getting things done, a very relatable kind of thing all true individuals must accomplish, at times.

Alas, Joe does not find Peggy while he is posing as Rudy, setting up a great scene in the basement room where Peggy is being imprisoned. Sadly, this is one of two episodes of the DVD releases where something went wrong with the master, or with the digital re-mastering, of the episode. The other is "The Deadly Madonna," from season 7, an episode that almost appears to have not been restored. But I can live with a lesser quality "Deadly Madonna" much more easily than I can with a lesser quality "Walk on the Blind Side." The episode is still very watchable, and I am so grateful to have it back at all. But this is one of those episodes where subtle expressions on faces matter so much, expressions fans waited six years for after they were first shown, expressions that lit me up when I first watched this episode.

After Joe, posing as Rudy, departs, Peggy's kidnapper brings her some tea, and starts to do some chit-chat with her. Then, almost abruptly, he asks her, "What's he look like?" Peggy does not know what the heck he is talking about and answers "Who?" The kidnapper replies, "The guy you work for, Mannix." Peggy shrugs, seeming to need to think about it some, and goes on to describe Joe in an offhand way. "He's about 6-2," she says. Then she thinks a bit more, looks up in the air and, seeming to conjure him in her mind, adds, "180 pounds." The kidnapper goes on, "Color of his eyes?" Peggy answers, "Brown. Brown hair." The second part comes from her own thinking about Joe, just her reflection upon him, not in reply to a question. When it comes, you see her nod and smile, as if she is someplace else when she is thinking about Joe—sweet. She is conjuring someone who isn't there, someone whom, at that moment, she has every reason to believe she will never see again, because she has, presumably, been presumed dead. Even just thinking about him affects her, changes her mood, moves her. You want to see Peggy's face in this scene, and it's painful that the episode's quality on DVD isn't as clear as the others.

The kidnapper goes on to ask, "What kinda car does he drive?" Peggy starts to answer, but something dawns on her in mid-reply. "Blue... a gray hardtop," she says, substituting the color gray for blue at the last second. His car really is a blue hardtop this season. But the kidnapper realizes this is a lie, saying, "You mean blue, don't you?" Peggy looks sort of attentive now, hopeful. The kidnapper goes on to say, "Well, he was here." Then Peggy has this moment of recognition on her face, one that transforms her emotions almost in an instant, in an explosion-like change in mood from resigned to ebullient, "Oh, he knows I'm alive!" The scene goes on, with the kidnapper becoming angry, suspecting Peggy might have put something like a note in the coat, and telling Peggy that when Joe visited, he "didn't see a thing." After the kidnapper leaves the room to answer a knock at the door, we see Peggy's face. No words are spoken. But her relief that Joe knows she is alive is all over her face. She sort of sighs, really just breathes, "Oh!" and puts her head down.

No words needed to be spoken. We know these characters too well by now. We also know that they know each other too well by now. We know that Peggy knows that since Joe was not fooled by the bullet in the coat, and he is out looking for her, he is not going to stop until he finds her. And once he pursues something, he has quite a track record of success. He is Joe Mannix, after all. What that means in her situation is all over her face. She may have good reason to have faith in him finding her. But it is still faith. When you know these characters so well, it is faith that makes perfect sense.

The episode ends with a great scene where Joe and Art kick the door in, at the very last minute, if not the very last second. Myth tends to include this last-minute kind of timing, where the hero makes it just in time. Since time is a major reason why we often cannot find answers through reason, at least in time, faith and timing seem strongly related.

After the bad guy gives his final nutty speech and dies, in this case the victim of a bullet wound from other bad guys, Joe goes over to Peggy who falls into his arms in a way we never see in any other episode of the entire series, in a way we have waited for. It is, finally, a warm embrace between a white man and a black woman that *Mannix* made possible in the first place, by breaking ground six years prior, and all along in-between. It would also be the last such embrace in the series.

The depth of emotion between these characters is conveyed on their faces in the briefest of moments, again making it all the more poignant. And it happened all throughout the series.

My favorite piece of evidence is in season 5's "Catspaw." This is the only episode in the entire series where Peggy quits working for Joe. Here is the obligatory "friend-quits-on-friend" storyline. In other series, more dominated by soap-opera think, this situation would have lasted at least one entire episode, if not several episodes. But when it happens in *Mannix*, it all happens so fast. The set-up is where the bad guys get to Peggy because she had a cold. They use a fake doctor who gives her an injection, a truth serum that forces her to give up the combination to Joe's office safe. When Joe comes back the next morning, after a trip to Fresno, he expects to see a letter, a potential piece of evidence, in the safe. After all, Peggy called him the day before and told him she was putting it in there. Even she expected it to be there. When it is not, a visiting cop from Fresno accuses Peggy of selling out, since the safe was clearly not broken into and only she and Joe know the combination. Joe, being Joe, looks like he is going to punch the Fresno cop at this point, and Art has to stop him. But when Joe goes to question Peggy about what the heck might have happened, she gets angry and quits on him! In this scene, after she walks out of Joe's office, Joe looks somewhat upset, but mostly just frustrated and confused. It gets better.

After Peggy manages to find out that a switchboard operator is involved and finds this woman murdered, we cut to Peggy talking with Art. Joe walks up. He is subtly but poignantly different. When he shows up, he, very noticeably for *Mannix* fans, says hello only to Art, and does not acknowledge Peggy! For her part though, Peggy is clearly visibly moved by Joe's presence; she actually stands up a lot straighter the moment she sees him. Joe does glance over at Peggy at this point, and when he does, the look on his face is worth freezing the DVD and examining. Here is yet another one of those complex, completely visually expressed emotions—part sad, part confused, and part hurt, because, after all, Peggy just quit on him. Here comes the dialogue, surrounded by sublime facial expressions, especially on the part of Connors.

Art: "Peggy, out of curiosity, who did you call first, him or me?"

Peggy: "I called him right after I called you, Art. I thought he ought to know."

Wow. Peggy is not acknowledging Joe either. She's talking to Art like Joe isn't standing right there, just referring to Joe as "him"! This scene does not mean as much to people who are not familiar with these characters. But for those who are, it is touching. Somebody has to make the first move here. Fans know this conflict will be resolved, which makes it all the more amazing that the resolution is not the least bit self-indulgent or overblown. The first person to make the move is Joe, and you can see, right on his face, how he assesses and processes the situation. His reasoning is not expressed in words, but it is all over him.

When Art leaves, taking the dead body with him, Peggy turns around to get her purse, slowly, very slowly, putting it on her shoulder, with her back turned to the doorway the entire time. She has no way of knowing if Joe is still there, or if he left with Art. She seems to not want to turn around to even look. Whatever is going to happen is going to happen. She quit on Joe, after all, and she can't very well beg for her job back now. She has dignity as well, which only lends dignity back to Joe when we see him through her eyes. Joe, sensing her dilemma, a conclusion you can actually see him reach, with no words at all, seems to sequence through a half dozen emotions within a few seconds time. He is initially sad to see that Peggy has not turned around, then he seems curious about what is going on with her, then he seems to be thinking about what to do about it, followed by resolve, punctuated by a step you can actually hear him take with his foot which Connors could not presume would ever have been audible, since it likely wasn't audible on the TV sets used during the series' first run. That step was just a part of his being that much in character and letting himself be moved by the fact she quit on him, as well as witnessing her difficulty dealing with it.

These emotions quickly morph, one into the other, until he winds up with a classic Joe Mannix half-smile on his face after he both realizes what is going on with Peggy and has decided what to do. Then he simply says, "C'mon, Peggy, I'll drive you home." When he says this, you can see his confidence level go down just a bit, because he isn't 100% sure what she is going to say. He waits. Then Peggy turns around, gives her own version of a half-dozen emotions, including surprise that he would ask, joy that he has, and winds up in a kind of a giving over, almost as if to say, "You know I'm coming." But she never does actually say it. She just walks over to take his outstretched arm and they walk away, arm in arm.

This whole scene takes only seconds. Never mind that what Joe said makes no sense. Why did Peggy need a ride home? Did she take the bus to the apartment of the switchboard operator? How would Joe even know that, if she did? And what does "home" even mean? Is he referring, symbolically, to 17 Paseo Verde? We never find out, and the logic does not matter. There is a greater truth going on here.

The next scene has them together, in Joe's green 'cuda, pulling up to a red light.

Peggy: "I guess I was kind of a pill yesterday."

Joe: "As a matter of fact, you were."

Peggy: "Well, I feel much better now."

Joe: "Good."

Never mind that Peggy's reference to "yesterday" does not make any sense either. She is dressed in the same outfit as she was when she quit, and so was Art in the previous scene. Joe changed his clothes, but that made sense since he was coming in from travel. This is a mistake, but we don't tend to notice it, unless we have watched the episode more times than we care to report. We overlook lapses in logic when something else matters to us more.

As they continue on in the 'cuda, the look on Peggy's face is one of pure joy, in stark contrast to an earlier look on her face in her apartment when she was thinking about the implications of having quit Joe for good, yet another brief and wordless complex expression. That's all there was to Peggy's quitting Joe; no overblown, dragged out thing. The light touch ultimately made it all the more moving.

Yet another of my favorite episodes of the series, a tough list I will never actually make, is "A Pittance of Faith," from season 2. This episode comes relatively early in the series, during that transition between the periods when Peggy was calling her boss "Mr. Mannix" and her coming to call him Joe, during that time she generally did not use his name at all when speaking directly to him. It contains the last time she referred to her boss as "sir" in the normal course of events, as if it was expected. The episode opens with a young woman being thrown from a balcony at night, something we know is not suicide, but the police do not. Lt. Kramer, played by Larry Linville during seasons 2-4 prior to his role as Major Frank Burns on *M*A*S*H* (CBS-TV 1972-1983), ends a short scene where he is investigating the supposed suicide of a fashion model, Gina Lardelli. He reads the suicide note aloud, "Pray for me," to which he adds, "Okay Gina, we're praying." We cut, quickly and directly, to see Peggy, actually singing for the only time in the entire series, really sort of humming as she is happily doing small things around Joe's office. An older man, a professor, comes in to ask Peggy for Joe's services to investigate the death since he does not believe that Gina committed suicide, which was the conclusion of the police. The professor convinces Peggy to believe him. Peggy nods agreement and calls Joe, who is "just across the Paseo."

From here, we cut to a scene in a bar where Bobby Troup is playing a song on the piano, "Girl Talk," with a bass violinist accompanying him. The song is, in and of itself, evocative of something, a kind of comfort and ease, bridging Peggy's singing in Joe's office to this bar where Joe is working. Joe enters the scene by walking over to the bar, drink in hand, presumably after having taken the call from Peggy. He almost glides into his seat at the bar, utterly cool, somehow perhaps the single *coolest* scene in the entire series.

Joe is writing in a small notebook, with Albie—his sometimes fellow PI friend who appears mostly in season 2 (and once in season

6, played by a different actor)—beside him. Joe is clearly enjoying the music, even nodding his head to it, with a smile. Peggy walks in, down some stairs, with the prospective client. She sees Joe, sort of looks down and softly smiles when she does, coolly signifying recognition, makes sure the professor is seated at a table, and glides over to Joe. When she says "hi" to him, he acknowledges her in a cool, pleased, almost offhand way and says, "Oh, hi, Peggy." She points out the potential client. Joe looks over at him and says to Peggy, "And you believe?" She nods and says to him, "I believe." Admonishing Peggy for this belief, Joe informs Peggy that Lt. Kramer does not make mistakes like that. Notice how Joe and Peggy have switched roles here, albeit temporarily. Now Peggy is the believer and Joe is the doubter. Belief seems to always have to face doubters. Since it is not based upon systematic reasoning and cannot be proven, what would the alternative be?

Joe, of course, indulges Peggy, and goes over to at least meet the professor. The professor tells Joe that he has proof that Gina Lardelli did not commit suicide. Joe guesses correctly that the professor, Gina, and the members of the society that is actually hiring Joe, are all Catholic, further correctly surmising that the reason they want to hire him is because Gina cannot be buried in consecrated ground if she committed suicide. Joe asks what proof the professor has. Joe is given monetary "pittances" from the association, as proof, since the members of the association are mostly poor. We see Joe hold up a collection of small bills, and he is clearly, visibly, moved by them, saying with some irony, "And it shall move mountains," referring to himself as the mountain. He asks Peggy to obtain the police report. She softly smiles (but not for Joe to see), then nods and says "Yes, sir" in a very business-like way as she goes off to do it. When the professor goes to thank Joe, Peggy stops him, from behind Joe's back, knowing that Joe does not want this to turn into something sappy. This is not the last time in this episode, and far from the last time in the series, we see Joe visibly moved without it becoming the least bit sappy.

This is also far from the only time Joe works for less than his advertised rates, which are already presumably far less than what he is really worth to the people that need him. He worked for kids offering their pittances in episodes like season 1's "Make Like It Never Happened," season 4's "The Crime That Wasn't," season 6's "The Upside Down Penny," and season 7's "A Question of Murder," even though he was never known to take their meager offerings in return. The subject of

Joe's paltry bank account comes up in a fun scene early in season 4, in "One for the Lady," and then in the very next episode to air, in a sweet exchange between Joe and Peggy at the opening of "Time Out of Mind," one of the few episodes in which Joe winds up working for Peggy for free because she asks him to, as opposed to his just doing it for her. That dialogue is the last time in the series where mention is made that Joe once worked for someone else, because Peggy threatens that if he does not do something about accounts receivable, he is going to "have to go back to work for someone else," something Joe relates to a hit below the belt. He promises to do better "from this moment on" until the phone rings and a relative of Peggy's needs help, for free.

Curiously, this attitude towards money—the very attitude that was mentioned as being so far-fetched when Steven J. Cannell discussed how he came up with the supposedly more evolved and more realistic concept for *The Rockford Files*[2.2]—would seem to have the most concrete basis in reality. Connors' father, who emigrated from Armenia after the genocide there, was a lawyer who practiced in Fresno. William Sayoran, the author, was also Armenian and knew Connors' father, describing him in a *TV Guide* article in a way that brings the Atticus Finch character from *To Kill a Mockingbird* to mind.[11.1] Connors once described his father as taking payment in kind, telling his family that monetary things would just work themselves out, somehow.[11.2] Connors brought that reality to Joe Mannix, a reality that was attacked by Cannell as being unreal, thus spawning a very different kind of follow-on myth.

Later in the episode, the father of the twin girls in "A Pittance of Faith" expresses grief over how Gina, the one who was supposedly dead, led her life. Maria was the "good" twin, and Gina the one who went bad, at least in the father's eyes. We discover that it is really Gina that is still alive, and she tells her story near the end of the episode, with much sadness and regret, because her sister was murdered instead of her, due to mistaken identity. During the telling, Joe is seated behind his desk with Peggy standing at his side. The father walks into Joe's office. He looks only at Gina, his only surviving daughter. He knew which daughter was still alive all along, which is why he was resisting Joe's investigation. Gina was still a target.

When the father walks in, Joe slowly, extremely respectfully, stands to honor him. Aside from Gina, who was seated by his side, Joe was the only other person seated in the room. He stands in such a way that he does not even seem to be consciously aware of it. He is simply moved to do so. Gina is crying, and goes over to her father. Her father takes her in his arms, and simply says, "Enough. Enough. Maria understands, and forgives." Then, they walk out of Joe's office, together.

Joe looks down and sighs, as if in awe and near disbelief. When we are moved, the first test that seems to have to be passed is our own, internal, disbelief. Joe is clearly, visibly processing what he just witnessed, and moved by it. As usual, it is unspoken, but all over his face. Peggy, perhaps because she is more used to being a witness, and who is now standing beside Joe, tries to sum it up. She says, with her own sense of awe, "And it shall move mountains." Joe looks over at her and smiles warmly, conveying mutual understanding. Lt. Kramer is still trying to process what just happened and, not being able to, says, "What?" Joe responds to him with a smile, saying, "Faith, Kramer. A pittance of faith."

Joe places his right hand on Peggy's shoulder and they smile the smile of recognition when you simply get something that defies logical explanation.

You just get it, the way Peggy gets Joe, the way fans get Joe. The frame freezes and goes into the classic *Mannix* grid with Peggy looking at Joe, with a great smile of admiration on her face. She knows something we are forced to consider, if we bother to pay enough attention to these characters, to this scene. The best heroes display the courage to be individuals, to defy the odds, and to move the world according to the way they see it, living out the personal struggle between reason and faith. But they can only really move us if they also display the courage to be moved, themselves.

Chapter 12
Let's Go

The title of this book is evocative of a moment. We describe moments as mere instances of time, infinitesimally small, too small to measure. We must infer their existence by observing the change that surrounds them, a sharp difference in the way we viewed our experiences before and after, a change in context, a change in interpretation, a change in meaning of events otherwise casually sequenced in time. Moments give us a sense that we have the power to change ourselves just by changing the way we view and evaluate our experiences. In turn, we change what we do with our experiences.

The title of this book refers to a collection of moments that, in retrospect, taught me at a very early age that such moments existed in the first place. I watched *Mannix* over its entire eight-year first run on CBS, during an era when viewers had to pay close attention to what was happening on the screen, or they were going to miss it. This was prior to the ability to record episodes by any means, before VHS or Betamax, let alone the DVR capability to automatically record series, go back and view the previous few minutes of something that just aired, or wait just a few days before episodes are available for download or "on demand." If viewers missed something during the first run of an episode of a series like *Mannix*, the only remotely certain opportunity to see it again was during summer reruns six months later, if the episode happened to rerun (not all did). Syndication was far from a certainty for many series back then, and its tendency to over-edit episodes to accommodate more commercials meant some key scenes would seemingly be lost forever. Loyal fans wanted to see every second of a series they loved as soon as it first aired. And so they had to pay attention, focusing on what they were watching at the exclusion of pretty much all other thought.

In those days, when a commercial break ended and a program was about to begin again, the network announcer would say, "And Now, Back to (the name of the program)." This tended to happen in hour-long dramas, in which a seemingly endless series of commercials aired at the halfway point of every episode. The FCC (Federal Communications Commission) had rules about how many consecutive commercial minutes could occur in a row without going back to the episode, but the networks had this trick of showing a still image that represented the show for a few seconds. In the case of *Mannix* this tended to be the colorful grid that symbolized the series, generally with the gold, all lower-case lettering of "mannix" on top, shown while the announcer would say "*Mannix* will continue." Then the network would go off and run a few more commercials before giving the announcement, "And now, back to *Mannix*" or the more verbally economical version, "Back to *Mannix*."

This brief announcement was really quite a courtesy, telling viewers to start to pay attention again, or they were going to miss something. During a long run of commercials, effectively the intermission of an hour-long drama, people did all sorts of things, like talking to others in the same room, making a run to the kitchen or bathroom, or just daydreaming, even about the first part of the episode they just saw. *Mannix* also ran in an era before remote control, so it made no sense to change to another channel for a few minutes, only to have to get up and change the channel back again. We also weren't external stimulation junkies back then, treating each moment of our day as an endless quest for information that we never seem to give ourselves the time to actually process. There weren't a whole lot of other channels to choose from anyway, so you just left the same channel tuned in but, in effect, tuned yourself out from the commercials. Then, the brief announcement signaled that the context was about to change from the obligations, back to the real reason you were there in the first place, back to the story.

January 2011 represented another such moment for me, one where I also found myself in awe of the way I paid such attention to *Mannix* when I was a kid. Even just having that hour to look forward to each week—an hour of blocking everything else out, seemingly losing myself and just focusing on those characters, along with the ability to have them in my head to think about during other times—gave me a sense that I could change the context, could control the way I viewed things. No drug could have been better for mental health. But why was *Mannix* so compelling to me in the first place?

Young minds, with still developing intellect, tend to sort things out more in terms of pleasure and pain, or punishment and reward. They also do not have a fully developed capacity for what has been called "emotional intelligence."[12.1] Some young people start to exhibit it when, for example, they choose to receive two candy bars if they wait an hour in lieu of receiving one candy bar immediately. Kids that make this kind of choice, called delayed gratification, tend to be more capable in their adult lives of pursuing careers that require a lot of up-front personal investment and risk before any, if any, societal reward is given in return. The capacity for delayed gratification turns out to be required for pretty much all creative and intellectual endeavors. Kids that don't take that candy bar up front sort out perhaps the most fundamental of all emotions—pain. They sort out the pain of waiting for an hour compared to taking the upfront reward but then knowing that, after an hour passes, they will have to endure the pain of always knowing they obtained less than they could have, had they only waited. Emotionally intelligent adults are not so different from kids, except that they sometimes have to have a lot of faith that the symbolic candy bars will eventually come. They can also come to realize that by delaying gratification, they wind up being rewarded with something entirely different than that which they originally sought.

The greatest myths help us to sort out pain, doing so by showing us how to change the context of the pain we experience. They do not take pain away. They do not mislead us, unlike lesser myths, into believing that a successful life can be lived while seeking to avoid pain, effectively denying its existence and eliminating the need to make painful choices. We come to act badly when we cannot sort out how to deal with pain and this includes when we put a great deal of effort into trying to avoid it. We also act badly when we deny its existence, such as when we subscribe to myths that portray that the world is somehow more perfect than it really is and likely ever will be. The greatest heroes do not deny pain and are not ruled by it either. Rather, they tend to choose the potentially immediately painful consequences over the longer-term insidious ones. The greatest myths show us why it is better to choose to be tough rather than weak, courageous rather than cowardly, vulnerable rather than detached, energetic rather than depressed, alone rather than subsumed, individual rather than common.

If the single biggest feature that distinguishes *Mannix* is the level of physical and emotional punishment its hero took, and let himself be open to take, over so many situations and so many choices, then *Mannix* also stands alone in portraying perhaps the most fundamental of emotional dilemmas we all must face, the sorting out of how to deal with pain. His very dignity seemed to come from his ability to face pain up-front and in so many situations. That was simply fascinating to me then, and it still is now.

Mannix was groundbreaking and hugely successful in its day. It resulted in Mike Connors being one of the highest paid actors in Hollywood, and the syndication of the show in over seventy countries during its first run.[1.3][12.2] The show's very success was the reason CBS put it up against juggernaut schedules on competing networks in its last three seasons. That success also led to its premature cancellation, since ABC wanted to run it during late night (so that it would have been running on two different networks), had CBS renewed the then-Top-20 show for a ninth season.

The Rockford Files, part parody of *Mannix*, part parody of itself, and part parody of life, a show that never had the success *Mannix* did during its first run, became a darling of the Baby Boomers. *Rockford* was ranked the top TV detective of all time by a survey of viewers in a 2000 *TV Guide* article, while *Mannix* came in at #12.[12.3] The Top 10 list included a collection of what could be considered cerebral, politically correct, wise guy, Peter Pan and gimmicky detectives, or some combination thereof. One could make the argument that *Mannix* made these shows possible in the first place.

The preference for *Rockford* over *Mannix* would seem to be a generational shift, from one labeled the "greatest" because of what it endured, fought, overcame and built, to its arguably less impressive offspring. The series were virtual contemporaries and yet *Mannix* was far more successful in its first run. *Rockford*'s first season was 1974-1975, overlapping the final season of *Mannix*. In that season, *Rockford* ran on Fridays at 9:00 p.m. on NBC, and came in with a seasonal ratings rank of #12, overall. But in each subsequent year, the show experienced a steady decline in the seasonal ratings rankings, coming in at #32, #41, #46, #59 and (does not apply), respectively, over its five and a half-year run. During its final season *Rockford* was canceled in mid-run. This initial precipitous drop followed by a steady decline occurred despite the show holding the same timeslot over all of its tenure (Fridays at 9:00 p.m.), for all or part of each of those seasons. During its final two seasons it also experienced some airtime on Thursdays at 10:00 p.m., a solid weeknight timeslot for a crime drama, and even Saturdays at 10:00 p.m., *Mannix's* old timeslot.[12.4] It seems reasonable to conclude that, when *Rockford* first ran, viewers liked it less the more they saw it.

By contrast, *Mannix's* overall seasonal ratings rankings during its eight-year run are, by season:[12.5]

#58
#42
#30
#17
#7
#42
#31
#20

The first four seasons of *Mannix* aired on Saturdays at 10:00 p.m. and ratings steadily improved each year.[12.5][12.6] The series ultimately wound up in the Top 20 during its fourth season, despite airing in what was normally considered a graveyard timeslot. When it was moved to its best timeslot of Wednesdays at 10:00 p.m. during its fifth season, it wound up in the Top 10, a category *Rockford* never achieved.

Then, after its fifth season success, CBS ran *Mannix* on Sunday nights for its final three seasons. There, it went up against the *ABC Sunday Night Movie*, which during those years gave viewers the first and only opportunity to see such blockbuster movies as *Patton* and *Love Story*, after those movies left theatres. Network TV was where theatrical movies went after their theatrical runs. At that time there was no ability to record those airings, buy or rent movies, or watch two shows that aired on TV at the same time. Movie night was event night. Against ABC's Sunday evening movie, NBC ran its *NBC Mystery Movie*, which featured *Colombo*, *McMillian and Wife*, and *McCloud*, among others, each developed to be more like mini-movies than episodic TV. Running ninety minutes each, fewer of these "series" episodes were produced per year than those of a traditional TV series.

Mannix, still working under the grind of weekly episodic TV but competing with movies airing on the only other two commercial networks, had Sunday night start times of 9:30 p.m. and even 8:30 p.m. during those years. At 9:30 p.m. its start time was after movies on the other networks were already in progress.[12.6] It also suffered from weak lead-in series that did not pull viewers away from starting to watch those movies. (For example, during the hour that preceded *Mannix* during the fall of 1972, CBS ran *The Sandy Duncan Show* and *The New Dick Van Dyke Show*, each half-hour sitcoms.[12.6] *The Sandy Duncan Show* ran only thirteen weeks before being canceled.[12.7] *The*

New Dick Van Dyke Show was in its second season, but during its first season its ratings were much lower than the three other sitcoms that surrounded it on Saturday nights. Those ratings became much worse during the fall of 1972.)[12.8] Furthermore, when *Mannix* started at the absurdly early 8:30 p.m. start time, it just felt wrong. *Mannix* had a mood normally reserved for a later hour of the day, one also normally less associated with family-oriented viewing, which Sunday night programming targeted in those days.

The re-tooled version of *Mannix*, from its second season onward, never dropped below #42 in the ratings, regardless of what the series was up against. Still, normally television series that experience a sharp ratings decline so not see those ratings rebound. But after it was moved to Sunday night viewers discovered *Mannix* a second time.

Presumably as a means of trying to go up against longer dramas and movies, CBS started to package *Mannix* with *Barnaby Jones* in something called the *CBS Mystery Double Feature*. This "package" even had its own title sequence and a mini-theme song. Its opening featured a black cat named "Midnight" that was presumably some kind of jewel thief, since it wore a diamond collar and pranced around like it had obtained the jewelry on its own without actually earning it. The cat-based introduction went into a cartoon silhouette, black on blue, which led into the Bond-like silhouette of Joe that opens seasons 6-8 of *Mannix*. This extra packaging required airtime which CBS certainly wasn't going to accommodate by sacrificing commercials. Consequently, *Mannix's* first-run main title sequence was shortened, including the classic Lalo Schifrin theme. Beyond that, the producers actually had to shorten the running time of *Mannix* episodes they delivered to the network by a full minute, something that can be seen, to this day, in the season 7 episodes, which come in at under fifty minutes instead of just over fifty minutes, unlike every other season of *Mannix*. The shortened opening title sequence never did make it to the DVDs. Instead, both seasons 6 and 7 have the full-length opening title sequence that was used for the first part of season 6, presumably because there was no full opening for season 7 to be had, making them the only seasons of *Mannix* with completely identical openings on the DVDs (season 4 added the gold lettering to the teaser).

I distinctly remember watching the "cat packaging" of *Mannix* and thinking, even in my young mind, that it was absurd. *Mannix* was paired with another detective drama, but what else did *Barnaby Jones* really have in common with *Mannix*? It was like saying that *All in the Family* and *The Brady Bunch* (if they had been on the same network) should be packaged together as the 'Family Comedy Double Feature' because they are both sitcoms about families.

Mannix survived the black cat, rebounding to #31 during its seventh season. Incredibly, its ratings experienced yet another increase, enough to take the Top 20 again during its eighth season, despite remaining on Sunday nights and viewers not being aware that this was to be its last season, something that still amazes. In that final season CBS took away the "black cat packaging" and gave *Mannix* its full opening back, with updated arrangement of the full theme and two new scenes for the "m-a-n-n-i-x grid," making it possible for me to stand the sight of black cats again. A ninth season of *Mannix* didn't happen because ABC bought the syndication rights from Paramount and wanted to run the show on *ABC Late Night*, right at 11:30 p.m., against *The Tonight Show Starring Johnny Carson* in the years before *Nightline* premiered, itself the product of nightly news reports about Iranian hostage crisis in 1979-1980. CBS balked at a series running on another network while were they paying for new episodes of it to be run in prime time. They thought the late-night airings would siphon viewers away. To this day, I still can't think of another series that would have had episodes airing from different seasons on two networks at the same time, not just in different syndication runs but on competing networks, which would have been the result. When CBS and Paramount could not reach an agreement about those late-night airings, presumably because the show was already sold by Paramount to ABC and CBS would not back down, the show was canceled, even though it was back in the Top 20. It would seem CBS was wrong. *Bronk* (starring Jack Palance) and *Delvecchio* (starring Judd Hirsch) ran in *Mannix's* timeslot over the next two years, each unmemorable detective series that were canceled after a single season. Furthermore, the summer reruns of the eighth season of *Mannix* on CBS, which ran in its best, fifth-season timeslot of Wednesdays at 10:00 p.m., reportedly finished in the Top 10 and reached as high as #3 for the week.[12.9]

Mannix can be thought of as having two epochs during its first run, the first one being seasons 1-5 and the second being seasons 6-8. During its first epoch, when it ran on Saturday nights for its first four seasons and then was moved to Wednesday night for season 5, its ratings steadily increased. During its second epoch, when it ran in various timeslots on Sunday nights and faced all sorts of challenges, it struggled at first but then its ratings steadily increased again, ultimately regaining the Top 20.

Comparing the first-run of each series, in stark contrast to *Rockford*, it seems reasonable to conclude that the more viewers saw *Mannix* the more they liked it—not once, but *twice*.

It seems safe to assume that more of the "Greatest Generation" watched both *Mannix* and *Rockford* during their first run compared to people who answered the *TV Guide* poll in 2000. Since the two shows are basically contemporaries of each other, one cannot simply conclude that we prefer more modern settings. And they are both about PIs, with *Rockford* described by more than a few as an "evolution" of *Mannix*, an appealing argument on the surface of things, considering *Rockford* seemed to accomplish as much as Joe Mannix, only without the vulnerability and pain. Then again, Baby Boomers do seem to have quite a track record of giving a lot of attention, time and money to trying to find ways to avoid pain, while the Greatest Generation, one that actually did have to deal with quite a bit of pain in their formative and young adult years, and who were not known for trying to avoid risk and pain in their prime adult years, didn't find *Rockford* nearly as interesting as *Mannix*.

Then again, evolution seems to require regression, sometimes making it hard to distinguish if something that seems more evolved is really a step forward or a step backwards. The phrase "three steps forward two steps back" can apply, metaphorically, to pretty much any progress measured over seconds, minutes, days, years, or generations. *Mannix* was progressive, some might even argue revolutionary, in that it portrays an utterly responsible, post-romantic, highly individualistic hero, one who deals with pain in an emotionally intelligent way, portrayed symbolically at the level of life-and-death struggles. But he wasn't a cowboy kind of individual, off in the wide open spaces because no building or town could contain him. He was an individual who belonged to and was engaged in the world. His desire to be so engaged was the very source of his more immediate forms of pain, but choosing those forms of pain gave him a kind of dignity that made his life seem, overall, that much more rewarding. He did not do good deeds as the by-product of any circumstances, organization, team, buddy, gimmick or superior, above-it-all, wise-guy kind of attitude.

If you really paid attention, *Mannix* made you think and might even have affected you in ways you never fully realized. Then again, things that affect our subconscious do tend to run deeper. They also tend to surface in ways which, like moments, can be difficult to measure directly; they must be inferred.

Despite *Rockford* overtaking *Mannix* in the Baby Boomer generation popularity contest, an image of Joe Mannix graced the page that introduced the article in the same issue of the *TV Guide*. And in early February 2011, the PBS *Pioneers of Television: Crime Drama* put an image of Joe and Peggy on its main website page, the primary image used to advertise the special. Furthermore, *Mannix* has been mentioned quite a bit in popular culture over the years, arguably in a far more diverse collection than other series, like *Rockford*. *Mannix* has been mentioned in movies and TV shows as diverse as *All in the Family, Californication, Boston Legal, Caroline in the City, Everybody Loves Raymond, House, Mad About You, Men in Black II, Men of a Certain Age, Monk, Seinfeld, The Simpsons* (in multiple episodes, including one of its featured Halloween episodes as well as a reference as recent as 2012), and *Saturday Night Live*. Many of the references occurred in only the past fifteen years, and some are very recent, with ten in 2011-2013, alone.[12.10][12.11] Most references are subtle, seemingly included out of a kind of reverence for the way the series is such a deep part of Americana, one that also seems to hearken back to days when we weren't as dug in and self-protective. Curiously, if Ellen DeGeneres and Bill O'Reilly were representatives in Congress, they might not agree on much, might not seem able to find any common ground, typifying our current divided government. But they could strike up a conversation about *Mannix*, since both are fans. Katie Couric could interview them, since she mentioned "I used to love *Mannix*."[12.12] When Couric gave her comment, she added "I don't know why."

Mannix can so easily seem to be about something other than what it really is all about, unless you think about it in terms of matters of character, something we seem to value so much less than we used to. Ric Myers' *Murder on the Air*[1.9] included several incorrect descriptions of the series in the chapter on *Mannix*, the worst of which is when he describes Joe as an ex-cop who went to work for a private detective agency (Intertect) in order to avenge the death of his ex-partner, Peggy's husband! This would also seem to be the source of the error in Gail Fisher's obituary in the *New York Times* that mentions that Joe knew Peggy's late husband cop.[12,13] In terms of matters of character, this is a serious misconception. The very foundation of the show was Joe Mannix's individualism—he would never have been a cop. Furthermore, his character did not come as a reaction to something that happened to him, like the death of a friend; real heroes come to conclusions on their own, symbolic of the heroism that is self-awareness. The series more than suggests that Joe did not know Peggy before her husband was killed. Reference is made in season 5's "A Walk in the Shadows" to Joe's instincts because he hired Peggy "five minutes after you walked through that door." Season 3's "Medal for a Hero," where Joe investigates the alleged corruption of Peggy's late husband, stops well short of establishing that Joe knew him. The relationship between Joe and Peggy, an important part of the series, means so much more because Joe chose her when she walked through his office door, despite no prior relationship, and despite her race. Myers' book goes on to err that the subject of race was never brought up in the series, which is not only completely wrong, it fails to give the credit the show deserves for its unique way of handling race during a time when other series were ignoring it. *Mannix* had the guts to include some racial conflict between Peggy and Joe ("Last Rites for Miss Emma" from season 2) and Peggy's race came up in a collection of other episodes as well.

Once it got past season 1, *Mannix* was almost completely devoid of gimmicks of any kind, and it seemed unafraid to take on anything—race, nude art, and faith included. *Mannix* also had no gimmicky catch phrase like "Who loves ya, baby?" or "Book 'em, Danno," the latter of which was used as a signal for the ending of episodes of *Hawaii Five-O*. *Mannix* also had no voiceover announcer to close its episodes, telling us, for example, that the fugitive on the run would have to keep on running. It did not tend to end its episodes in warm, comfy comradery, unlike so many other buddy and team-oriented shows did, with happy reunions that seemed to ooze privilege. Many of the endings of *Mannix* are not actually even happy, ending on a note of sadness, or with signature *Mannix* mixed feelings, since people often did get hurt, after all. Peggy was not even in every episode of the seasons she was in, let alone all of the closing scenes of the episodes she was in.

Mannix did not consistently end its episodes on any kind of note, be it comfortable, humorous or series-formulaic, even though gentle humor tended to be included as the seasons went on. Some episodes include a lot of humor, such as season 6's "A Matter of Principle," which is really well done, leveraging knowledge of the characters so that loyal viewers experience a little bit more, a *Mannix* style. Some of my favorite episodes for humorous, albeit brief, closings are season 4's "The Crime that Wasn't" and season 8's "The Survivor Who Wasn't." The latter is an episode that includes some great scenes between Connors and Fisher where the series pokes a little fun at Joe's track record of demolishing cars, hitting the sweet spot while stopping well short of self-parody. That episode ends with Joe and Peggy in an elevator, the doors about to close, with Joe about to tell Peggy what just happened to her car, something we never do find out. He had just borrowed Peggy's car against her initially strong objections since he just demolished two previous cars, on the same case. The frame freezes before we see what happens next. Your imagination is practically forced to fill that in.

The series was more likely to end on completely serious notes, often abruptly, leaving the viewers wanting more, always closing with a *Mannix* grid and the words "Executive Producer Bruce Geller." But since *Mannix* was far more about matters of character than formulae, it also ended on some time-consuming long shots as the camera pulls up and back, into the sky, into the ages. Among my favorite is the beautiful ending of season 2's "Edge of the Knife" where, after recovering a kidnapped boy and re-uniting him with his parents, Joe simply walks away, to an ever-widening shot as he, alone, departs the joyous reunited family. It left a big impression on me, another example that seemed to drive home that some heroes were bigger than others. The family, a doctor and his wife, were heroic in their way. But Joe is the one who got their son back, risking his life in the process and becoming emotionally involved in what he was doing, as he always seemed to. He was worth far more to those parents than his fee. He was the one doing more than just trying to preserve what he already had. Even more importantly, in the end, he simply walks away, all alone, and onto the next thing, while the family rejoiced.

If there is a set of words that tends to be uttered the most, at or near the end of *Mannix* episodes, it is probably the simple phrase, "Let's Go." This is a kind of all-purpose phrase often used to convey that the bad guy had been identified and caught, and so it's time to get this guy to the police, and move on to the next case, move on to the next opportunity to experience pain, in full recognition that the pain of not doing so is far worse. *Mannix* was far from the only show during that time to repeatedly use this simple phrase, designed to be common enough that you barely even notice it. But it conveys that, while a given episode is over, it is just one episode of a much longer adventure. It seems to say, "Let's go on to the next thing" more than it says "Let's go home and relax for the rest of our lives now" or "Let's go have a beer because us buddies sure do deserve it." The bad stuff in life goes on as sure as pain is a part of life.

But "Let's Go" wasn't always used only to get the bad guy to move. It was also used in two episodes that closed with Peggy. One of them was season 8's "Walk on the Blind Side" where, after Joe and Art bust the door in, and Peggy winds up in Joe's arms, the only words Joe utters to Peggy in that entire scene are "Let's Go." Those simple words are filled with emotion befitting the experiences of the characters in the six previous years.

In just the previous season, "Climb a Deadly Mountain" had Joe in an airplane accident, a classic *Mannix* episode with a little bit of everything. The episode brought all sorts of action back, early in an action-packed season 7. With less action in season 6, reportedly due to pressure from CBS after Congressional hearings on violence on television, *Mannix* seemed to hearken back to its roots in season 7. The episode also included lots of location shooting, where Joe and an escaped convict, played by Greg Morris (co-star of *Mannix's* recently-canceled sister series, *Mission: Impossible*), need to make their way down a mountain with some bad-guy prison guards chasing them and wanting to kill them. It has Joe trusting this ex-convict, an innocent black man who helped pull him out of the wreckage of the airplane after Joe nearly fell out of the sky on top of him—pretty symbolic, right there. It has Joe hurt, and limping around, but still moving. It has Art going out of his way to find Joe. And it has Peggy knowing something is wrong with Joe, because he went off in this small airplane and did not call in when he said he would. This results in some scenes with Peggy where the previous five years of her witnessing Joe being Joe are all over her, and you sense on her face that the potential loss of Joe is far more than just the loss of a friend. It gives us some more of those scenes like the one in "Death is the Fifth Gear," where Joe's presence seems all the more when he is not even physically there—beautifully illustrating why character is the most spiritual part of our being, cutting across all professions and all other accomplishments.

"Climb a Deadly Mountain" also has a great ending.

After Joe says goodbye to the Greg Morris character, he pivots to see Peggy. He is surprised, because he is, after all, in the middle of nowhere, having crashed on this mountainside. When he sees her, he walks towards her and says, "Hi, Peg" with a great smile (another one of Connors' "best of the series" smiles—and it's just too bad it is so far away). Complete with torn shirt, bloody arm and bandage, Joe walks, limps actually, towards Peggy. She is clearly overjoyed to see her boss and friend, but trying to hold it back so much that she is actually quivering. She does not return Joe's smile. Instead, she simply says, "Joe," as a way of almost coldly acknowledging him. She goes on to say, "You cost me a fortune in babysitters. I was worried sick." When we are overjoyed to see someone who means that much to us, and whom we were so worried about, we do tend to get a little angry at them. We feel somewhat indignant that they caused us such concern in the first place, even if the reason was not their fault. Here is yet another small but significant detail that gets things right, one of many that made the series well worth your complete attention.

Joe has walked up to her at this point, and looks—in yet another classic, complex emotion that was the very hallmark of *Mannix*—simultaneously confused and concerned. And then he seems to figure out what is going on with Peggy. He thinks a bit, then says, "I'm sorry I didn't call, Peg." He takes a beat to think about it some more, and in this era well before cell phones, he gives one of the very few expressions ever used in *Mannix* that could be considered to be dated, "I just couldn't find a phone." This line was used, mostly by men, during the pre-cell phone days as a catch-all excuse for not calling women when they promised they would. When Joe says this line, he smiles with a charming, self-effacing kind of self-satisfaction for having come up with it, and the pitch is perfect. Peggy, sensing this, seeing his playfulness with the situation, and his typical verbal underestimation of the peril he was in, lets out all of her emotion at this point, and just puts her head down in a combination laugh and sob of relief. This is someone she just spent days imagining was dead, and not only does he come back, but at his first opportunity he gives her evidence of just how much she would have missed him, had he been lost. Then, sensing her emotion, and trying to assess it, he looks at her, tilts his head down to see her better, and upon her nodding to him that she is okay, he simply says, "Let's go." Each with an arm on the other, they go off, into the car that will take them down the mountain together, as another long crane shot takes us, simultaneously, up and on to the next thing, all scored to some of that great *Mannix* music. We can only imagine what happens next.

Each episode of *Mannix* was so tightly edited, and the expressions on faces so tightly cut, scenes seemed to be crammed into episodes that were trying to be movies packed into fifty minutes. This is one of the few scenes where we get to see all of that great expression and warmth between these two characters in an episode that seemed to have equal parts action and emotion. It came after the series was into its seventh year, and its sixth with Fisher. When it came, we wanted to see it, had practically imagined something like it before. But what we saw was always somehow better. In each scene, in-between scenes, at the end of the episodes, and at the end of the series, we are left wanting more. Fans who pay attention to the series, who give themselves over, just a bit, to these characters, are given the gift of not only having these characters inside their heads in the first place, but of practically forcing their imagination to answer, "What happened in between? What happens next? What would happen if?"

That is the way myth that is compelling—which does not merely confirm our being less, but which inspires us to be more—both entertains as well as works on us, ultimately giving us the energy and courage to work things out for ourselves in our own lives, to become individuals as we face some fundamental truths about life. Myths give us the impetus to ask questions in the first place, the courage to endure the often painful consequences of coming up with our own answers, and the insight that we are the least alone when we are in concert with them, which is really the same as being in concert with matters of character. In the process, we can come to associate the cost of doing the right thing, of accepting immediate forms of pain instead of waiting for the insidious ones, with beauty. But unlike beauty that is merely granted to us, it is the kind of beauty we can achieve by paying attention and changing the context.

Once we experience them, myths like that never really end. They are in us without our even realizing it, unless we look back and discover them there, in all of those moments of decision, where we could choose to be so much less than our potential, but for them. They seem to be with us always, making us feel least alone when we are most alone. They are not real, not material, but seem to come from the realm of spirit, that which we can only imagine. And yet, that is the realm we seem to yearn to belong to, if we could only find the means to view our lives in a spiritual way, as character in timeless story.

Let's go.

and now, back to mannix

References

[0.1] Neely Tucker, "Mannix was the man," The Washington Post, November 18, 2007, http://www.washingtonpost.com/wp-dyn/content/article/2007/11/16/AR2007111600181.html.

[0.2] Mark Wyckoff, "Final season of 'Mannix' is out on DVD," Ventura County Star, December 27, 2012, http://www.vcstar.com/news/2012/dec/27/final-season-of-mannix-is-out-on-dvd/?partner=RSS.

[0.3] Mike Connors, "Good Scripts is Mannix Problem," Toledo Blade, July 11, 1969, http://news.google.com/newspapers?id=RMowAAAAIBAJ&sjid=sQEEAAAAIBAJ&pg=3248%2C3228609.

[0.4] Joseph Campbell and Bill Moyers, Joseph Campbell and the Power of Myth (PBS broadcast, 1988; PBS DVD, 2011).

[1.1] "Which is Which??" Chicago Tribune TV Week (November 30, 1968).

[1.2] "Mannix," CrimeTV.com, accessed February 28, 2013, http://www.crimetv.com/page/tv/action/mannix/880.

[1.3] "Success Comes to Mike Connors" TV Guide (June 24, 1972).

[1.4] Coyne Steven Sanders and Tom Gilbert, *Desilu: The Story of Lucille Ball and Desi Arnaz* (New York: Quill, 1993; re-issued by New York: HarperEntertainment, 2001).

[1.5] "How old is Mike Connors?" TV Guide (September 30, 1967).

[1.6] "Six Authors in Search of a Character," TV Guide (October 31, 1970).

[1.7] Pioneers of Television: Pioneers of Crime Dramas (PBS broadcast, 2011).

[1.8] "Michael Connors," Turner Classic Movies, accessed February 28, 2013, http://www.tcm.com/tcmdb/person/38005%7C111373/Touch-Connors/.

[1.9] Ric Myers, *Murder on the Air: Television's Great Mystery Series* (New York: Mysterious Press, 1989).

[2.1] Joseph Campbell, *The Hero with a Thousand Faces* (New York: Pantheon, 1949).

[2.2] Bill Carter, "Stephen J. Cannell, Prolific TV Writer, Dies at 69," The New York Times, October 2, 2010, http://www.nytimes.com/2010/10/02/arts/television/02cannell.html?_r=0.

[2.3] Amy Chozick, " Stephen J. Cannell: Some Final Words With 'The A-Team' Creator," The Wall Street Journal, October 1, 2010, http://blogs.wsj.com/speakeasy/2010/10/01/stephen-j-cannell-some-final-words-with-the-a-team-creator/.

[2.4] Carl G. Jung, *Psychological Types: The Collected Works of C. G. Jung, Vol. 6* (Princeton: Princeton University Press, 1976).

[3.1] Karen Armstrong, *The Case for God* (New York: Anchor, 2010).

[3.2] Thomas S. Kuhn, *The Structure of Scientific Revolutions* (Chicago: University of Chicago Press, 1962.

[4.1] Carl G. Jung, *Man and His Symbols* (New York: Doubleday, 1964).

[4.2] Michael Polanyi, *Personal Knowledge: Towards a Post-Critical Philosophy* (Chicago: University of Chicago Press, 1958).

[4.3] Thomas Wolfe, *The Face of a Nation* (New York: Charles Scribner's Sons, 1939).

[4.4] Viktor Frankl, *Man's Search for Meaning: An Introduction to Logotherapy* (Boston: Beacon Press, 1959).

[5.1] "My mother is a very strong lady," TV Guide (October 19, 1968).

[5.2] Nichelle Nichols, *Beyond Uhura* (New York: Random House Value Publishing, 1996).

[5.3] "Gail Fisher,"The Internet Movie Database, accessed February 28, 2013, http://www.imdb.com/name/nm0279500/bio.
[5.4] Peggy Hudson, *TV 71* (New York: Scholastic Book Services, 1970).
[6.1] Joseph J. Ellis, *Patriots: Brotherhood of the American Revolution* (New York: Barnes & Noble Portable Professor Series, 2004).
[6.2] The TV Collector (No. 85, Sept-Oct 1996).
[7.1] The Internet Movie Database, www.imdb.com.
[7.2] Mark Phillips,"Impossible Magician," STARLOG (September 1995).
[8.1] Ayn Rand, *Atlas Shrugged* (New York: Random House, 1957).
[8.2] Thomas L. Friedman, *The World Is Flat: A Brief History of the Twenty-first Century* (New York: Farrar, Straus and Giroux, 2005).
[8.3] Douglas Hofstadter, *Gödel, Escher, Bach: An Eternal Golden Braid* (New York: Basic Books, 1979).
[9.1] Mario Puzo, *The Godfather* (New York: G. P. Putnam's Sons, 1969).
[10.1] "Mannix,"The CBS Syndication Bible, accessed March 17, 2013, http://syndicationbible.cbstvd.com/.
[10.2] "energy definition" Google Search, accessed January 23, 2013, https://www.google.com/#q=energy+definition.
[10.3] M. Esther Harding, *Psychic Energy: Its Source and Its Transformation* (Washington, DC: Bollingen, 1947).
[10.4] "The Apollo Flights,"The National Aeronautics and Space Administration, accessed March 17, 2013, http://www.hq.nasa.gov/office/pao/History/apollo/welcome.html#chart.
[10.5] The TV Collector (No. 84, Jul-Aug 1996).
[10.6] "Patti Cohoon-Friedman letter," Mike Connors Guest Stars/Crew, accessed February 27, 2013, http://17paseoverde.tripod.com/id3.html.
[10.7] "The Driver Didn't Walk Away,"TV Guide (August 10, 1968).
[10.8] "It was the closest I've ever come. The day a Mannix stunt went out of control,"TV Guide (September 15, 1973).
[10.9] "A long fall on Mannix,"TV Guide (December 5, 1970).
[11.1] William Saroyan, "I'll tell you who Joe Mannix really is,"TV Guide (July 13, 1974).
[11.2] "A Victim of Discrimination," Modern Screen (February, 1971).
[12.1] Daniel Goleman, *Emotional Intelligence: Why It Can Matter More Than IQ* (New York: Bantam Books, 1996).
[12.2] Paramount Press Release for the fall premiere of Mannix (Paramount Studios, 1974).
[12.3] "It's Murder Out There,"TV Guide (July 8, 2000).
[12.4] "The Rockford Files,"Wikipedia, accessed February 17, 2013, http://en.wikipedia.org/wiki/The_Rockford_Files.
[12.5] CBS Programming Research Department (via National Academy of Television Arts and Sciences).
[12.6] "Lists of United States television network schedules,"Wikipedia, accessed December 14, 2013, http://en.wikipedia.org/wiki/List_of_United_States_network_television_schedules.
[12.7] "The Sandy Duncan Show,"Wikipedia, accessed December 14, 2013, http://en.wikipedia.org/wiki/The_Sandy_Duncan_Show.
[12.8] "The New Dick Van Dyke Show,"Wikipedia, accessed December 14, 2013, http://en.wikipedia.org/wiki/The_New_Dick_Van_Dyke_Show.
[12.9] "[Mannix] Why was Mannix cancelled?" Mannix Yahoo Discussion Group,

thread started July 16, 2011, http://tv.groups.yahoo.com/group/Mannix/.

[12.10] "Mannix Connections," The Internet Movie Database, accessed February 17, 2014, http://www.imdb.com/title/tt0061277/movieconnections.

[12.11] "[Mannix] A 'Mannix' reference on a contemporary show," Mannix Yahoo Discussion Group, thread started February 20, 2011, http://tv.groups.yahoo.com/group/Mannix/.

[12.12] Katie Couric, Archive of American Television (comment is about 11 minutes into the interview which was conducted in 2010), accessed February 17, 2013, http://www.emmytvlegends.org/interviews/people/katie-couric.

[12.13] Lawrence Van Gelder, "Gail Fisher, 65, TV Actress Who Won Emmy for 'Mannix,'" The New York Times, February 20, 2001, http://www.nytimes.com/2001/02/20/arts/gail-fisher-65-tv-actress-who-won-emmy-for-mannix.html.

www.ingramcontent.com/pod-product-compliance
Lightning Source LLC
Chambersburg PA
CBHW062007220426
43662CB00010B/1258